The Completion of the Project of the West, And Its Romantic Sequel

The Completion of the Project of the West, And Its Romantic Sequel

Essays in the History of Western Culture

By

Patrick Madigan, S.J.

SCRANTON: THE UNIVERSITY OF SCRANTON PRESS

Library of Congress Cataloging-in-Publication Data

Madigan, Patrick, 1945-
    The completion of the project of the West, and its romantic sequel : essays
in the history of western culture / Patrick Madigan.
        p.cm.
    Includes bibliographical references and index.
    ISBN 1-58966-018-8 (hc) – ISBN 1-58966-019-6 (pbk.)
        1. Christianity–Philosophy–History. 2. Philosophy and religion–History. I.
Title.

BR100.M26 2002
909'.09821'001–dc21
                                                                      2002071973

Distribution:

University of Scranton Press
Linden Street & Monroe Avenue
Scranton, PA 18510
Phone: 1-800-941-3081
Fax: 1-800-941-8804

PRINTED IN THE UNITED STATES OF AMERICA

CONTENTS

So all the people took off their earrings
and brought them to Aaron,
who accepted their offering,
and fashioning this gold
with a graving tool, made a molten calf.
Then they cried out,
"This is your God, O Israel,
who brought you out of the
land of Egypt."

Exodus, 32, 3–4

INTRODUCTION

"Erant gigantes in diebus illis" ("*There were giants in those days*"). Or so it seemed to us who began our philosophic studies a generation or two ago. There was A.J. Ayer, whose *Language, Truth, and Logic* launched a new age of logical positivism, there were the projects of the earlier and later Wittgenstein, there was Heidegger, as well as a pantheon of lesser deities: Carnap, Russell, Sartre, Frege, and Husserl, among others. Marx and Freud continued to command an allegiance whose fervor bordered on the religious. A sea change, however, has occurred; no one commands such loyalty today. Too many programs have gone bankrupt; too many masters have turned out to have feet of clay. Not only are there no such figures today, no one even aspires to such status. Richard Rorty debunks philosophy's pretension to have any "truth" to tell beyond that conveyed by the particular sciences. We live in an overcritical and dispirited age, dispelling its own boredom by ridiculing its former pretensions, soothing its wounded nerves and disappointed expectations by making fun of the inflated agenda of the modern period. Pomposity and arrogance are out of fashion, but with them also has departed a bit of ambition. We were introduced to philosophy as manifesto and revelation, and now we realize that if we are to have it at all, we must retrieve it as archeology. We no longer expect truth to assault us from the future; rather, we realize we may well have to dig whatever we can of it from the past.

And yet this is not the end; it is only the beginning. This book chronicles a series of historical failures, progressively more serious. The Hebrew and Olympian covenants went bankrupt, and the Aristotelian philosophy proved incomplete against its own criteria of adequate explanation; in trying to redress this deficiency, the Plotinian synthesis overshot the mark and posited an ultimate principle which necessarily expands and thus absorbs its world. On the political or human level, Jesus was clearly a failure. Within the Cartesian project to respond to the arch-skeptic, which defines the modern period, the Leibnizean-Kantian strategy to impress space and time as forms of phenomenal intuition into a guarantee against ultimate "noumenal" disorder, rests upon an illusion, a "distinction without a difference." Nevertheless, their project paved the way for the Romantic "victory" which leaves

ix

everything exactly as it was found, a victory that is ultimately indistinguishable from defeat; in other words, this Romantic "solution"—our current settlement—consists of a violently heightened awareness or expression of ordinary realities, which similarly cannot bear the metaphysical weight placed upon them, as one Romantic poet after another, responding to the "anxiety of influence," attempts to "play god," to displace his predecessors into the oblivion of "belatedness" and achieve ultimate "anteriority." Further, the "sublime" expansion of the Romantic sensibility becomes indistinguishable from the sterile climax of pornography. Thus our current insecurity and instability, our swings between exaltation and depression, with no more ground for the one than for the other. It is Nietzsche who keeps us honest, who brings this Cartesian project to its limit, and forces us—ironically through Wittgenstein—to retrieve this suicidal project of absolute "foundationalism" for reconsideration.

We live in a "postmodern" age which has succeeded the "modern." The Enlightenment project to purge the mind of "unclear" ideas and live "according to reason," where reason is understood in a primarily critical sense, is over, its assumptions the victim of its own radical program. If Socrates has said that "the unexamined life is not worth living," as early as Hume, who in some ways may be viewed as the patron of the Enlightenment, it was announced that "the examined life *cannot* be lived"—or in Hume's own words, "reason is, and ought to remain, the slave of the passions."

With the buildup of mathematical science, freedom had appeared more and more suspect—an "unclear idea"; yet freedom was the deepest assumption of the Enlightenment, the indispensable engine for a whole array of projects, but specifically the project to cleanse the mind of unclear ideas, thereby to rise from the trough of ignorance, superstition, and fanaticism in which Western man was supposed to have lain bound and immobile for over a thousand years. With the physical world consigned to determinism, only a critical act could demonstrate the freedom the Enlightenment thinkers needed to ground their project; but how should criticism now orient itself toward freedom? Reason understood as rigorous or maximal criticism seemed to land the Enlightenment in a lived or existential contradiction; paradoxically, to attack freedom was to demonstrate her; to deny her (as a more critical act that need not have happened) was to show her to be real. Contradiction seems to disqualify an idea, however, by indicting it as definitively "unclear." Imagination, the former villain of the piece, was enlisted to become the new champion during the Romantic phase of the modern period. In the wake of Hume's and Kant's results, if a deeper region of reality defeats reason's assault and attempt to extract a "clear" idea of it, perhaps imagination, free to combine ideas in ways that violate our conscious or *a priori* ways of ordering experience, may allow us finally to fashion a more adequate, a less distorting experience of this reality, and would thus deliver the "clear and distinct" idea that will lift us up, bring about a change, and thereby demonstrate decisively the freedom this project needs. This phase reaches its culmination in Nietzsche, whose "*Übermensch*" demonstrates the value of his life by being able to embrace the deliberate fiction of the "*Eternal Recurrence of the Same,*" that is, the vision of his life as without value, and this repeated endlessly. The contradiction is not removed, but is merely played out as a perpetual migration between mutually unacceptable alternatives.[1] Pascal described this fate prophetically at the outset of the modern period:

> Limited as we are in every way, this state which holds the mean between two extremes is present in all our impotence . . . This is our true state; this is what makes us incapable of certain knowledge and of absolute ignorance. We sail within a vast sphere, ever drifting in uncertainty, driven from end to end. When we think to attach ourselves to any point and to fasten to it, it wavers and leaves us; and if we follow it, it eludes our grasp, slips past us, and vanishes forever. Nothing stays for us. This is our natural condition, and yet most contrary to our inclination; we burn with desire to find solid ground and an ultimate sure foundation whereon to build a tower reaching to the Infinite. But our whole groundwork cracks, and the earth opens to abysses.
>
> *Pensées, # 72*

This theme is fundamental in what follows in the article "Lonergan and the Completion of American Philosophy." The "antifoundationalism" that has become a characteristic feature of the "postmodern" philosophical program means that the project that had defined the modern period from Descartes to Nietzsche is over, bankrupt, and abandoned. One consequence which one sees in Rorty is that philosophy has become embarrassed and confused about what it should be doing. It has been so long since it has done anything *but* the Enlightenment project that when this project is called off, philosophy is at a loss how precisely to justify itself. One promising and currently fashionable response in Anglo-American philosophy is the project to explain "consciousness." Lonergan indicates the direction in which a philosophy of the inquiring subject should be developed that builds on the contributions of Anglo-American philosophy during the last century of the millennium; he leads philosophy beyond physiological psychology by encouraging reflection on the operations of breakthrough, testing, and confidence that characterize our progress in knowledge and which are more distinctively human than mere "consciousness."

As part of the postmodern critique, the Enlightenment view of the relation between Greek philosophy and Christianity must be revised. Since the eighteenth century, it has been a fundamental axiom of the Enlightenment mentality that Greek philosophy offered an autonomous and complete explanation of the world (in several modalities: atomistic, Platonic, and Aristotelian) which Christian thinkers vandalized, dismembered, and appropriated to their foreign purposes; the columns of the free-standing Greek temple were removed and transported to become pillars within the new cathedral. While no claim can be suggested that a divine intervention or revelation is in any way pointed to by Greek philosophy, the disinterested observation may still be permitted that the dominant forms of Greek philosophy were seriously flawed, that the Aristotelian program in particular (in many ways the most impressive) was systematically incomplete, that is, that it suffered from a serious omission that prevented it from providing an efficient cause for the universe—and demonstrated a form of bad faith by attempting to cover this omission by simply declaring the universe eternal, which hardly solves the problem because dependent substances cannot have brought themselves into existence; and that only an "activist" or dynamic view of the highest substance, allowing him to know and care about beings other than himself, could remedy this deficiency. In some ways an accidental historical fact, such a view of the highest substance was presented by the emerging Judeo-Christian tradition. On this revised view, Christianity did not distort or pervert Greek philosophy, but rather removed the impediment that had stymied Greek philosophy, thereby ironically allowing it for the first time to complete its self-given project of providing an adequate explanation of the world.[2]

The papers brought together in this collection extend the points made above. Specifically, Part I examines the internal inadequacies of the Platonic-Aristotelian synthesis attempted by Plotinus, his revolutionary proposal to describe the One as "infinite," thereby finally overthrowing the Parmenidean convention of divine perfection which had hobbled Greek philosophy for seven hundred years. This allowed the West to advance in good conscience to a dynamic, "activist" view of the first principle, without seeing this step as necessarily a lapse back into mythological thinking. Collaterally, the biased Enlightenment view of the Hellenistic period as a whole and the origin of Christianity in particular are examined. One relevant observation from contemporary sociology of religion is that of the major role played by hellenized Jews in the spread of early Christianity over four hundred years. Thus, the Enlightenment view of the chief recruits to Christianity as *lumpen Proletariat* or emasculated slaves must be revised. The final reconciliation of the scandalous "good news" of the Christians with the Greek convention that love, divine or human, should be proportional to its object, occupied the West for a thousand years, coming to completion in the daring description by Duns Scotus of the human nature of Christ as the "perfect creature" and God's intention from all eternity, even before creation and apart from the foreseen sin of Adam. This position was combined with Christ's role as redeemer in the work of Lawrence of Brindisi.

The modern Romantic project, the "sequel" to the classical problematic of the West, is examined in Part II. The scholastic synthesis of Duns Scotus was lost during the Reformation, which again stressed the yawning, uncrossable chasm between human merit and divine grace, but, significantly, sought certainty of salvation in inner experience. The Enlightenment radicalized and secularized this project, seeking assurances of the unity and coherence of experience through the subject's inner resources. The search for such assurances in space and time is examined in the work of Leibniz and Kant. The shift of the source of "salvation" from outside to inside the subject is thematically executed in Romanticism, and Harold Bloom is examined as our most perspicuous exponent and simultaneous critic of this modern "solution." The danger of the Romantic internal "victory" as a compensation for external failure, as a "triumph" which makes no difference at all but leaves things exactly as they are, is piteously exposed by Nietzsche, the "unavoidable" modern philosopher and "bookend" to Descartes, who can be said to bring the modern Cartesian project to whatever "end" it is capable of. And with Nietzsche's critique of "herd morality" and a "revolt of the slaves," we come full circle and rejoin our own examination of the origins of Christianity. The study concludes with a reflection on the sense in which Jesus can be described as an expression of the "fidelity" of God.

Acknowledgments: Chapters 1 and 6 appeared in *Chiedza, the Journal of Arrupe College*, in May 2001 and 2000, respectively; Chapter 3 was given as the Arrupe Lecture at Arrupe College in October 2000; Chapter 7 appeared in the *Kant-Studien,* heft 1, 1976; Chapter 8 was first presented as a paper at the Jacobson Conference held at the University of Zimbabwe in November 1996; Chapter 10 appeared in *Tulane Studies in Philosophy*, vol. XXIV, 1975; Chapter 12 appeared in *Method: Journal of Lonergan Studies*, 19/1, Spring 2001. Permission to republish these articles is gratefully acknowledged.

Notes

[1]For a fuller exposition of this development, see my *The Modern Project to Rigor: Descartes to Nietzsche*, University Press of America, Lanham, MD, 1986.
[2]For a more complete exposition of this pont, see my *Christian Revelation and the Completion of the Aristotelian Revolution*, University Press of America, Lanham, MD, 1988.

PART I

CHAPTER 1

The "Degenerate Origins" of Christianity; The Enlightenment Critique of Hellenistic Society

I t was Edward Gibbon who said that the decline of the Roman Empire was accompanied by the rise of "barbarism and religion," but he was a bit ahead of his time. The Enlightenment critique of Christianity moved from contesting doctrinal issues during the eighteenth century to casting aspersions upon its origins in the nineteenth. Whereas Gibbon's contemporary, David Hume, disputed miracles, the existence and nature of the deity, and even personal identity, the later critique fell back to an agnosticism (a word coined by Thomas Huxley in 1869) on theological matters and contented itself with dismissing Christianity as a noxious weed which had luxuriated only because it grew from an unhygienic and pestilential swamp. The Romantic phase of modern thought, as is well known, began with optimism and rationalism in Schelling and Hegel, but by the mid-nineteenth century had fallen back to relativism and even pessimism in such thinkers as Feuerbach, Schopenhauer, Burckhardt, Dilthey, and later, Nietzsche.

Chateaubriand's *Génie du Christianism* (1802) was followed a half century later by the very different accounts of the life of Christ by Ernest Renan and David Strauss, and the novels of the apostate evangelist Marian Evans (George Eliot), later by Thomas Hardy, and still later by D.H. Lawrence. The rise of "psychology" and "sociology," as Nietzsche assures us, was intimately tied in with the rage of the "*untermenschen*" who could not tolerate contrast with the truly great, were determined to "strip the mask" of superiority from all the supposedly higher cultural achievements to reveal the mass of squirming maggots beneath, and as a consequence spun out theory after theory to pull the "great" down to their own level, showing how the "good" emerged from the "bad." For Nietzsche, their overheated imaginations indulged in an orgy of resentment and revenge, in an unfortunate and inappropriate manifestation of the "Will to Power." The

1

blatant reductionism or *ad hominem* character of this attack did not blunt its success nor shame its perpetrators; indeed, this was *ad hominem* raised to the level of theory, openly embraced and publicly proclaimed.

Most of us have at one time or another read Freud's account of the origins of Judaism and Christianity in *Totem and Taboo* and *Moses and Monotheism*, but find the postulation of the origin of Judaism in a parricide by the sons interesting, yet a bit too bizarre and exotic to be convincing. More persuasive has been Nietzsche's tracing of both to a rise of a "herd morality" against the superior but threatening stronger individual—probably because we recognize such tendencies in ourselves, and have no difficulty projecting such motivations onto the even more exposed and insecure denizens of technologically less advanced societies.

All these influences combine and coalesce to form a general, if usually unspoken, Enlightenment criticism of the origin of Judaism, but especially of Christianity, no longer by disputing their respective doctrines, but rather by viewing them as intellectual or psychological "crutches" by which the weaker members of society reconcile themselves to their painful or less privileged position; they are viewed as compensation mechanisms that function by postulating a vicarious, if unrealistic, "victory" in another world or against an alternative (and invisible) set of values. In short, they "move the goalposts" when they see themselves losing the game, or change the rules halfway through by announcing that "losing" now counts for "winning," and "winning" counts as "losing." This general Enlightenment criticism discredits religious doctrines at their root, or "behind" their logical assertions, by projecting unworthy, if hidden or unconscious, motives as the forces which have impelled their disciples to embrace them. Conversion, rather than being an indication of strength at having risen to discern the suasive power of theoretical arguments, is taken now rather as a sign of weakness, a failure of nerve or flight from reason, a capitulation before unworthy or irrational motivations. An upward roll of the eyes indicates everything; nothing more need be said.

This criticism slowly percolated into philosophical and classical studies, initially under the influence or in reaction to Nietzsche himself, but eventually because it could be used to bolster or reassure the modern Enlightenment mentality concerning its questionable superiority over the "Age of Faith." Thinkers framed a contrast between the "Hellenic" and "Hellenistic" ages of Greece (a distinction which, like that between

"Platonism" and "Neo-Platonism," did not exist before the nineteenth century), with a clear preference or favoring of the former over the latter. They viewed "Hellenistic" culture and the "Neo-Platonism" of Plotinus in particular, not as the "harvest" which brought together all that was best in Plato and Aristotle. Nor did they see it as a turning and implementation of the funded resources of earlier thinkers who had tackled the internal deficiencies of Greek philosophy with regard to its giving a complete account of the world. They saw it as inferior, derivative, syncretistic and dispirited, a kind of step-down or decline. They considered this sort of other-worldly flight as symbolic of evasion, weakness, and degeneration. They hoped to devalorize all that emerged from this disordered social and cultural condition. They thought this even of Christianity. They used an "argument by association" to privilege themselves as the modern heirs to the robust, rational "Hellenic" thinkers. They thus saw themselves as superior to these inbred, world-hating, irrational decadents. Since, in a rage, envy or pique, they had destroyed the glory of "Hellenic" culture and created centuries of obscurantism, they had to be gradually overcome by the "reenlightened."

Already Gibbon had contrasted the Neoplatonic philosophers with "the ancient sages [who] had derided the popular superstition" by the accusation that they "converted the study of philosophy into that of magic."[1] The "Hellenic" period is viewed as standing in as an earlier version of the modern Enlightenment, a proleptic, anticipatory version of the same thing, whose asserted superiority over the following "Hellenistic" period is appreciated as symbolic of the victory at all times of sober rationalists over wide-eyed hysterics. Thus this supposedly neutral or impartial "scholarly" distinction had as one of its general, if not always conscious, purposes that of justifying existing power relationships, and incidentally also did useful duty in criticizing Christianity by impugning its origin. This may be termed the "Nietzschean myth" or way of understanding Greek Culture, and it is today still so entrenched and widespread that it is often felt not to stand in need argument or defense; it is rather taken as supplying the matrix of assumptions *within which* all discussion must take place.[2] Only in our own time has this "Nietzschean myth" come up for re-examination and serious reevaluation.

In this paper, I would like to examine the continuation of this "Nietzschean myth" is two influential contemporary thinkers who wrote forty years apart: the English classical scholar Gilbert Murray, and the American cultural pragmatist John Herman Randall. Both accept the myth in its general outline, but work such changes upon particular parts as to raise a question of whether the myth survives with any integrity. Both men embrace the myth, but they so qualify or complicate it as to rob it of its force. As a consequence, it begins to fall apart in their hands, a victim of its internal contradictions. They resist junking it completely, however, first because they have no alternative they find acceptable with which to replace it, and second, because this would call for too serious a revision of the dominance of Enlightenment culture.

In 1925, the English classical scholar Gilbert Murray published a book entitled *Four Stages of Greek Religion*, to which he added a fifth stage in the edition of 1930.[3] Murray clearly shows the influence of the Nietzschean myth—his chapter on the post-Olympian, Hellenistic stage of Greek religion is entitled "The Failure of Nerve"—but at the same time his honesty prevents him from overlooking the limitations of the earlier "Hellenic" stage. As with the famous Mexican muralists Orozco and Rivera, their criticism of the Christianity imposed by the Spanish does not lead them to romanticize the earlier, pre-Christian Aztec religion, which had practiced human sacrifice. Murray's integrity as a scholar impels him to the same honesty.

First, the acceptance of the Nietzschean myth. Early on, Murray informs us that the fourth or Hellenistic phase

> was based on the consciousness of manifold failure, and consequently touched both with morbidity and with the spiritual exaltation which is so often the companion of morbidity. It not only had behind it the failure of the Olympian theology and the free city-state, now crushed by semi-barbarous military monarchies; it lived through the gradual realization of two other failures—the failure of human government, even when backed by the power of Rome or the wealth of Egypt, to achieve a good life for man; and lastly the failure of the great propaganda of Hellenism, in which the long-drawn effort of Greece to educate a corrupt and barbaric world seemed only to lead to the corruption or barbarization of the very ideals which it sought to spread. This sense of failure, this progressive loss of hope in the world, in sober calculation, and in organized human effort, threw the later Greek back upon his own soul, upon the comparative neglect of this transitory and imperfect world for the sake of some dream-world far off, which shall subsist without sin or corruption, the same yesterday, today, and for ever. (18)

We notice that even here, at the outset, Murray speaks of the "failure" of the Olympian theology, and this contributes a note of melancholy to his general treatment, a lingering *fin-de-siecle* aestheticism and *Weltschmerz* which seems to hold that our choice is only between a variety of illusions. "Truth" is unavailable or a non-starter. In any case, what came to be called "truth" had a weakening or debilitating effect; it undermined the robustness, exuberance, and vitality of life, and so was to be excluded on aesthetic grounds. Only those life-giving illusions that lift the *élan vital* to a higher level are to be accepted; this is the only standard that matters, the only criterion there is. Still, these earlier mythological portraits of the deity had certain inadequacies in the form of logical difficulties and pernicious effects that cannot in good faith be overlooked.

Murray's theory is that in the formation of the Olympian pantheon,

> the kings and gods of the Heroic Age were transfigured. What had been really an age of buccaneering violence became in memory an age of chivalry and splendid adventure. The traits that were at all tolerable were idealized; those that were intolerable were either expurgated, or, if that was impossible, were mysticized and explained away. And the savage old Olympians became to Athens and the mainland of Greece from the sixth century onward emblems of high humanity and religious reform. (79)

This Olympian set of deities lifted Greece above her neighbors:

> The Olympian movement swept away also, at least for two splendid centuries, the worship of the man-god, with its diseased atmosphere of megalomania and blood-lust. These things return with the fall of Helenism; but the great period, as it urges man to use all his powers of thought, of daring and endurance, of social organization, so it bids him remember that he is a man like other men, subject to the same laws and bound to reckon with the same death. (84)

However, this elevation of kings and heroes to mythological status had certain negative theological consequences:

> In this respect the Olympian Religion did not merely fail: it did worse. To make the elements of a nature-religion human is inevitably to make them vicious. There was no great moral harm in worshiping a thunderstorm, even though the lightening strikes the good and evil quite recklessly. There is no need to pretend that the lightening is exercising a wise and righteous choice. But when once you worship an imaginary quasi-human being who throws the lightening, you are in a dilemma. Either you are worshiping and flattering a being with no moral sense, because he happens to be dangerous, or else you have to invent reasons for his wrath against the people who happen to be

struck. And they are pretty sure to be bad reasons. The god, if personal, becomes capricious and cruel. (90) Again, to worship emblems of fertility and generation, as was done in agricultural rites all through the Aegean area, is in itself an intelligible and not necessarily a degrading practice. But when these emblems are somehow humanized, and the result is an anthropomorphic god of enormous procreative power and innumerable amours, a religion so modified has received a deathblow. The step that was meant to soften its grossness has resulted in its moral degradation. (91)

Surprisingly, Murray can even cast a wistful eye toward the more logical, if less robust, religion which replaced it:

Thus a failure in the moral expurgation was deepened by a failure in the attempt to bring intellectual order into the welter of primitive gods. The only satisfactory end of that effort would have been monotheism. (91) Certainly Greek monotheism, had it really carried the day, would have been a far more philosophic thing than the tribal and personal monotheism of the Hebrews. But unfortunately too many hard-caked superstitions, too many tender and sensitive associations, were linked with particular figures in the pantheon of particular rites which had brought the worshiper religious peace. (92) Unlike many religious systems, it generally permitted progress; it encouraged not only the obedient virtues but the daring virtues as well. (95)

We will have more to say shortly about the form that Greek monotheism actually did take in Plotinus, and the price it paid, out of deference to Parmenides, for *not* making the god personal.

Stoicism, Skepticism, and Epicureanism, the forms of philosophy which developed during the Hellenistic period, are all described as simplistic and world-escapist ideologies for a defeated people:

There is a rise of asceticism, of mysticism, in a sense, of pessimism; a loss of self-confidence, of hope in this life and faith in normal human effort; a despair of patient enquiry, a cry for infallible revelation; an indifference to the welfare of the state, a conversion of the soul to God. (155)

And when Christianity finally arrived, it came

like water in the desert to minds reluctantly and superficially enlightened, but secretly longing for the old terrors and raptures from which they had been set free. (176) Just for a few great generations, it would seem, humanity rose to a sufficient height of self-criticism and self-restraint to reject the dreams of self-abasement or mega-lomania. But the effort was too great for the average world. (186)

The Columbia naturalist John Herman Randall, in a late work, *Hellenistic Ways of Deliverance and the Making of the Christian Synthesis*,[4] carries forward the same Nietzschean myth. He brings forth a wealth of information, and carries the argument forward to the Greek and Roman Church Fathers, without substantially altering the picture Murray has given; rather, at the beginning of his chapter on the Hellenistic period, he quotes Murray's diagnosis of a "failure of nerve" with approval (100). If anything, the myth is cruder in Randall; he writes in terms of simplistic, snappy oppositions: Greek-Oriental, monistic-dualistic, moral-mystical, "motive" vs. "mastery" in ethical theory, etc., which he elevates to a condition of mutual exclusion and applies with the presumption of automatic correctness. Besides bull-dozing his way past contrary data, and hilarious this-worldly inter-pretations of the doctrines of the trinity and the incarnation, his deepest failure remains the same as Murray's: a rejection of the "personal" as applied to the deity, as a sign of weakness and other-worldly escapism (126). Ironically, he castigates the Stoics for developing an ethic of impartial, universal service, but stopping short of *loving* mankind, for this would imperil their peace of mind and freedom of soul (54). Yet by denying that god is personal, Randall has removed the foundation for any practice other than the one best calculated to preserve inner peace and freedom from anxiety. More deeply, this denial or withholding of the category of the personal from the deity betrays a total failure to appreciate the internal development of Greek philosophy from Parmenides to Plotinus.

Both Murray and Randall seem innocent or tone-deaf to the dynamic propelling Greek philosophy; they seem to view philosophy as a pale, colorless *simulacrum* of Greek mythology, a copy at one remove and with all the charming aspects removed, whereas the philosophers saw it the other way around, that philosophy was extracting and salvaging the few items that were of value and worth preserving from the fanciful anthropomorphisms that make up the overwhelming bulk of mythology. Both are silent on the paralyzing defect of "Hellenic" philosophy—that after defining God as "changeless" with Parmenides, no account of the emergence of a changing world was possible. They are thus forced to view Plotinus as a "decline" rather than turning courageously to face the central difficulty created by Parmenides' con-tribution and exploiting all the resources available from the Greek tradition to attempt to resolve the problem, short of calling into question the central "Hellenic" convention that true reality, "perfection," or the deity must be changeless. Insensitive to the logical forces propelling philosophical reasoning, these two thinkers can see this change only as a capitulation to overpowering and unhealthy emotions, rather than the only solution to an inescapable problem.

Parmenides nearly closed down the new explorations (later called "philosophy") by the Milesian scientists by his rationalist announcement that Being cannot change; thus reason was declared to be an inadequate instrument for exploring our changing world. His pupil, Zeno, tried to show by his "paradoxes" that the project of "philosophy" should be given up. In a sense, Greek philosophy never recovered from this challenge; all later "philosophers" tried to make their candidates for "true being" live up to Parmenides' criteria, and still explain a changing world. They all failed.

The Atomists tried to explain the changing world as a conglomeration of changeless atoms, but their descriptions failed to satisfy our criteria of adequacy or fullness to the free, purposeful actions going on around us. Plato posited a set of static "Forms," but his device of "participation" to explain how the Forms cause sense individuals failed to satisfy even himself. Aristotle blushed to admit that his "unmoved mover" could function only as a "final cause" of the universe. His fourfold explanation of the world thus had to limp along on three legs; there could in principle be no "efficient cause" of the world. Aristotle tried to explain away the embarrassment by saying the world was eternal, but this hardly solved the problem. Even if the world is eternal, as a realm of dependent substances, it still requires an efficient cause. Strictly speaking, in Aristotle's theory there should be only God knowing himself. Nothing short of a broadening of the criterion of "perfection," the introduction of the category of the "personal" as *above* rather than *below* substance, the suggestion that there could be forms of "motion" not based on need or lack, but rather on overfullness and generosity, could solve the problem. Plotinus came as close as one can to solving this problem without challenging the convention by an ingenious combination of the received traditions; the fact that he did not challenge it is ultimately responsible for the contradictions that blemish what is still without doubt the most magnificent, successful, and satisfactory Greek philosophy.[5]

On the "origins of Christianity" as well, the "Nietzschean myth" is today in need of serious revision. After the destruction of the Temple in

AD 70, the future of Israel was up for grabs. All that was known was that the Temple priesthood and the Saducees were gone; what the future would bring, no one knew. There were several contenders, each claiming to carry forward the authentic traditions of Israel; chief among these were the Pharisees and the Christians. Matthew's gospel may be viewed as the brief for the Christian side. The question was not "Who is the true Christian," but rather "Who is the true Jew," for as yet no one knew what a "Christian" was, and Judaism had all the cachet and tradition. It was by no means assured that the Pharisees would win; in a sense, the dispute is still going on in our own day. Synagogue Judaism had developed during the Babylonian captivity and could be defined as the "condition of the Jewish people in exile," that is, when they did not have access to the Temple, which according to classical Judaism was the only place where proper worship to God could be offered.

Christianity was the "Reform Judaism" of its time, chiefly among hellenized Jews in the diaspora, that is, outside of Palestine, who were growing weary and disenchanted with the numerous obstacles which even a moderate observance of the Jewish Law placed between them and their non-Jewish colleagues.[6] Such devices created an onerous exclusionist atmosphere; also, it was becoming difficult to believe that God would be true to the promises made to Moses and renewed to the prophets, as these were traditionally interpreted, in terms of an independent Jewish nation state, and freedom of worship in the Temple, especially after AD 70. Could Judaism be "streamlined," systematically overhauled, and re-imagined from within with a new "center of gravity" for a new era where the old glories now looked like encumbrances and where there appeared to be no going back politically to a national Jewish homeland or a reconstruction of the Temple?

We know from recent scholarship that Christianity was founded, and supported for several centuries, not by gentiles seeking escape, but by Jews seeking continuity in changed circumstances.[7] They were convinced that God would not be deaf to their plea. He was still alive and cared for them. Christ himself seems to have been conspicuously a Jew of this cast. We do not intend to deny the theological dimension, but historically considered the Christian revolution within Judaism was a this-worldly solution to a this-worldly problem. What made life difficult for the Jews was an embarrassing and anachronistic Law inherited from the past, not belief in God *per se*, which was rather a step forward and, in monotheism, a giant breakthrough. The revolution or reform that occurred around Christ introduced simplification, economy, practicality, and an enormous release of the built-up tension within the institution of Judaism. We have no reason to believe that Jesus initially intended to set up another religion besides Judaism; it was only gradually that even he realized that he would not be accepted by the powers of the institution.

For the Hellenistic Jews chafing under the yoke of the Law, like St. Paul, this revolution threw open the gates to a better future in *this* world, rather than opening the possibility for a pretend "victory" in an alternative world. That this revolution incorporated gradually elements from the mystery religions around the figure of Christ is incontestable; but, given the circumstances surrounding his demise and belief in the significance of the change he had wrought (viz., that he must have been at least the equal of Moses), this can hardly be a surprise and must be viewed as a legitimate "development of doctrine," rather than an aberration, a concession to irrational forces, or a decline from an imaginary "initial purity" that was later corrupted by institutional Christianity. Just as the French Revolution was propelled by the twin ideologies of Rationalism and Romanticism, otherwise opposed, but which united to call for a critique and revision of the existing institutions, so Jewish nationalism and Hellenism, otherwise at odds, united to put forward Jesus as the "new thing" the God of the covenant had done for Israel, and now for all peoples as well. The nascent Christian movement rode the swell of the surprising and unprecedented combination of waves; Jesus was the Hegelian "synthesis" in which the previous "thesis" and "antithesis" were *aufgehoben*.

The other factor that must be mentioned in explaining the phenomenal increase of the Christian sect in all parts of the empire is opposition to the Roman Empire itself, with its cruelty that was seen as tied to the deification of the emperor. The "Kyrie Eleison" used in the mass was probably originally a way of addressing the emperor himself. The extraordinary behavior of the many Roman martyrs, from all social classes and all walks of life, is otherwise difficult to explain, and is testimony to the surprising opposition *from within* to the form the empire itself was taking. Just as the old Jewish covenant had to go, the Old Roman Empire had to go as well. It was a revolution on several fronts, but always against the *form* of the past while professing to carry what was *important* in the past forward, to salvage what was essential.

Murray and Randall, and the Nietzschean myth in general, can be said to commit the "fallacy of excessive self-doubt," or "motive-scrupulosity": the fact that there might be a *bad* reason for doing something does not mean that there is not also a *good* reason for doing the same thing. People talk themselves out of many worthwhile projects by imagining all the improper motives that might lead them to such a project, or improbable consequences that might devolve from it. This is a temptation to which our age seems especially vulnerable, because what passes for "intelligence" in the modern period is a mind that goes to excess in the abstract critical dimension. We could trace this tendency back to René Descartes' decision to alter the method of philosophy and to make combat with the *malign genie* the project of philosophy; specifically, it functions here to argue that, if there could have been a bad (irrational, escapist) motive for accepting Christianity, this must have been the *actual* motive that led people to embrace it. As a mode of reasoning, this is clearly facile, simplistic, and erroneous; indeed, it is an insult to the serious thinker and investigator. As a historical phenomenon it has created, understandably but unfortunately, the fashionable "Nietzschean myth," which is only slowly and painfully being corrected in our own day by more responsible scholarship.

Notes

[1]Edward Gibbon, *The History of the Decline and Fall of the Roman Empire*, ed. J.B. Bury, London: Methuen, 1896–1900, vol. 1, pp. 392–393.

[2]The problem is not in drawing a distinction between life-affirming and life-denying philosophies or religions, but in associating Christianity almost always with the latter. The otherwise impressive four-volume *History of Western Philosophy* by W.T. Jones is marred by passages like the following. Jones is discussing the rise of the mystery cults in connection with Pythagoreanism: "The new religious movement, introducing the worship of Dionysus, sounded a very different note [from Homer]. Here the primary motif was a yearning for immortality, motivated by a profound discontent with what was felt as the finitude, the defeats, and the inadequacies of this earthly life. This was a religion of redemption—the religion of a savior god who draws his worshiper to him in complete and joyful union." *The Classical Mind*, Harcourt, Brace & World, Inc., NY, 1969, p. 32. "Redemption" and "savior" are not terms which come down to us from the Dionysian cult; they have other associations in the collective Western consciousness.

[3]Gilbert Murray, *Five Stages of Greek Religion*, Columbia University Press, NY, 1930.

[4]John Herman Randall, Jr., *Hellenistic Ways of Deliverance and the Making of the Christian Synthesis*, Columbia University Press, NY, 1970.

[5]See my *Christian Revelation and the Completion of the Aristotelian Revolution* (University Press of America, Lanham, MD, 1988) for an extended treatment of this thesis.

[6]Hellenized Jews were prominent in the first or earliest Christian community, as we know from ch. 6 of the *Acts of the Apostles*, where the "Greeks" complain against the "Hebrews" that their widows are not receiving their fair share in the daily distribution. This was the occasion for the apostles setting up the institution of deacons.

[7]See, for example, Rodney Stark, *The Rise of Christianity: A Sociologist Reconsiders History*, Princeton University Press, Princeton, NJ, 1996, especially ch. 2, entitled "The

Class Basis of Early Christianity," which argues that Christian converts came largely from the *middle* and *upper* classes, and ch. 3, entitled "The Mission to the Jews: Why It Probably Succeeded." Stark notes that the scholarship contesting the traditional view that the Jews rejected Christianity goes back at least as far as the two-volume work by Johannes Weiss, *Earliest Christianity: A History of the Period A.D. 30–150*, Harper, NY, first published in 1914. Similarly, W.H.C. Friend, in his magisterial *The Rise of Christianity*, Fortress Press, Philadelphia, 1984, agrees with Adolf von Harnack on "the overriding importance of the Jewish Dispersion (Diaspora), not only in molding the early Christian mission but in providing the basis for its steady expansion throughout the Greco-Roman world" (p. 1). Indeed, "Greek-speaking Jews may already have shown an interest in Jesus' teaching before the crucifixion (John 12:20)," p. 86. On Paul's success being primarily among hellenized Jews and "god-fearers," see pp. 99–100.

CHAPTER 2

The God of the Temple Who Failed, Versus
The Failure Who Became The Temple of God

This article might be subtitled "the ultimate victory of anti-Davidic forces, both in Rabbinic Judaism and in Christianity, over the Davidic and priestly victory in classical Judaism expressed in national loyalty to Jerusalem and the centralization of cult in the Temple, after the latter's destruction in 70 C.E." A secondary but related claim is the surprising role played by hellenized Jews both in the initial spread of Christianity and (not so surprisingly) the later recoil from Rabbinic Judaism in the face of the latter's disappointing behavior and response to the destruction of the Temple. The hellenized Jews, especially of the diaspora, were interested in producing a non-centralized, simplified or streamlined form of Judaism more suited to a Jewish population moving freely about the empire, with no very profound desire to relocate eventually in Palestine. Christianity filled this description admirably. A third claim, and contrary to an earlier impression, is the easy commerce that persisted for centuries between church and synagogue, even after the expulsions and mutual denunciations at the official level in the wake of the loss of the Temple and consequent blame allocation, exposure to Roman persecution, and score settling—a traffic which came to an end, ironically, only when Christianity became the official religion of the empire under Constantine and the relationship between the two survivors of classical Judaism was reversed.

Christianity was created by Jews and was sustained by Greek-speaking Jews for at least the first three centuries. Hellenized Jewry was the "wind beneath the wings" of the young bird of Christianity. Ironically, the Christian mission to the Jews might have been even more successful had Christianity not become the official religion of the empire. This added an artificial external pressure which caused the Pharisaic claimants to the mantle of classical Jewry to dig in their heels and cut short any further dialogue. As in Aesop's fable about the contest between the wind and the sun to relieve the traveler of his cloak, the wind is powerful, but the sun is ultimately stronger. The Christians paid for their political victory with an interrupted dialogue and an indefinitely postponed reconciliation. By 400 C.E., civil authorities, now almost fully Christian, had begun to enact anti-Jewish penalties, often with the support of Christian leaders. The consequent alienation and mutual distrust led, not surprisingly, to a gradual decline and finally to a virtual extinction of commerce and communication between the squabbling heirs to classical Judaism.

I

Advances in the field of the "Sociology of Religion" over the past few decades have cast a novel spotlight over the history of Judaism and early Christianity, not denying the divine influence that may have been at work, but uncovering surprising, not at all obvious connections, and suggesting all too natural motivations behind developments that until now appeared swathed in otherworldly obscurity. Gerd Theissen,[1] Rodney Stark,[2] Wayne Meeks,[3] and Jack Finegan[4] are only a few of the researchers who have made signal contributions to our understanding of the forces that led Christianity from being, in 36 C.E., one of hundreds of minor sects competing within the religious bazaar of the empire, to being, 300 years later, the dominant rival to the official Roman pantheon. Consensus is far from complete and all is not clear, but enough has been accomplished to flesh out dramatically and alter a few of the landmarks in the traditional picture of the early stages of Christianity.

The most striking factor to rise in prominence is the condition of hellenized Jewry under the Seleucids, the Hasmoneans, and later the Romans. What has to be explained about Jesus is not so much Jesus, but rather the acceptance and response to Jesus. Here we must make reference to a significant reservoir of discontent among (especially, but not exclusively) the hellenized Jews of the period over the centrality of Jerusalem and its Temple, together with the dynastic Temple priesthood, in the ritual observances, and hence identity, of the Jews. While easy generalization is irresponsible, it is possible to notice in various groups a growing resentment and bid for independence from the Jerusalem Temple. The Essenes had already presumed to offer sacrifice on their own, and hence were excluded from Temple services; their belief in an afterlife owed more to Greek philosophy than to Jewish tradition.[5] Judaism at this stage was a proselytizing religion, though many God-fearers, like St. Luke, seem to have passed through Judaism and gone on to Christianity.

The spread of Christianity followed the main Jewish populations; even St. Paul always went first to the local synagogue. For almost a century, indeed, Christians were viewed by the gentile population as a species of Judaism. The splits within Palestinian Judaism between Pharisees, Saducees, and Essenes, between Galilee and Judea, between Syria, Samaria, and Israel, the obvious and embarrassing political corruption of the Temple high priesthood, together with the pressure of the occupying hellenistic culture, accentuated the messianic strain within first century Judaism, even—or perhaps especially—beyond Palestine; Apollos in Alexandria as well as the group of twelve who Paul encountered in Ephesus had first become followers of John's disciples, and John preached a baptism of repentance to prepare for the coming of the messiah.

Further, Christianity offered hellenized Jews a simplified form of allegiance to the God of Israel which made them stand out less and made them less exclusionary toward their gentile neighbors; it removed their embarrassment over a national epic and centralization of worship in the Jerusalem Temple that made them appear provincial and backward in the cosmopolitan *melieus* of Alexandria or Rome, especially in philosophical circles.[6] These factors made hellenized Jews a natural audience for the Christian announcement, as is clear from the description of the Jews who were converted at the first Pentecost—hellenized Jews in Jerusalem on pilgrimage—and who even before that Pentecost were attracted to Jesus.[7] Before we can go into this topic with any understanding, however, we do our best to make a few preliminary remarks about the powerful but problematic influence of what we may call the "Davidic strain" within classical Judaism.

II

David is the second most important figure for classical Judaism after Moses, because it was David who was considered the ideal of the monarchy, who established the capital at Jerusalem, and who commissioned the Temple. However, sufficiently important differences exist between David and Moses to render the former a problematic figure for Judaism. Whereas God himself forged the covenant on Mt. Sinai with Moses, God was opposed to the institution of the monarchy and curtly ambiguous on the suggestion of building a Temple. When David proposed to build a house for God, God deflected the suggestion somewhat indignantly by asking whether he *needed* a temple and responding that rather *he* would build a "house" for David—meaning an enduring dynasty (2 Samuel 7, 5–14). In other words, the Temple was man's idea, not God's.

Second, modern treatments of David have tended to accentuate his shrewdness over his piety—a "piety" which he seems rather to have used strategically for political purposes. He joined the Philistines to engage in banditry against Saul, but stopped short of actually laying hands on Saul ("It is not right to strike the Lord's anointed"), perhaps because he wanted to invoke the same privilege later. Saul's center had been in the north; David was resolved to control the northern tribes so that no upstart would later arise from that region. David brought the northern tribes south, but not to Bethlehem in Judah, which would have been unacceptable to them, but rather to a neutral city, Jerusalem, which he had recently conquered. He decided to make this his capital, so as not to favor any one tribe over another. David resolved to build a Temple in his capital and himself appointed the high priest, whom he could then control. David ensured that the Ark of the Covenant was placed in the Temple, since then all pilgrims would have to come there and nowhere else—and he could tax them. David has a relatively good press in the Bible primarily because the Book of Kings was written by official court historians. However, not all Jews accepted David—the northern tribes and later the Samaritans were hostile to Jerusalem and the Temple. Nor was the Jerusalem Temple or its priesthood universally popular, especially among Jews of the diaspora. Reciprocally, the Jerusalem Temple authorities and Saducees were easily threatened, which only made the situation worse.[8] The Jerusalem high priest had attacked the Samaritan temple on Mt. Gerizim. Jews who had emigrated into Egypt had built a temple of their own at Elephantine, and their priest had a better high priestly lineage than did the priestly caste in Jerusalem. The high priest of the Jerusalem temple connived with the Egyptian government to have the temple at Elephantine destroyed.

The Davidic strain in Judaism is significant because it suggests that the monarchy and the Temple were important to God—a claim which can find only an ambiguous foundation in scripture. It makes clear how crucial was the division between the "Hebrews" and the "Greeks," that is, between the Palestinian and the hellenized Jews, on the issues of primary loyalty to Jerusalem, the Temple, what the "kingdom" might be, and what the "messiah" would look like or be expected to accomplish. On these issues the two groups looked in very different directions. In particular, it makes clear how much was at stake in the Jewish revolt against the Romans in 66 C.E. and its culmination in the destruction of the Temple and expulsion of the Jews from Jerusalem. For those who identified the religion of Israel with worship of the one God in the Jerusalem Temple, and further identified God's "fidelity" or support of Israel with the city and the Temple, this result was devastating. The unsentimental Jewish priest Josephus (like St. Paul, he wrote all his works in Greek) put his own opinion into the mouth of King Herod Agrippa II: God had deserted Palestine and migrated to Italy, and the emperor Vespasian was the world ruler foretold in Hebrew prophecy.[9] If God's interests were identified with defense of the Davidic city and the Davidic Temple, that God had failed. For the second time in its history, the center of the Davidic form of its religion was removed. "Classical" Judaism was over, and it has not yet come back. The likelihood is that it never will.

III

Jesus did not extend the David strain in Judaism, except in an inverse or contrived sense so as virtually to deny the original; it would be truer to say that Jesus went back to God's first intention, which was opposed to the monarchy. If Jesus went through the scriptures with the two disciples on the road to Emmaeus explaining how they pointed to himself as messiah, this would not have taken a long time, for the only passages which really prepare us for the Jesus event are the Suffering Servant verses from Second Isaiah, the prophecy from Deuteronomy 18 about a "prophet like Moses," psalms 22 and 69, the first 30 lines of the second chapter of the Wisdom of Solomon (a late book written in Greek only a generation or two before the birth of Jesus), together with a few instances of how prophets had been badly treated. Nothing in the Mosaic or Davidic tradition prepares us for how God was being "faithful" to Israel in the Jesus event. Its attraction, therefore, especially to hellenized Jewry, had to lie elsewhere. It's "fulfillment" of the kingdom lay precisely in the fact that it *gave up* the notion of the kingdom, at least in a political sense.

All the Mosaic and Davidic precedents consist of deliverance of Isreal *from* her enemies, whereas Jesus was delivered *over to* his enemies. The only meaning that could be salvaged from this apparent disaster had to lie in the new "covenant" which Jesus deliberately pronounced the night before he died—an act which put him, daringly but consistently with some things that he had earlier said about himself, at the level of Moses at least. This act, together with his relaxation of the Law and his ambiguous relation to the Temple, was apparently sufficient for the hellenized Jews to seize upon as establishing his relevance to their complaints, grievances, and desire for an altered form of Judaism.

IV

It is wrong to view the Roman occupation of Palestine on the model of the Israelite bondage in Egypt. The Jews were not being "oppressed" by the Romans; on the contrary, the Jews had been slaughtering each other for centuries, and the Romans were invited in, largely to restore public order. In 90 B.C.E., the Pharisees invited the Seleucid Demetrius III to aid them in an insurrection against the Maccabean king Alexander Jannaeus, the great-grandson of Mattathias; when Jannaeus was able to put down the insurrection, he had eight hundred Pharisees crucified, after having their wives and children slaughtered before their eyes. When the Pharisees themselves came into power around 76 B.C.E., they took their revenge in turn by having the counselors of Jannaeus (he was already dead) crucified.[10] In the time of Jesus, Herod (an Idumean who married into the Hasmonean high priestly family) killed many Jews, including members of his own family. The Romans ruled Judea from 2 to 39 C.E., and left the Christians largely alone. For four years, however, from 39 to 44, another Jewish King, Herod Agrippa I, a friend of Caligula and Claudius, ruled Judea; it was he who started the persecution in which James, the brother of John, was killed. In 44, the Romans returned, but the governors became increasingly corrupt. In 62, during the absence of the Roman governor, the high priest Annas II had James, the brother of the Lord, killed. When the Roman governor returned, he had Annas removed for having exceeded his authority. When Josephus later raises the question of why God had allowed the Temple to be destroyed, he does not mention the Romans, but says rather that it was "because we hated one another and failed to keep His Law."

The first persecution, that which followed the martyrdom of Stephen, was crucial, because an indirect effect was that the first Christian missionaries beyond Jerusalem were hellenized Jews who had accepted Jesus. Chapter 6 in Acts shows a powerful and unassimilated group of hellenized Jews within the very earliest Jerusalem Church. The "Greeks" were unhappy because their widows were not receiving their share in the daily distribution of food. To forestall rebellion, Peter appointed seven "deacons" from among their own group. A misunderstanding here must be corrected; these "deacons" were leaders in the fullest sense—the equivalent of later "bishops," not "food servers" or manual laborers. Among them is Stephen—the Greek word means "crown"—who gives a powerful speech against the Jews with a noticeable anti-Temple animus (Acts 7:48–50). His death sparks the first persecution, which drives out not the apostles or the Hebrews but the "hellenists" from the city. This first persecution thus has the important consequence of making hellenized Jewish-Christians carry the new faith into Judea and Samaria.

It is only in John's gospel that Jesus goes into Samaria; indeed, in the synoptics, he avoids Samaritan towns and expressly forbids his disciples from going into Samaria (Matthew 10, 5). Scholars now feel that the exchange between Jesus and the Samaritan woman at the well in John's gospel may well be a an epitome of the kind of "gospel" the first generation of missionaries preached when they reached Samaria:

> Believe me, woman, the hour is coming
> when you will worship the Father
> neither on this mountain nor in Jerusalem . . .
> The hour is coming—indeed is already here—
> when true worshippers will worship the Father in spirit and in truth.[11]

Thus, acceptable worship of God need not take place in the Jerusalem Temple, but could in principle take place anywhere. This is precisely the kind of gospel one would expect to hear from a hellenized Jew who had become a Christian. Impatience with the centralized cult and elaborate dietary laws characterized the hellenized Jew's stance toward his own faith, and Jesus' message on both counts would have been viewed as positive.[12] At Acts:11, 20, Luke tells us that it was the Hellenists—not the apostles—who first preached Christianity to the gentiles.

V

The gospels themselves show strong hellenizing tendencies.[13] First of all, it is now the general scholarly opinion that none of the gospels was written by an eyewitness to Jesus, that they were all written in Greek, that Mark and Matthew were hellenized Jewish Christians, Luke was a Gentile who had probably been a "god-fearer," and that even John's gospel received a final redaction by a hellenized Jewish Christian —probably in Ephesus—before it attained the form in which it has come down to us. Further, "Q"—the body of the sayings of Jesus that is thought to have been a common source for Matthew and Luke— was used by them in a Greek edition. The author of the first gospel, Mark, was a cousin of Barnabas, and thus a Jew of the diaspora, perhaps also from Cyprus. Mark is a Greek name, and Mark is sometimes confused about Palestinian geography. Further, the intended audience was most likely the community of Greek-speaking Christians in Rome (whether originally Jewish or Gentile) who has originally been evangelized by Jewish Christians.

If Matthew the apostle—and tax-collector—had been the author of the gospel which bears his name, we would not be surprised to discover the viewpoint of an alienated Jew fully at home in the Greco-Roman world of his masters, and with scant respect for the Temple authorities, who long before had made their own comfortable accommodation with the occupying forces, and yet looked down upon such persons as tax-collectors as not able to fulfill the Law, ritually unclean, and thus not worthy to participate in certain Temple services. As it happens, however, scholarly opinion is almost unanimous that the author of Matthew's gospel was a *diaspora* Jew, probably of Antioch, for the use of the Antiochean Church which had been mostly Jewish-Christian but was becoming increasingly Gentile in composition. Antioch had been first evangelized by hellenized Jewish-Christians fleeing Jerusalem after the martyrdom of Stephen, and it was in Antioch that these missionaries for the first time preached directly to Gentiles. Also, it would be Antioch, and not Jerusalem, that would sponsor Paul's missions to the Gentiles, to found "little Antiochs." There are indications in Matthew that, after the Jewish Rebellion and the destruction of Jerusalem, the Jews turned angrily against their Jewish-Christian relatives for not standing with them. The latter were "scourged" and "thrown out of the synagogues." Thus, such Jews who remained with the Antioch Christian community had to break not only with the Temple but also with the synagogue, and thus turn increasingly to the Gentile world. Matthew has the Magi coming from the East, he adds the story about Jesus healing the Centurion's serving boy, and he has a strong "replacement" theme by stressing parallels between Jesus and Moses.

Luke is the only Gentile evangelist, and his Greek is better than the others. He was also from outside Palestine, probably Syrian Antioch. He accompanies Paul on his second, and perhaps third missionary journey, his return to Jerusalem, and his final trip to Rome. Luke had perhaps been a "god-fearer" for some years before he became a Christian; he knows the Septuagint, but perhaps not Hebrew or Aramaic. Luke's two-volume work is intended to assure the churches descended from Paul's mission about the authenticity of their foundations and against calumnies stemming from the non-Jewish, hellenistic world. In Luke's gospel Jesus is open to Samaritans, shepherds, and other groups marginalized by the Law. Acts ends in Rome, symbolically the center of the Gentile world, and the last lines (28:25–28), attributed to Paul, indicate that the future of the gospel lies with the Gentiles, not with the Jews. In the Acts, both Peter and Paul have powerful experiences which "open their eyes" to the fact that the Law has been abrogated in view of the "new thing" God has done. Peter has a vision of a cloth descending from heaven on which are various foods prohibited by the Law, but he is told to "take up and eat." Then Peter is taken to Cornelius, a Gentile, and witnesses that the Holy Spirit, God's gift to the Church after the departure of Jesus, has been poured upon Cornelius and his family as well. Paul similarly is transformed from a diaspora Jew fanatical about the Law to a Christian convert whose position is so latitudinarian as to strike Peter, James, Barnabas, and perhaps even "Matthew" as shocking and excessive.

John's gospel has had the most complicated development. The "beloved disciple" was probably a minor figure in the entourage of Jesus during his ministry, certainly not an "apostle," a term which never appears in John. The beloved disciple made early contact with Jews of an anti-Temple bias who made converts in Samaria (John 4). The Samaritans were Jews who rejected the work of David; for them Moses was the salvific figure *par excellence*. Jesus became the new Moses, the pre-existent Wisdom of God, who did not have to go "up" to receive the tablets from God because he was already in God's presence, and thus only needed to come down. This led the beloved disciple to develop a scandalously high christology, identifying Jesus not only with the "Son of Man" who would return at the end of the ages to judge the world, but also as the "*Logos*" of God present with him before the creation of the world, mentioned in Sirach 24 and Wisdom 9. Only in John's gospel does Jesus explicitly claim to be God. The gospel in this form was most probably written down by a follower of the "beloved disciple."

Not surprisingly, after the Jewish council of Jamna, this led to long debates with the Jews, and to John's community eventually being expelled from the synagogues. The community then moved to the Greek-speaking diaspora, perhaps Ephesus, where the gospel went through a final redaction by a hellenized Jewish-Christian. There was the introduction of a universalistic horizon, and a harsh depiction of the Jews as the "Pharisees." There is also a strong replacement motif of all things Jewish with Jesus and the Church. The Johannine community, however, with its high christology bordering on the docetic (denying the human nature of Jesus) and its weak, anti-authoritarian structure basing everything on love, was unstable and soon fell apart. What remained of it was absorbed by the greater Church.

VI

The Pauline Settlement Paul is remembered by many Christians for having stared down Peter when the later came to Antioch and preferred to observe Jewish dietary laws when eating with Jews, but in fact Peter's behavior exemplifies perfectly the Pauline latitudinarian ethic, based on a "freedom" that Christians have won over the Law through Christ, together with a sensitivity to the limitations of those with whom we find ourselves, such as those who object to eating meat that has previously been sacrificed to idols. Paul won a major concession from James and the Jerusalem Church by being allowed to accept gentiles as Christians through baptism without circumcision; that is, gentiles could become Christians without first becoming Jews. This seemed strange to James and the Jerusalem Church, and in a sense they were right: Why would anyone be interested in accepting Jesus as the messianic fulfillment of the Jewish expectations, if they were not first seriously interested in Judaism? Christianity would only be of interest or appeal to people who took the Jewish religion seriously; if you accept Jesus as the fulfillment of the promises, don't you have to accept the promises as well?

Nevertheless, they eventually, if reluctantly, granted Paul his freedom in return for certain minimal concessions—avoiding irregular sexual attachments, not eating the meat of strangled animals, etc. What is often overlooked is that, in return for this signal change in the conditions for entering the Christian community, Paul allowed a great freedom in the extent to which the proselytes could carry on Jewish practices—up to and including full observance of the Law. Indeed, when Paul went back to Jerusalem, he himself went to the Temple to give indications that he observed the Law (Acts 21:26). In short, he behaved exactly as had Peter when the latter came to Antioch, except, of course, that Paul was then no longer in a mixed company, where his "Judaizing" behavior might give offense.[14] In other words, the significance of the Pauline settlement is that Paul was able to maintain fellowship (*koinonia*) with the more traditionally Jewish Jerusalem Church, winning a relaxation on the issue of circumcision by simultaneously tolerating a wide variety of Jewish practices. While these were not necessary to salvation, and Paul himself preferred to do without them —witness his reaction to the "super-apostles" who came to Corinth from Jerusalem preaching a more "Jewish" form of Christianity, which was the typical attitude of a strongly hellenized Jew from Tarsus!—still he was tolerant of almost any practice which some Jews converted to Christianity might wish to carry forward.

Thus, in the 50s and 60s, there was undoubtedly a wide variety of practice among the Christian communities of the eastern Mediterranean, but all would have appeared far more Jewish than anything we would recognize today as a "Christian liturgy." Paul is significant for insisting upon an exclusively "Christian" theology, where Christ replaces the Law and Temple sacrifice as our means of salvation, but also for allowing a wide variety *of practices* in which the key issue remains pastoral sensitivity to people's needs and expectations. If a large number of converts in a Christian community had formerly been Jews, then one would tolerate a greater continuity with Jewish practices. We know, in fact, that judaizing sects of Christians, successors to the Syrian "Ebionites" mentioned in patristic literature, such as the "Quarto-decimans" and the "Athingani," persisted well into the Byzantine empire.[15]

VII

According to Eusebius, the Christians did not participate in the Jewish revolt against Rome, which began in 66 C.E. Instead, they left the city. After the Temple was destroyed in 70, we are told that the Jewish leaders blamed their "Jewish" brothers who accepted Christ as the messiah as at best cowards, and at worst traitors, and turned against them in two ways: various synagogues expelled the Christianized Jews from their midst, and some informed the Roman authorities that Christians were now a group distinct from the Jews and should no longer benefit from the Jewish privilege of being free from the obligation to emperor-worship. This had the effect of exposing Christians to Roman persecution.

It is not difficult to imagine the effect on Christianized Jews this behavior by the Rabbinic authorities would have had. This response would have appeared disappointing on several scores: First of all, they saw the acceptance of Jesus as the messiah as no betrayal or defection from Judaism, but rather as the fulfillment of their Jewish faith. Second, after the destruction of the Temple, the center and core of classical Judaism was removed. It is difficult to exaggerate the significance of this event for the Davidic strain of Judaism—which was essentially the same as classical Judaism, since David had commissioned most of the historical books, and the priestly authorities had "edited" most of the others to make sure they favored the monarchy and the Temple. For the

Davidic wing of Judaism, the center was now void, there was nothing to go back to; however, rather than accepting this change and moving "forward," the synagogue authorities seemed resolved to act as though nothing had happened and to remain set in their ways. As a comparison, one is reminded of the old schoolyard tag: "Aside from that, Mrs. Lincoln, how did you enjoy the play?" To many hellenized Jews, Rabbinic Judaism seemed resolved to enter into a pathetic charade based on denial and self-delusion. However, certain changes were too significant to overlook. As an example, the most sacred day in Judaism is Yom Kippur, the Day of Atonement. Strictly speaking, there has been no atonement in Judaism since the year 70, because for atonement to take place, the high priest must enter the Temple and throw blood upon the alter. This has not happened since the year 70.

This recalcitrance, not only in the face of Jesus' message but equally before the decisive later loss of the Temple, caused the hellenized Jews who had accepted Jesus to throw up their hands in exasperation. They retaliated against their expulsions from the synagogues by instituting a program for a full-scale replacement in the Christian liturgy of the Jewish elements.[16] The Pauline settlement was over; the wide variety of Christian practice, ranging from full observance of the Jewish law and participation in synagogue services to relatively minimal observance, was slowly done away with, as the hellenized Jewish-Christians now realized they had to develop both a theory and a practice which emphasized Christ as the legitimate replacement for the Law and the Temple.

The lines hardened; people on both sides dug in their heels. Stubbornness and intractability took the place of reason and insight, masquerading as courage. Dialogue and growth came to an end. Both sides settled down to a protracted standoff, each side nursing memories of outrage and injustice, in place of reason, to justify its present posture. Had the other not been there, it would have been impossible for each side to continue in its stance without appearing ridiculous and a mockery even in its own eyes. We carried on out of spite, if for no other reason, so as not to give the other satisfaction.

However, the so-called "Council of Jamna" in 72 C.E., by which the Pharisee party consolidated its hold over the future of classical Judaism, did not bring about a cessation of contacts between the Christian and Jewish communities. Almost exactly the opposite took place, because for many hellenized Jews, Christianity was the legitimate heir to the mantle of classical Judaism; Matthew's gospel presents the Christian brief in this debate. In the face of later denunciations between the two groups, individual Jews continued to migrate freely back and forth between the two camps.

Of course, hellenized Jews were not the only source of new "Christians"—a name first used in the Antioch community which admitted gentiles. There was clearly dismay in certain Jewish-Christian communities, such as the Jerusalem community, at the influx of gentiles into the new "way." That there was "envy of the Jews" by the gentiles, in the sense of admiration for their monotheism, their solidarity and social values, and their steadfastness under persecution, is undoubtedly true. At the same time, in the face of the Jewish revolt of 66 C.E., which brought unprecedented suffering to Jews in Palestine, and the later failed revolt of Bar Kochba in 132 C.E., there was also exasperation felt toward classical Judaism—and not only by gentiles. The non-violence of Hillel, which became normative for later Pharasaic Judaism, was not characteristic of classical Judaism. Indeed, later Pharasaic Judaism was accused of being too passive, and Jews were looked upon almost as apostles of Gandhian non-violence. Again this is the opposite of the way Jews of the time of Christ were regarded. Clearly a decision was called for, personal and painful. Even for those who remained Jews, there was a marked change; in its attitude toward violence, later Pharasaic Judaism had more in common with Christianity than it had with classical Judaism.

Viewed as opposed from within, from without the two groups appeared to have as much in common as they had differences. Only gradually did Christians separate from Jews in public perception. The benediction in the Talmud calling down a curse upon the Nazarene and his followers was only inserted in the fifth or sixth century—after the civil authorities had begun to enact anti-Jewish penalties.

VIII

It now seems safe to say that, without hellenized Jews, Christianity would never have expanded from being a small sect of the Nazarene in the year 36 to become the dominant rival to the traditional cult of the pagan gods by the year 300. Hellenized Jewry seems to have been like a super-saturated chemical solution, awaiting only the introduction of a catalyst for crystals of a new form to begin to precipitate out. The Christian message was that catalyst, and the reaction was swift and strong. It begins with Paul and continues unabated for several hundred years. Christianity was in fact a rather unimpressive catalyst. After all, by any human measure, Jesus had failed. Jesus' public ministry had been barely three years, and had ended confusedly and inauspiciously as regards his followers, all of whom fled, after the leader, Peter, had denied him three times. No one could have predicted a strong afterlife for this sect. However, Jesus' interests coincided sufficiently with the complaints and grievances of hellenized Jewry, both inside and outside Palestine—in fact, expansion to a "gentile church" does not seem to have been part of Jesus' intention—that many hellenized Jews responded with alacrity and enthusiasm to this, admittedly minimal, token of direction and leadership. Jesus' martyrdom was no handicap; violence at the hands of the Roman rulers was a daily occurrence, and the fact that their own Temple authorities had connived in his arrest and execution only added to his attraction, since opposition to the centralization of cult in the Jerusalem Temple, as well as to the corrupt Temple authorities, was a major complaint and point in their program for a "streamlined" Judaism that would be more suited to an outward-looking, expanding, cosmopolitan Jewish population.

The ironies that result from this situation are prodigious. First of all, most modern Jews have thrown off the Davidic strain from classical Judaism as completely as have the Christians. That is, most contemporary Jews do not want to see the Temple rebuilt and the return of Judaism to its classical form. Rabbinic Judaism, apart from the extreme orthodox interpretation, is an expression of the victory of the irritation and chafing of hellenized Jewry over a primary loyalty to Jerusalem and the centralization of cult in the Temple as completely as is Christianity. The two siblings have more in common with one another than they have with classical Judaism. The emotions are the greater because what divides them is so small.

Second, as said, the Christian "mission to the Jews" (carried out primarily by hellenized Jews) was much longer and more successful than is generally imagined, and more deeply, might have been even more successful had not Christianity become the official religion of the empire under Constantine. This added an artificial external pressure that shifted the issue and skewed the discussion from a response to the "new thing" God had done, to a loyalty to tradition under persecution, that spoiled the disinterested openness in which the discussion could have been carried further. The Christian option was a creation by Jews and for Jews as a response to their own tradition; apart from that, it makes no sense. Now that the West has no "official religion" in a sense, perhaps, with that artificial pressure removed, the discussion can resume and move on in the direction of a more satisfying conclusion.

Notes

[1] See Gerd Theissen, *Sociology of Early Palestinian Christianity*, Philadelphia: Fortress Press, 1978; also *The Social Setting of Pauline Christine: Essays on Corinth*, Philadelphia: Fortress Press, 1982.

[2] See Rodney Stark, *The Rise of Christianity; A Sociologist Reconsiders History*, Princeton University Press, Princeton, 1996.

[3] See Wayne Meeks, *The First Urban Christians*, New Haven: Yale UP, 1983; also with Robert L. Wilken, *Jews and Christians in Antioch in the First Four Centuries of the Common Era*, Missoula: Scholars Press, 1978.

[4] Jack Finegan, *The Archeology of the New Testament*, rev. ed., Princeton: Princeton University Press, 1992.

[5] See G.A. Williamson, *The World of Josephus*, London: Secker & Warburg, 1964, pp. 97–98.

[6] See Rodney Stark, *The Rise of Christianity; A Sociologist Reconsiders History*, Princeton: Princeton University Press, 1996, ch. 3, "The Mission to the Jews: Why It Probably Succeeded," esp. pp. 57–68.

[7] See John 12:20–22.

[8] F.E. Peters sees the opposition between Pharisees and Saducees as essentially a conflict between a "classical" Judaism of the Temple and an emerging Judaism of the Law: "The Saducees' narrow body of Scripture freed them from assent to the evolving form of post-exilic Judaism that was at the heart of the Pharisees' program . . . With the exile, history had taken the temple from the hands of the priests. In the place of the temple now stood the Law, and in the place of the priests, the scribes, a new class unconnected with priestly pedigrees. The scribes became the custodians fo the new Jewish City of God, whose constitution was set down in the Torah but whose understanding was encompassed in the oral tradition." See F.E. Peters, *The Harvest of Hellenism: A History of the Near East from Alexander the Great to the Triumph of Christianity*, NY, Simon & Schuster, 1970, pp. 289–90.

[9] Josephus, *The Jewish War*, tr. Williamson, Penguin Books, Harmondsworth, 1959, pp. 149. As G.A. Williamson puts it in *The World of Josephus* (London: Secker & Warburg, 1964, p. 57), "It is no doubt true that as the Christians believed that in rejecting Christ the Jews had forfeited their privileges as the people of God, so Josephus would have his readers believe that in rebelling against Rome his countrymen had finally and for all time offended the Deity, and driven Him as it were into the camp of their enemies." On Josephus' view that Vespasian was the messiah, see. p. 65.

[10] See Elias Bickerman, *From Ezra to the Last of the Maccabees: Foundations of Postbiblical Judaism*, NY: Schocken, 1962, pp. 168–169.

[11] John 4, 21–24; Jerusalem Bible.

[12] On the role of hellenized Jews in the formation of John's gospel, see Raymond E. Brown's reconstruction of this process in *An Introduction to the New Testament*, Doubleday, NY, 1997, pp. 373–76.

[13] All the material presented in this section on the composition of the gospels can be found in Raymond Brown's magisterial final work, *An Introduction to the New Testament*, NY: Doubleday, 1997.

[14] Raymond Brown even speculates that, had Paul had a son, he almost certainly would have had him circumcised. Circumcision is not necessary for salvation, but according to Paul, even in the new dispensation, Jews enjoy certain "privileges," and Paul would undoubtedly not have wanted to deprive his son of these traditional privileges. See Raymond E. Brown, *Introduction to the New Testament*, Doubleday, NY, 1997, p. 438.

[15]See Cyril Mango, *Byzantium: the Empire of New Rome*, NY: Charles Scribner's Sons, 1980, p. 103.

[16]Christian scriptures from the '90s of the first century showed a marked anti-Temple of anti-Jewish animus over writings from the '60s; for example, the gospel of John, the letter to the Hebrews, and 1st Peter. John's gospel shows a more hostile attitude toward "the Jews" than do the synoptics, and refers to Christians being "thrown out of the synagogues" (John 16, 1–4; see also 15, 20–25). The letter to the Hebrews builds an elaborate comparison on the priesthood and Temple, but now the emphasis is on the *heavenly* temple which God revealed to Moses, on which the earthly temple is based and from which it is derivative. More deeply, Jesus replaces the Jewish cult. 1st Peter is written to gentiles, whom it informs: "You who were not a people are now a people." In the Jewish understanding, there is only *one* people, the Jews themselves, made so by God. By contrast, now 1st Peter can tell the gentiles "You are a chosen people" (1st Peter 2, 9–10; see also 4, 12–17).

CHAPTER 3

Plotinus' Pyrrhic Victory

With Plotinus we approach one of the most interesting and attractive figures in the unfolding dialectic of Western thought. He was long neglected because of his difficult style and because his period—the mid-third century—falls between the centers of gravity of Greek philosophy and medieval philosophy, respectively. He is compelling because he recognized the central deficiency within the Platonic-Aristotelian tradition—its failure to explain why there is a world—and he mobilized the full resources of their common philosophical tradition to come up with a solution within the conventions of divine existence which this tradition recognized. He supplied the two devices that later scholastic philosophy would develop to meet the objections stemming from the Greek convention of perfection both to the Christian "good news" as well as to why there is anything besides God: that in knowing himself, God could simultaneously know the world as his effect or as a possible likeness to himself, and that in loving himself most intensely, God would naturally be led to want to share this goodness with others.[1] In other words, there is no necessary opposition between God's *egotism* and his *altruism*, to use words from a later era; they are directly, and not inversely, related.

Unfortunately, Plotinus did not exploit these devices to the full but, under the influence of the Parmenidean-Aristotelian convention, chose to see the "One" as unable to attend to beings outside itself; each level of reality is produced necessarily as the proper consequence and reflection in a lower order of the one above it, and the entire world below the "One" is produced to give full amplitude in the lower orders to the One's glory, but (by default) without intention or knowledge. If the One were to know the world, it would automatically fall to the lower level; thus it must be held aloof. However, by also carrying forward the "subversive" Platonic tradition of the Good as inherently overflowing, generous, and dispersive, Plotinus pushed the Parmenidean-Aristotelian convention of perfection dangerously close to the notion of "person," with its connotations of interaction, reciprocity, and mutuality, thereby making significant practical concessions to the portrait of God being insistently promoted by the rising Judeo-Christian tradition, concessions that perhaps stop just short of representing, by the identity of indiscernibles, capitulation and surrender.[2] Thus Plotinus' "victory" may have in the long run been "Pyrrhic."

The central and most difficult doctrine for the reader to grasp is the unity of creation, determined existence, and salvation in Plotinus. Each hypostasis or level of reality follows the pattern of the One. Each "thing" produces an indeterminate "matter," which only attains form and determinate existence when it "converts" or turns back and contemplates its source. It then is "saved" insofar as it can be, attains form or specific existence, is filled with the One or the "Good" insofar as it can be, and spontaneously becomes creative itself.

Salvation is not all things rising to one level, the highest level; rather it is each thing rising to its *appropriate* level, which is the level of its determinate existence. There it becomes as full of its particular goodness as it can be, and then follows the law by which each thing in its mature form, following goodness itself, seeks to diffuse itself and also imitate the highest reality by producing others like itself, thereby achieving a kind of immortality. Creation is good, not evil; there are no evil layers of creation, not even the lowest, weakest, unformed matter, which is unable to turn back toward its source. Each thing thus becomes a miniature version of the One, saved and creative at the same time, although the latter does not have to undergo a process to achieve this. Salvation, determined existence, and creativity coincide; we become creative *only* when we are saved, and in contact with the forms above us. Each thing creates, not only the One above, and each thing creates only the level immediately below it. Further, each thing creates for the best of possible motives, the good's natural desire to share or diffuse itself; there is no rebellion or jealousy in this creation. That way the entire universe is filled up, and everything is as it should be. You don't have to die to go to heaven; you are already there.

What is striking from a Christian point of view is how ingeniously Plotinus mobilized the resources of Greek philosophy to engineer a means of "salvation"—that is, of conversion, ascent, and ultimate union with the One—in a world without grace, that is, without a notion of the highest cause as a person. Knowledge makes a metaphysical difference for the Greeks; as Aristotle puts it, in the act of knowing, knower and known become one.[3] This means in practice that one rises or falls to the level of the object one is contemplating. Knowing the wrong kinds of objects has been responsible for our fall; our souls turned from respectful attention to the Forms at the level of the Second Hypostasis, or Intelligence, because of an ambition to rule their insubstantial copies in the realm of matter, and automatically fell to their level.[4]

Our presence here is good for matter, but bad for us. Matter cannot be "saved" or organized beyond a certain level, despite our best efforts; further, this administration can be more expeditiously and (for ourselves) less injuriously carried out at the level of the Third Hypostasis, World Soul, where the soul would "save" matter as far as it can be saved without becoming distracted from its primary activity of contemplating what is above it. Thus, our "salvation" consists of exploiting knowledge to *reverse* the direction of our first independent foray or initiative into reality, and thereby to correct this minor blemish or "hitch" we have introduced into the cosmic pattern. Otherwise, everything is well; the world is the best it can or could be, because it gives maximal expression to the goodness of the One. By "converting" or turning our gaze to objects above us, we can pull ourselves hand over hand back whence we have fallen, with no "help" from grace. The One was oblivious to our fall, and will be equally indifferent to our salvation. The latter is something that *we* arrange, and is of interest only to ourselves; it is definitely *not* of cosmic significance. The harmony, balance, and perfection of the universe are maintained essentially the same after as before, no matter what we do. Everything is as it is and has to be. The best is the best, and everything after that is as good as it possibly can be. Nothing could be better.

Plotinus adds a special device beyond Plato to aid us in this ascent, because he must dispense with divine assistance, which would violate the Parmenidean/Aristotelian conventions of perfection. For Plotinus, our "higher soul" has never really fallen into matter, but is even now faithfully maintaining its position at the level of World Soul, gazing upward into Intelligence. This may serve as a "piton" or Archimedian fixed point by which we can direct our ascent. Its presence establishes a kind of "elevator shaft" by which we may hoist ourselves up to the precise point we occupied before, again emphatically under our own power. Salvation or union with God happens just as in the Christian view, except that there is no grace. Luckily, there doesn't have to be. Knowledge is sufficient. It has to do it all, because there is nothing else. Without it, there would be no salvation.

Plotinus may be said to produce an impressive but unsurprising synthesis of Platonic and Aristotelian philosophy, which became the common ambition of his successors Porphyry, Iamblichus, and Proclus, but with three remarkable additions. These additions lead into one another; they start with one that may be viewed as a permissible and legitimate extension of Plato's description of the Form of the Good, and move on to conclusions that are progressively more surprising and foreign to anything for which Plato or Aristotle have prepared us. The first seems innocent enough, but imperceptibly we are led into territory very different from the Platonic-Aristotelian philosophy, and finally into a landscape that is indiscernibly different from the Judeo-Christian tradition, or more accurately, helped to *create* the landscape of the Judeo-Christian tradition after the first three centuries.

Plato had described the Form of the Good as "above Being," that is, as higher than the unchanging type of existence that for him characterized the Forms. In the *Republic*, VI, 508, he describes the Form of the Good as similar to the sun in the visible world, responsible for our ability to see correctly the world around us, and perhaps for there being a world at all. For the Greek tradition up to this point, finitude had been a synonym and necessary attribute of perfection; what was "infinite" was unbounded, unshaped, unfinished, indefinite, and ugly. For Aristotle, "Infinity" was more a characteristic of matter than of form. Following the Parmenidean tradition, Plato reserved the term "Being" for the kind of existence characteristic of the Forms, in contrast to the "Becoming" which characterized the objects of the sense world. Thus changelessness and finitude would be defining attributes of the realm of "Being."

However, as said, Plato seems to elevate the "Form of the Good" (or the "One") to a position of preeminence over the other Forms, and even gives it the puzzling description of "above Being." Given this Platonic background, it is not illegitimate, though certainly innovative and a bit daring, for Plotinus subsequently to describe the One as "infinite." This move may be defended in a Platonic spirit as a way to mark its difference or preeminence over the other Forms, but it is daring in calling into being a new sense for "infinite," this time as meaning a type of perfection *above* that of the Forms, besides its previous sense as a type of existence *below* the Forms. This is Plotinus' first addition to his otherwise impressive but unremarkable synthesis.

The second is a corollary of the first, and is even more surprising. It is a thesis Plotinus returns to again and again: that the One is *immediately* present to every soul below it, even those which have fallen into "matter."[5] This is an unexpected departure from the hierarchical pattern and system of relationships which have characterized both the

Platonic description of the levels of reality in the allegories of the Cave and Divided Line, as well as Aristotle's description of his "unmoved mover" as engaging is self-contemplation and moving all things by attraction, itself unmoved and unattracted by any of them. Because Plotinus has previously described the One as "infinite," it is theoretically *possible* for the One to relate to other beings directly, in a manner outside the hierarchical structure, without going, so to speak, through the normal "command structure," but it certainly represents a departure from and apparent violation of the previous Platonic-Aristotelian tradition to hold that it does so. Even Plato, in stating that the "Good" is naturally dispersive, generous, and desires to share itself, develops this theme not to suggest the possibility of a personal relationship, but rather to explain the production of other levels of reality below the "One" or the "Good." His new doctrine of a higher "infinity" has been used here by Plotinus to break down the walls of finitude and proportionate love that had until now been a cardinal element and defining feature of the Platonic-Aristotelian tradition.

In this tradition, the higher never stoops or inclines toward the lower; rather, it is for the lower to "convert," to reorient itself, and thereby to ascend to the higher.[6] Love should be proportional to its object; it is wrong, indeed obscene, to love an object above or below its merits. This doctrine creates a problem when it comes to explaining why there is a world at all, or at least a world below the divine. According to Aristotle, the divine must be engaged in the highest activity, and that directed to the highest object. In other words, the divine must be self-preoccupied. While Aristotle officially has a difficulty explaining why there is a world—his "unmoved mover" can function as a "final cause" for the universe, but not as an "efficient cause"—Plotinus fixes upon another tradition Aristotle brings forward in his "unofficial" doctrine that every being, when it reaches its term or perfection, naturally attempts to bring into being another like itself (*Meteorology* 4, 3, 380a12 ff)—in other words, Aristotle's way of carrying on Plato's doctrine that the Good is naturally dispersive. Plotinus develops this "subversive" Aristotelian doctrine to explain the necessary but unintended production of the lower levels of reality from the One: This happens primarily in the Fifth *Ennead*, which begins thus:

> If there is anything after the First, it must necessarily come from the First; it must either come from it directly or have its ascent back to it through the beings between, and there must be an order of seconds

and thirds, the second going back to the first and the third to the second. For there must be something simple before all things, and this must be other than all the things which come after it, existing by itself, not mixed with the things which derive from it, and all the same able to be present in a different way to these other things, being really one, and not a different being and then one; it is false even to say of it that it is one, and there is "no concept or knowledge" of it; it is indeed also said to be "beyond being." For if it is not to be simple, outside all coincidence and composition and really one, it could not be a first principle; and it is the most self-sufficient, because it is simple and the first of all: for that which is not the first needs that which is before it, and what is not simple is in need of its simple components so that it can come into existence from them. (V.4; tr. Armstrong)

Plotinus continues:

Now when anything else comes to perfection we see that it produces, and does not endure to remain by itself, but makes something else. This is true not only of things which have a choice, but of things which grow and produce without choosing to do so, and even lifeless things, which impart themselves to others as far as they can: as fire warms, snow cools, and drugs act on something else in a way corresponding to their nature . . . How then could the most perfect, the first Good, remain in itself as if it grudged to give of itself or was impotent, when it is the productive power of all things. (V.4. I.27–38)

There is a three-beat syncopation to the production of each subsequent level of reality:

In each and every thing there is an activity of the substance and there is an activity from the substance; and that which is of the substance is each thing itself, while the activity from the substance derives from the first one, and must in everything be a consequence of it, different from the thing itself: as in fire there is a heat which is the content of its substance, and another which comes into being from that primary heat when fire exercises the activity which is native to its substance in abiding unchanged as fire. So it is also in the higher world; and much more so there, while (the One) abides in its own proper way of life, the activity generated from the perfection in it and its coexistent activity acquires existence (*hypostasi*) since it comes from a great power, the greatest indeed of all, and arrives at being and substance, for that is beyond being. That is the productive power of all, and its product is already all things. (V.4. 2. 28–39)

As Professor Gatti explains the procession beyond the One:
(T)he generation of the intelligible hypostases and, in part, of the physical cosmos . . . beyond the two activities mentioned, includes a further activity that is equally essential, namely, the *epistrophĕ*, that is, the return to the contemplation of the generating principle. . . . In many passages of the *Enneads* Plotinus has highlighted the metaphysical return of the generated to the generator, owing to which the first acquires its own determination. We see, for example, this return in the passage from the first to the second hypostasis. The power that comes from the One does not directly generate *nous*, but rather an indeterminate and shapeless intelligible matter, that determines itself and becomes the world of forms only as a result of contemplating the first principle. . . . In this derivative procession the determining element is the return or conversion rather than the flowing . . . Plotinus has in large part anticipated Proclus, presenting a circular triadic law that unfolds according to an articulation of stability, that is, immanent activity in each hypostasis; progression, that is, activity that derives from each hypostasis; finally, turning and return, that is, conversion to the preceding hypostasis. In the process of the derivation from the One, indeed, there was no question of a flowing of the substance of the first principle, but of its potency, much less a kind of physical necessity, but a necessity that follows from the supreme act of freedom, the self-willing of the first hypostasis.[7]

As said, this production is unintentional, does not involve a distraction of the higher from its essential self-preoccupation, nor is the higher "diminished" by this production. All the Parmenidean-Aristotelian conventions of perfection are observed; yet Plotinus has managed to inject Plato's doctrine of the naturally dispersive Good into the highest principle by making self-contemplation naturally, even if unintentionally, productive.

The third addition is related to the second: By turning to contemplate what lies above it, the human soul may ascend not only to the level of World Soul, from which it initially descended, but may even ascend *above* World Soul to Intelligence and even possibly to union with the One; Plotinus believed himself to have attained union with the One four times during his life.[8] Again this doctrine is grounded in the Aristotelian tenet that in knowledge, knower and known become one, and the distinctive Plotinian tenet concerning the permanent accessibility and availability of the One itself. (Augustine's theology shows a marked influence from Plotinus, and nowhere more than here: his description in *The Confessions* of Jesus as the "interior teacher" who is "closer to me than I am to myself"—*tu autem eras interior intimo meo et superior summo meo*, III, vi. 11.) Nothing in the earlier Platonic or Aristotelian tradition prepares us for this third addition; by its interiority alone, leaving aside its outrageous theology, it runs fundamentally counter to the extrovertish, politically oriented, and finitely grounded perfection for human beings described in all of Plato's and Aristotle's works.

Here one has to wonder whether Plotinus has not so modified the notion of divinity coming down to him, and which he defends as faithfully Platonic, as to make it indiscernibly different from the rival, activist, and personal portrait of the divinity proffered by the emerging Judeo-Christian tradition. Specifically, has not Plotinus in practice or effect thrown over the entire Parmenidean-Platonic-Aristotelian tradition, according to which true Being is changeless and, if personal, necessarily self-absorbed? It is Plotinus' official position that the One is not interested in a relationship with an individual soul, nor is this the reason the One produced a world. The reflection of his glory he receives at the level of World Soul is sufficient remuneration. Or expressed more stringently, the thinking and loving relationship with itself is so eminently satisfying and unparalleled that the attractions of a relationship with a derivative being pale by comparison. Such a relationship would violate the principle that love must be proportional to its object.

At most the One would be willing to grant a lower being such a share in its self-comprehension and self-love as the latter is able to attain, since then the universe is in good order and the One is getting back the glory from the created world it deserves; but the universe *as a whole* is the "reason" the One made the world, not any particular part of it, since the existence of the universe as a whole is necessary to fully express and reflect back to the only audience that matters—the One itself—the only message that matters, which is how good the One is. The One allows us to indulge in this as far as we may, but its enjoyment of itself is not enhanced thereby. The enjoyment by particular souls is tolerated, but not expressly desired. We gorge ourselves at God's table, a feast to which we have snuck in, uninvited. God is too far above us. His enjoyment of himself is a *nonpareil*, and nothing we can offer to him can possibly compare with it. When you've got steak at home, why go out for hamburger?

And yet, and yet . . . This is Plotinus' official view, fully in accord with the received Parmenidean-Aristotelian convention of perfection. The One is indifferent to any reaction or recognition it receives from without, and is interested in no relationship with a being lower than itself.[9] But the startling three innovations Plotinus has added to an otherwise conventional synthesis of Plato's and Aristotle's philosophies tell a different story. One might put it this way: his lips say "No, No," but his philosophy says "Yes, Yes." For can we say after the serious modifications that Plotinus has worked into the traditional Platonic-Aristotelian philosophy that the One is really not interested in a personal relationship with individual souls? Even if we ascend by our own efforts, the One has done everything he can to remove every obstacle from our path, and even made himself directly and immediately available, not just through his lower hypostasis of World Soul or even Intelligence. Reciprocally, Plotinus could say that those (few) individuals who work their way up through contemplation to union with the One show thereby their superiority over other souls, and that they are thus worthy to be absorbed, by the identity of indiscernibles, *into* the One, which is equivalent to being worthy objects of the One's attention and approval—in other words, that this kind of relationship involves no necessary violation of the principle of proportional love.[10]

Behind such a naturalistic "screening" of candidates, it seems Plotinus' deepest mind that the One *is* interested in grooming worthy *individual* souls with whom to enter into a relationship—souls able to appreciate his goodness, as all creation does, and reflect it back to himself. At least everything happens in Plotinus' new arrangement of the Platonic territory to suggest that this is the case. Further, this way Plotinus gets to have it both ways: he can arrange it *as if* the One is interested in a relationship with individual souls, and yet still maintain that, since we make all the effort to close the gap ourselves, his depiction of the deity does not violate the traditional Parmenidean-Aristotelian conventions. Any divine "initiative" toward us is effectively camouflaged, neutralized, or rendered indistinguishable from his remaining in splendid isolation, moving others by attraction, himself unmoved.

Plotinus evidently intends the two portraits to blend or blur together, as indeed they could if he had more explicitly exploited the two devices mentioned at the beginning of this article which he has at his disposal: that, in knowing himself, God could simultaneously be aware of all other beings as either his effects, or (in the Christian framework of a free creation), as *possible* likenesses to himself; and second, that if his love for himself is intense enough, it would not constitute an impediment to his altruism, but rather would well up, make the latter possible and even almost inevitable, as a deeper unfolding of the subversive (anti-Parmenidean) Platonic motif of the Good's natural tendency to disperse itself. The two are directly, and not inversely, proportional. These motifs were ingeniously uncovered and in a revolutionary way exploited by Duns Scotus almost a thousand years later, when the apparently opposing Greek conventions of necessary divine self-absorption and the desire to share itself in a relationship were for the first time successfully reconciled.

It seems clear why Plotinus did not so exploit devices he had himself discovered: the resulting portrait of the divine would have been indistinguishable from the personal God being vigorously promoted by the emerging Judeo-Christian tradition, against which in part he had conceived the project of mobilizing the resources of the Platonic-Aristotelian tradition to produce an alternative explanation for the existence of the world. He failed; his world is not truly independent from his God. More scandalously, he opened the door to the possibility of a mystical union with God which, if anything, was in advance of the thinking of contemporary Christian theologians, but which was in surprising fundamental accord with both their project and their portrayal of the divinity. Thus Plotinus' "victory" was at best Pyrrhic; on all important differences between the two portraits, Plotinus made surprising and even decisive concessions. Over the next five hundred years, Christians would grudgingly come to admit the truth contained in the Greek convention that love should be proportional to its object, and that God must in some sense be self-absorbed. By the time we reach Duns Scotus, the gap has been effectively closed, *les extremes se touchent*. What is relevant to say regarding Plotinus, however, is that, trying to deliver a stunning blow as an enemy, he succeeded instead in delivering a traitorous breakthrough from a secret, if perhaps unintentional, friend. It is on a Plotinian framework that Duns Scotus was later able to elaborate his successful—and probably the only possible—reconciliation without needing to make any fundamental structural alteration.

Notes

[1] See Plotinus, *The Enneads*, III.8.4; VI.8.15.
[2] At V.8.12, God, although "self-intent," is described as "rejoicing" in his offspring, which includes the World Soul, but also what is below the World Soul.
[3] Plotinus makes the same point at V.1.4.
[4] See V.1.5 and VI.4.16.
[5] For the immediate presence of the One to particular souls, see *Enneads* V.I.II; VI.5.5; VI.6.12; VI.8.16; VI.9.4; VI.9.7.
[6] See VI.9.8.

[7]Maria Luisa Gatti, "Plotinus: The Platonic tradition and the foundation of Neo-platonism," in *The Cambridge Companion to Plotinus*, L.P. Gerson, ed., Cambridge: Cambridge University Press, 1996, pp. 30–31.
[8]See V.9.1 & V.9.2; see Porphyry's *Life of Plotinus*, #23.
[9]See V.5.12; VI.4.7; VI.5.3; VI.9.8.
[10]See V.5.8; VI.4.11; VI.9.4.

·

CHAPTER 4

Scotus, Luther, and the
Yawning Gap of Perdition

The paring in this title will strike most readers as puzzling. Could one imagine two more different historical personalities, two more opposed psychological profiles, or two more divergent fates in terms of their lasting influence? For while the modern history of Europe is incomprehensible without Luther, whether we view this approvingly or askance, Duns Scotus seems to have virtually disappeared without a trace, to have come into existence merely to provide one late mote, together with Ockham, in the declining beam of degenerate scholasticism. Scotus seems to give the occasion for Luther's reformation; if Scotus had not existed, the Reformation would have had to invent him. For wasn't Scotus precisely what Luther was revolting *against* (together with Church corruption)—and *triumphing over*—an overrefined and irrelevant (not to say unbiblical) scholastic theology? Psychologically as well, compared with the robust earthiness of Luther, Scotus, insofar as he is known or imagined at all, appears other-worldly and emaciated—a sallow and ineffective English headmaster flailing in vain to keep order in the classroom while his students gleefully tear up his notes and roll them into the infamous "dunce" caps for each other to wear. We grant his brilliance, but it seems excessive, overly subtle, adding an epicycle to an already overburdened and outmoded epicycle, and symptomatic of a nervous, perhaps neurotic personality—similar to that other overwrought figure who admired Scotus, the poet Gerard Manley Hopkins.

In the event, this caricature is far from the reality. Only two hundred years separate Luther from Scotus, and as far as the material conditions of life are concerned, comparatively little had changed between 1300 and 1500. The major alterations in technology and lifestyle were to occur later. But much indeed had changed on the historical and psychological landscape—the failure of the crusades, the great plague, the corruption and schism of the papacy, including the Avignon exile, a consequent rise in a never-abated nationalism among the crowned heads of Europe, and class antagonism, resentful of the taxation needed to support the aristocracy and their armies, as well as against the indulgence-selling pope in Rome. While none of these issues has a direct bearing on theology, they did arouse and betoken passions that were pushing for expression. Theology, as the main legitimating discourse or "master narrative" of the era, was put under enormous pressure to deviate from its thousand-year project to fashion an ever better and ultimately satisfying reconciliation between Christian belief and the best that the (rival) classical tradition had to deliver on the same subject, to producing validating grounds for the particular historical and psychological agenda of the day. Thought no longer led passion; rather passion put a ring through thought's nose and led it where it would.

This tragedy is the greater in that Duns Scotus had recently achieved what could be described as the deepest synthesis and mutual accommodation between Christian belief and the apparently opposed position on God by a neutral and unafraid (or unmanipulated) reason. The tragedy of Duns Scotus is that he was *made to appear* a tragedy; his triumph was clouded over and obscured by a theological *putsch* which succeeded in having its own preoccupations pushed to the top of the cultural agenda and all other projects vilified and swept from serious consideration. His position is subject to caricature and distortion, and in fact is burdened with the precise failure of the opposing Reformation view. In him are fulfilled the conditions of the maximum of injustice, or the "perfection of injustice" as this is described in Plato's *Republic:* the Reformation position has concealed its own setback, while investing scholasticism and Scotus in particular with precisely its own deficiencies—a God even more distant, more outrageous to reason, more transcendent and hence fearful and unpredictable than anything to be found in Augustine, the father of "Original Sin."

It is a measure of the triumph of Reformation (and its rebellious offspring, Enlightenment) thinking that Scotus and Luther are rarely studied together, as if the results of such a comparison should be obvious (since Luther has already given them to us implicitly in his critique of scholasticism) and hence otiose to any rational person. However, I propose that they must be put together if the age is to be understood at its deepest level. Otherwise, we are limited to comparing Luther with contemporaries like Thomas More or Erasmus, and lamenting the loss of sympathy, humor, and a well-rounded, polyvalent "humanism" in the former, without knowing precisely what that humanism refers to. Only by studying the two of them directly does the "map" of that period suddenly snap taut, the wrinkles disappearing, and we take in the dimensions of what has been lost—a whole project, and perhaps its best solution—and what replaced it, and the consequences of this exchange. Whatever advances in biblical scholarship were obtained, this exchange saddled the West with a disastrous fall-back position, a God even more authoritarian, transcendent, and fear-inspiring than Augustine's or Anselm's (and a consequent setback and postponement of serious theology for several hundred years), to which the Enlightenment apathy and rejection were both a justifiable and ultimately unavoidable reaction.

The Problem

The "stumbling block" of Christian belief to Greek philosophy had always been not the "cross" as Paul believed but the Incarnation itself—the belief that God could touch matter and still remain God—or what the "cross" represented, that God could care passionately about the human race—about anyone else but himself, in fact—of which belief the "cross" is merely the extension, intensification, and for the Greek philosophers the *reductio ad absurdam* and over-the-top indulgence in Romantic sentimentalism. This had always been the crux of the difference between Athens and Jerusalem—for Athens, the basis and fundamental assumption of Judaism consists of a "myth" which must be overturned at the *beginning* of any true philosophy—before any real philosophy can get started. The eminent Jewish scholar Abraham Heschel states that the Old Testament is the story not of a people's search for its God but rather of a God's search for his people.[1] This degree of concern in "God" is for the Greeks the first but fatal error of Jewish belief. Christianity, by its own admission, is merely the extension and fulfillment of this belief. Both owe their origins, the Greeks believe, to a fatal indulgence in wishful thinking and self-pity. When one has correctly analyzed what God must be like—if there are grounds for thinking there is any reality which may be correctly characterized as a "God," which both Plato and Aristotle think there are—one sees that any such concern in God for anything beyond his nature is simply impossible; not only *did* it not happen, it *could* not have happened. It is in principle impossible. The Greek city states had a number of myths recounting the dying and rising of a savior god, usually tied to the cycle of seasons; however, correct thinking simply banishes such myths, it replaces them with a rational account of God's nature, and makes us see them for what they are: wishful thinking on our part. The Jewish belief is not orthodoxy; it is blasphemy. It is the Greek philosophical theology that defines orthodoxy. When one has correctly understood the canons of perfection, one realizes that God is not, *cannot* be like that, and one adjusts one's attitudes correspondingly.

The Greek "masters of suspicion" (Ricoeur) needed no help from Nietzsche, Freud, and Darwin to "disenchant" their world, even if the degree of their disenchantment was not as severe as these modern champions of "rigorous" thinking would achieve. We can still come close to God (the goal of all "salvation" or "redemption"), but we do so by doing what God does—exercising our highest faculty upon the highest object. We direct our thinking to God, who is "thought thinking itself," and by the "identity of indiscernibles" we *become* what we know and love, we coalesce and become "like unto God"—as far as any moving, and hence imperfect, substance can. As the first letter of John says, in the afterlife we shall know Jesus, and then "we shall be like him, because we shall see him as he is"(3:2). Any other account has to be treated as an allegorical version of this rational truth. That is what philosophy *is*—giving up mythical thinking for a rational account that is universal and necessary. The Jews have not taken the first step in philosophy, and cannot take the first step until they give up their national myth. Until that time a "Jewish philosophy" is impossible; *a fortiori* the same is true for a "Christian philosophy."

This objection to the basic assumption of Judeo-Christianity is an expression of another Greek principle, that love must be proportional to its object. It is wrong, indeed obscene, to love an object above or below its merits. This comes out most forcefully in Aristotle's discussion of the virtue of "great souledness" (*megalopsychia*), and of friendship between unequals in books 4 and 8 of the *Nicomachean Ethics*. With the common people the "great souled" individual affects an easy camaraderie and is indifferent to their opinion of him; from his peers, however, he expects his excellence to be recognized and is sensitive to being overlooked or to any sign of disrespect.[2] Aristotle subscribes to a rigid social hierarchy, but one based on character, not on family or wealth. He would find the modern cult of egalitarianism puzzling, unnatural—certainly not empirical. In a friendship between unequals, Aristotle asserts that it is only natural for the superior to receive more than the inferior, since he is "worth" more. He does not normally receive it in the same "coin" as the inferior, however, but in the acknowledgment and praise of the latter.[3] When the gap is too wide, however, a friendship between the two becomes impossible, because there is nothing that the inferior can give that is of any value to the superior. It is like the attitude of the "great souled" individual to the common people; he affects an easy exchange with them, but their opinion of him means nothing to him. That is why, in contrast to John's gospel, Aristotle asserts that a friendship between God and man is impossible.[4] For the Greeks, the superior never "inclines" or "stoops" to the inferior; such would be improper, morally wrong—even metaphysically impossible. Rather it is for the inferior to "convert," to reorient himself and concentrate upon the superior, to take in his excellence, become like him, and thereby return acknowledgment and glory to him. The Greeks originated the notion that the highest form of praise is imitation.

It is not surprising that the Greeks had difficulty explaining the existence of the world at all. Strictly speaking, it should not be here. There should be only God knowing and enjoying himself. The existence of anything outside of God is a rational surd, a small pebble upon which their efforts to give a full account of the world foundered. Not only *did* God not make the world; he *could* not have, and still remain God. It would have represented a decline from his pure activity and absolute perfection. Either the world is an illusion, or it is an unintended but necessary side effect, and thus part of the divine nature. One finds both solutions in Plotinus, who produced the last and most impressive attempt to bring the full resources of Greek philosophy to bear on this problem. For Plotinus, man's "higher soul" has never really fallen into the realm of matter, so that even now our "true" self is aloft, contemplating the Forms in the Divine Mind, which is the true world, of which the things we see around ourselves here are an insubstantial copy. But then where are we—here or "above"? This flaw shows up as an inconsistency in his other solution, making the realm of matter a necessary emanation in the unfolding of the divine nature, succeeding Mind and Soul. This solution makes matter part of the divinity, and yet, being in motion, it is necessarily imperfect and hence, for the Greeks, far from the divine.

This insistence that love should be proportional to its object is the deepest Greek objection to the Christian good news. The two outlooks differ on fundamental assumptions, so one cannot exist or be entertained seriously in the thought world of the other. Greek philosophy cuts off Christian good news even before the latter has had a chance to make its announcement, as St. Paul found out when he tried to preach on the Areopagus. The history of Christian "theology" consists of considerable measure in a gradual acknowledgment and grudging accommodation with the truth contained in the Greek philosophical theology and psychology of loving, the attempt to reconcile and coordinate the two in an encompassing, harmonious conceptual edifice. So different and opposed did these seem at the outset that the project could be compared to squaring the circle—an impossible task. The history of Christian theology shows repeated swings to one extreme or the other. One of the high points of synthesis—perhaps the highest that is possible—occurred with Duns Scotus. One of the major setbacks occurred with Luther.

An Evolving Integration

From what has been said it should be clear that the Greeks would have greeted with alarm and rejection the supposedly more "humanistic" (compared with the more juridical theory of atonement) theory of divine condescension or *kenosis* (self-emptying or self-abasement) to explain the "Incarnation." The gap was simply too wide, the fall too great, to permit a God to take on more than the "appearance" of being human, and still remain God. The early hymn quoted by Paul in Philippians, which summarizes the Christian belief that

> His state was divine, yet he did not cling
> to his equality with God, but emptied himself
> to assume the condition of a slave, and became as men are;
> he was humbler yet, even to accepting death,
> death on a cross.[5]

would have been greeted, not with awed respect, but with howls of indignation and hoots of laughter.

Here is not the place to discuss the aptness and progress involved in the eventual Christian replacement of "substance" with "person" as an ultimate metaphysical category, one which allows certain forms of "motion" and response which are an indication of *superiority*, and not of *inferiority*, to what is without motion or change. The point is rather the gradual recognition and assimilation by the Christian community of what validity there is in the Greek canon of divine perfection, especially as this is applied to the psychology of loving. This process took place over centuries, for it required a slow cultivation of the psychological ability to test and question the received expression of the faith, to risk trespass and disapproval and to break taboos, to hold the Christian notion of God up against the secular portrait the Greeks insisted applied to him, to lose gradually their fear of disrespect and blasphemy, to have rather a growing faith in their own powers of reason, to accept and eventually to meld what was valid in the Greek insights into a more powerful, impressive, and finally acceptable notion of the divinity. This integration evolved over centuries, suffered setbacks and strange digressions, and reached arguably its highest expression in the work not of the encyclopedic Thomas Aquinas but of the more profound Duns Scotus.

Because of the sense of cultural depth and superiority permeating the Greek-speaking eastern half of the empire, the destabilizing effects of the barbarian invasions in the West, and perhaps because both Tertullian and Augustine had led licentious lives as youths and generalized their experiences to all humankind, the Church in the West accentuated the determining reality and lasting effects of what Augustine called "Original Sin" more strongly than did the Eastern Church. Whereas the Eastern Church was inspired more by the semi-mystical and contemplative writings of St. John, the West took its cue from the practical and sober assessment of the dire human situation St. Paul gives in his letter to the Romans:

> Are we any better off? Not at all: as we said before, Jews and Greeks are all under sin's dominion.

> As scripture says:

> There is not a good man left, no, not one;
> there is not one who understands,
> not one who looks for God.
> All have turned aside, tainted all alike;
> there is not one good man left, not a single one. . . .
> Sin *entered the world* through one man, and through sin death, and thus death has spread through the whole human race because everyone has sinned.[6]

When asked about God's motivation for the Incarnation, the Greek Fathers would typically answer: "God became man so that man might become God"—not literally God, of course, but so that man could participate more deeply in the economy of the divine self-love. By contrast, the West explained the Incarnation by the necessity of atoning for Adam's sin. One could claim this is merely the difference between calling a glass of water "half empty" or "half full," but it does make a difference which one emphasizes. As a general characterization, the West's stress, following Augustine, on the reality and serious consequences of original sin, however useful for evangelistic or homiletic purposes, widened the gulf between God and man, and made the interest and passionate concern of God for human affairs, even to the point of self-sacrifice, more offensive to Greek ears as an obvious violation of the canon of perfection. Acceptance of Christianity seemed to involve necessarily and unavoidably an outrage to one's reason. With Tertullian we would have to say, "*Credo quia absurdum est*," for Tertullian reason and faith were opposed, even though the same God supposedly stood behind both reason and revelation. This was a "biblical theology" with a vengeance, in the sense of rejecting any philosophical interference or admixture; but it paid the price of vilifying and demonizing human reason as a faculty infected with sin and "puffed up" by pride, as St. Paul puts it. It paid the further price of limiting the spread of Christianity to a vulgar audience which could be manipulated by guilt and fear. If the psalmist says, "The beginning of Wisdom is fear of the Lord" (111:10), this tradition concluded that the "end" of wisdom is *also* fear of the Lord. It showed no interest in exploring patterns of psychological and spiritual development or in doing justice to St. John's statement that "love casts out fear" (1 John 4:18).

The decisive influence of Augustine on this issue was only gradually overcome. A question began to appear in the disputes of the later middle ages in this form: If Adam had never sinned, would the Incarnation still have taken place? The first part seems an impossible hypothetical, for once God has given a creature freedom, it seems only a matter of time before some individual will misuse it, and a reign of sin will spread to enmesh all humankind. But something deeper is at issue here. The Bible presents a two-beat syncopation to salvation history, with God surprised and dismayed by the misuse man makes of his gifts. He several times considers destroying the creation which has gone so seriously awry, but in the end relents and mercifully forges a covenant and gives a law so as to form a people acceptable and pleasing to himself. The "kingdom" never fully comes about, however, and Christians interpret the phenomenon of Jesus as the surprising culmination and fulfillment of God's promises. The Jews are underwhelmed, while Christian theorists appear to be overwhelmed. There is still no visible "kingdom" in the political sense, but the notion of "one people" has been extended to cover both Jew and gentile.

God appears still to be surprised by the sinfulness of man, and Augustine interprets the suffering of Jesus as necessary to atone for Adam's sin. And yet another theme is now introduced. Through his notion of a "*felix culpa*" or "happy fault," Augustine suggests that our second state is (or will be) better than was the first in the garden of Eden. In other words, Jesus not only "brought us back," he brought about something fundamentally new—different and better than we had before or could ever have anticipated; specifically, we can enter into a greater knowledge and participation of the unanticipatedly intense love of God. In other words, God *used* the (foreseen) evil that would spread as a result of the gift of freedom to creatures to occasion a stupendous *disclosure* and *transmission* of a love whose true dimensions we otherwise would have had no way of properly measuring.

This debate continued throughout the Middle Ages, with most thinkers following Augustine's apparent position that, if Adam had never sinned, God would not have become man, because there would have been no "original sin" and hence no need. Thomas Aquinas considered both sides but eventually opted for what he took to be Augustine's position, because he interpreted the Nicene Creed's explanation for the Incarnation, "*propter nos homines et propter nostram salutem,*" as indicating atonement for sin. Thomas concedes, however, that although *in fact* God's motive was atonement for sin, he *could have* brought about the Incarnation even if Adam had not sinned.[7] However, there are theoretical problems with this two-beat presentation to the divine initiative. As mentioned, it seems to make God appear unintelligent, or not to know what is going to happen. More seriously, it seems to make the appearance of the greatest good for mankind dependent on his most regrettable and devastating embarrassment, his disobedience to God. Would God really have withheld the disclosure of his unanticipatedly intense self-love, which he wishes to open and share with a worthy and capable creature, from mankind merely because mankind had behaved *better* than Adam had behaved? Would we have been *rewarded* for better behavior by being *punished* with the loss of our greatest gift? Or did we first have to "fall" to have our "pride" become apparent and thence removed, hence a necessary first step before any "free" creature would be in a position to receive and appreciate the magnitude of what God had done for him, a disclosure and transmission which could have been made in no other way, and far more than could have been achieved with an "unfallen" creature who perhaps acted automatically and was thus not truly "free"? (Is this a subtle way of salvaging our pride or *réssentiment*, because, although we are "fallen," we are still "higher" than those creatures whose behavior is better?)

For various reasons it appeared to several thinkers that God's wisdom could be better safeguarded, and the principal elements in salvation history more economically preserved and presented, by positing a single unitary development to God's initiative, operating continuously through both creation and Incarnation. Here, surprisingly, the Greek canon of perfection (principally love being proportional to its object) could be respected and apparently reconciled with the principal tenets of the Christian interpretation of Jesus. Prominent in this innovative and stimulating line of speculation was Duns Scotus; specifically, he was able to reinterpret and tie off the apparently opposing notions of perfection in an interesting theoretical resolution.

Duns Scotus

Christian apologists were eventually forced to acknowledge the truth in the Greek convention that love should be proportional to its object, but they found a way to say that God could still be interested in a relationship with humankind. God's self-love could be so intense that He could be moved by a desire to share it with a creature worthy and able to appreciate it. The intensity of the divine self-love was the variable factor that Christian thinkers could "ratchet up" to remove the self-imposed impediment in the Greek project to explain the world. God does indeed know and love Himself most of all (and appropriately so). The Greeks interpreted this to mean that He found this self-love most satisfying, and they further concluded that divine attention to any other object would constitute a lapse and decline from this uniquely perfect activity. This made it impossible to explain where the world came from, except as an unintended offshoot of God's self-contemplation. Ironically, the Greeks produced an impressive and unimpeachable theology, but at the same time this insight destroyed their attempt at a complete philosophy. The Christian suggestion was that if this divine self-love is intense enough, it need not constitute an impediment to the (conscious) production of a world, but rather would almost imply such. For then God could be moved by the desire to share this love beyond the godhead, with a creature worthy and able to appreciate it. This would be a "motion" not based on need or lack, but rather on its opposites— goodness, over-fullness, and generosity—it would then constitute a perfection, and not an imperfection.

Within this general approach a novel device was discovered by which to close the gap between God's outsized love and the meager objective merits of humankind. In knowing himself, God can be said to know simultaneously all that follows as a consequence from his nature. As a further extension, God could be said to know how he could be imitated, however inadequately, by every possible "outside" finite creature, how he would appear or be viewed from every possible "outside" perspective (using spatial language to suggest ontological difference and degree). Thus, knowing other beings would not necessarily "distract" God from knowing himself, or cause him to "dip down" to their level (since, for a Greek, knowledge has a metaphysical effect on the knower, causing the knower to rise or fall to the level of the object he is contemplating). In wishing to share his goodness with other beings, God is naturally attracted to that being which would best imitate him, which would be maximally able to receive, comprehend, and appreciate this gift—thus giving back to God the acknowledgment, respect, and praise that according to the Greek conventions of friendship are due to the superior in any relationship. Divine egotism would not necessarily be opposed to divine altruism. Thus, creation can be "explained," in the sense at least of no longer appearing irrational—there is a natural desire of the Good to diffuse or share itself, and this can all take place along personal lines which respect the Greek conventions of God's necessary self-preoccupation and the psychology of loving. As a corollary, in loving us, God can be said to be attracted to our "true" selves, the imitations of his perfection he envisaged in creating us, our selves as we *should* be—not the actual selves which may occasionally fall drastically short of this ideal. In a sense, God loves us *toward* our ideal selves, our highest possibility. Thus his love for us need not seem excessive, exorbitant, nor an outrageous or flagrant violation of the Greek canon that love should be to the measure of its object.

It was Dun Scotus's further distinctive suggestion that this "highest creature" was the human nature of Christ. The Council of Chalcedon had declared that Christ was "true God and true man." His human nature was not just an appearance; rather it was the acme of creation because it was the unique human nature fitted to be united with the godhead. It is the possibility of this highest creature that would have drawn God's attention and desire "from all eternity" and justified the creation of the world, that is, made the production of the world interesting and worthwhile for Him. Scotus writes:

> Therefore, I argue as follows: in the first place God loves Himself.
> Secondly, He loves Himself in others, and this is most pure and holy

love. Thirdly, God wills to be loved by another who can love Him perfectly, and here I am referring to the love of someone outside God. Therefore, fourthly, God foresees the union between the Word and the creature Christ who owes Him supreme love, even had there never been the Fall. . . . In the fifth place, he sees Christ as mediator coming to suffer and redeem His people because of sin.[8]

This insight became a mainstay and permanent acquisition for Catholic theology. Francis de Sales (1616), the Doctor of the Love of God, follows Scotus in asserting:

(S)ince every well ordered will which determines itself to love several objects equally present, loves better and above all the rest that which is most lovable; it follows that the sovereign Providence, making His eternal purpose and design of all that He would produce, first willed and preferred by excellence the most amiable object of His love which is our Savior; and then other creatures in order, according as they more or less belong to the service, honor, and glory of Him. Thus were all things made for that divine man, who for this cause is called the *first born of every creature.* (Col. 1:15)[9]

This suggestion is a bit humbling or deflating to human vanity, because it moves mankind in general off center as the first object of God's attention, as the apple of God's eye; however, it is in surprising accord with the scriptures, especially with St. Paul. We are loved by God insofar as we become incorporated into the body of Christ; we are encouraged to "put off the old man" and to "put on Christ." As the preface for the seventh Sunday in ordinary time puts it: "May you see and love in us what you see and love in Christ." As in Aristotle's reconciliation of altruism and egotism in a friendship based upon character, God's perception would be "deceived" by the resemblance between ourselves and Christ, so his response to one becomes also his response to the other.[10]

Thus, it was God's desire to produce Christ "before" it was His desire to produce the world or even humankind. The world and mankind exist as God's "way" to Christ. The Incarnation was God's "end"; it preceded creation in the order of God's intention.[11] In a literal or very deep sense, the world exists because of and for Christ. The Incarnation would have taken place (in some form) even if Adam had never sinned (which is probably an impossible hypothetical). It was God's intention from all eternity, and is the reason there is a world at all. It was simultaneously God's genius to exploit the unavoidable appearance of human sinfulness—a species of "intellectual judo," or turning an apparently destructive blow to one's plan to an advantage—to occasion a disclosure and transmission of the intensity of His self-love to mankind, a disclosure that could have been made in no other way.[12]

This unitary approach abolishes the two-beat syncopation of the traditional (scriptural) approach to salvation history, and makes God look less surprised and dismayed by the appearance of sin among men. On the contrary, he foresaw and is able to exploit this development to occasion an epiphany of the extent of his love which he wishes to open up and share with a creature worthy and able to appreciate it. Christ both *discloses* the Father's love, and is also the perfect *response* to that love.[13] Further, this interpretation is in surprising accord with the Greek canon of perfection, where the greater is properly taken up with the greater. It makes the divine *kenosis* or "condescension" toward fallen humankind no longer the scandal or stumbling block, the violation of the canon of perfection or the psychology of loving, the mythological indulgence in self-flattery, self-pity, or wishful thinking it had appeared before to a Greek, as also to the modern Enlightenment sensibility. On the contrary and paradoxically, it allows us now for the first time to complete the Greek project to develop a "scientific" or rational account of the world's existence, insofar as this can be attained. The Greek problem or impediment is removed, not by *denying* the Greek doctrine of God's proper involvement with himself, his satisfying knowledge and love for himself, but rather by stressing, *intensifying*, and reinterpreting this. Surprisingly, this makes the production of a world not only possible; it seems almost to imply it.

Philosophy culminates in Theology, with the Greek convention of divine perfection respected at the same time as it is revised in an imaginative way. Not only the Greek project, but the Christian project, are brought to completion at the same stroke. In a sense, the Western enterprise is now complete. A final synthesis between Christian doctrine and Greek philosophy has been forged.

Luther

There is no such unitary pattern in Luther replacing the two-beat biblical presentation of salvation history; nor is there any attempt at a reconciliation with the Greek (and later Enlightenment) psychology of loving. In Luther's "theology of the cross" love falls out of the picture altogether. There is gratitude for Christ having covered over our sins with his merits; but rather fear at having provoked the divine wrath by our sinfulness and guilt for having occasioned such an egregious and exorbitant price from God himself as his sacrificial death on the cross, are the two chief emotions tapped to propel the individual toward repentance and, not so much a transformation or change of life, but accepting Christ's merits to do duty in place of one's own (impossible) merits. Thus the ultimate effect, and the deepest spiritual awareness that dawns within the individual, is the enormous gap that yawns between what God has done for him and what he actually deserves. The lavish inappropriateness of that love is precisely the mechanism used to disturb the (presumed) sinners and propel them out of guilt, not toward conversion or *metanoia*, which is impossible, but toward an acceptance of this gift, since any other response would constitute the height of ingratitude. The discrepancy between the outsized show of love and the actual worth of the object is thus not concealed, but rather paraded, emphasized, and exploited to create a sense of embarrassment in the sinners which is meant to propel them to the minimal step of accepting this colossal act which God has done not only for them, but on their part.

This is Augustine's anti-Pelagian position with a vengeance. This is the worst form of the atonement theory, the all too common homiletic strategy of inculcating an overwhelming sense of sin and its alarming consequences, raised to the beginning and end of theology. The "good news" seems to be shading into "bad news." The repentance doesn't have to be that great, for change, real conversion, is impossible. Before and after we accept Christ's merits, we form part of the *massa damnata*. Christ's merits cover our sins the way snow covers a dunghill. Thus the discrepancy, the embarrassment at the gulf between God's act of love for us and our actual worth, is not only not covered over, it is exposed, underlined, lifted up, and exploited as the centerpiece of theology and the central mechanism in the psychology of evangelization and pastoral care. In our spiritual progress, love does not cast out fear; rather, fear and guilt are renewed on a regular basis, for the only alternative envisaged is inattention to our spiritual condition and the apathy engendered by backsliding.

Luther shrugs off traditional objections that love should be measured to its object by openly espousing a theology of "paradox."[14] Contradiction is not a sign of error or rational breakdown, so much as an indication that the primary faculty in religious deliberation should not be reason but faith. Luther extends St. Paul's belief that reason "puffs up." It is more often than not the agency of pride, and is thus infected with sin. Luther associated the attempt to reconcile faith and reason, or Christian revelation with Greek reason—as scholasticism attempted to do—with the attempt to achieve salvation by one's own efforts or merits, rather than simply accepting Christ's sacrifice.[15] It is a "theology of glory," rather than a "theology of the cross," and is thus disqualified at the outset by Luther because of its unworthy psychological or spiritual origins.[16] The indifference to this criticism is also his way of showing contempt for the corruptions in the Church and its entire established tradition. A thousand-year project in the West is thus overturned; the theological insights of the Greeks are disallowed and their objections rejected.

This traditional project should be abandoned and replaced by a docile faith accepting none but biblical categories. We are saved by "grace," not by works—especially not by the works of reason. Even the notion of "grace" is different for Luther than it had been in earlier spiritual writers. Before—even in St. Paul—it had always been associated with some form of conversion, transformation, *metanoia* in *this* life. Grace is now associated by Luther rather with "justification," and theology is reduced to the worst form of the atonement theory whereby we are "justified" before the court of God's law by the merits of Christ, which leave the defendant, ourselves, the same before as after the court proceedings. We "appear" different to God afterward because of the merits of Christ, but underneath this appearance we are the same substantially as we always have been—*simul justus et peccator*. Again, the gap between God's outsized display of love and our actual worth yawns wide; rather than being concealed, it is emphasized and exploited to propel the individual to shame, repentance, and acceptance of Christ's gift.

Conclusion

After Luther, the universality of egotism and the propriety of self-love were reasserted with overwhelming force. The Duke de la Rochefoucauld found *"amour propre"* behind all our actions, even the so-called "altruistic," noble, or generous ones. A central strand of the Enlightenment, from Rousseau to Gibbon, from Hume to Marx, consists of a rejection of Augustine's emphasis on original sin and all attempts to arouse guilt or embarrassment because of it. As Mandeville wrote, private "vices" can become public "virtues," and Adam Smith showed how greed or selfishness can be harnessed for the benefit of the nation. In a sense, the Enlightenment simply secularized the Reformation's sense of overwhelming universal sinfulness, and ceased to feel embarrassed or guilty about it. In fact, it was now felt to be a natural and good thing. From now on, "altruism," in God or in humans, had to be shown to be compatible with a necessary and proper "egotism" (a possibility which Aristotle had already demonstrated, although with the need to "convert" to the vision of the "man of practical virtue"); this involved an implicit reassertion of the Greek principle that love should be proportional to its object, and a rejection of the notion that the higher can, or even should, incline or sacrifice itself for the sake of the lower.

Attempts to base theology or Christian apologetic upon an embarrassing or guilt-inducing "yawning gap of perdition," the discrepancy between the outsized display of God's love on the cross and the meager merits of its object, paid the price of again appealing only to a vulgar or uneducated audience. By an "enlightened" audience only too prepared and ready to detect any sign of manipulation or unscientific, irrational special pleading, such attempts were met with rejection and ridicule. As enlightenment values and sensitivity have filtered down to the population at large, the intellectual credibility of Christianity has appeared more and more precarious. Perhaps this would be an opportune moment to look back before the break of the Reformation and retrieve the most profound and sustained effort to achieve an integration of the Christian good news with what is legitimate and valid in these secular but irrepressible insights, in the theology of the "subtle" doctor, Duns Scotus.

Notes

[1] See Abraham J. Heschel, *God in Search of Man: A Philosophy of Judaism*, Farrar, Straus & Cudahy, NY, 1955.
[2] See Aristotle, *Nicomachean Ethics*, 112a5–15; hereafter "NE."
[3] NE 115825; 1163b1–5.
[4] NE 1158b35.
[5] Philippians 2:6–9; Jerusalem Bible.
[6] Romans 3:9–12; 5:12–13; Jerusalem Bible.
[7] Atoning for Adam's sin is responsible for Christ's *Passion*, but not specifically for the Incarnation. See *The Three Greatest Prayers: Commentaries on the Our Father, the Hail Mary, and the Apostles Creed by St. Thomas Aquinas*, trans. by L. Shapcote, London, Burns, Oates & Washbourne, 1937, pp. 54, 56. These were the Lenten homilies Thomas gave in Naples just before he died; they thus were his final thoughts on these topics. See also *Summa Theologiae*, III, Q.1, art. 3.
[8] *Reportata Parisiensis*, d.7, q. 4, n.5, Vivès XXIII 303b.

[9] *Library of St. Francis de Sales . . . , II: Treatise on the Love of God . . .* , London, 6th ed., pp. 76–77.

[10] NE 1166a30–35.

[11] See *Ordinatio* III, d. 32, q. 1, n.6, Vivès XV, 433a. Also *Reportata Parisiensia* III, d.7, q.4, n.5, Vivès XXIII, 98a.

[12] *Opus Oxoniense* 3.20. Scotus holds that Christ would have become man anyway as an expression and response to the Trinity's self-love, but he "would not have come as a mediator, as one who was so suffer, as one who was to redeem, unless someone had previously sinned." *Reportatio Parisienses* 3.7.5.

[13] For a good discussion of this, see Eric Doyle, *Duns Scotus and the Place of Christ*, Clergy Review, Sept.–Oct.–Nov., 1972.

[14] Paradox is a central term in Luther's theology. The theses Luther wrote for the *Heidelberg Disputation* of 1518 are entitled "theological paradoxes." See Martin Luther, D. *Martin Luther's Werke: Kritische Gesamtausgabe*, Weimar, Böhlau (1883–), vol. 1, p. 353. Line 11; hereafter "WA."

[15] A natural knowledge of God is possible according to Luther, but it has no soteriological power or significance. Luther associates reason not so much with the natural order of the world which God stands behind as the author of creation, but as part of the fallen condition of humanity. As such, its activity forms part of God's "alien work" (*opus alienum Dei*), God's works of wrath, or the suffering humans experience when they try to work out their salvation in any way but accepting God's disposition toward them through this wrath and accepting what he has done for them through Christ, and specifically his cross. The failure and frustration of such attempts are meant to prepare us for God's "proper work" (*opus proprium Dei*), which is the experience of mercy we feel when we have finally ceased these alternative efforts and simply accepted God's gift. Thus, there is a "two-beat syncopation" for Luther which typically characterizes the process by which an individual comes to redemption: his or her pride must first be beaten down or exhausted, before he or she will humbly accept what is offered, having tasted the bitter ashes of every other means of escaping this state of discomfort and frustration. Reason is inadequate for Luther, not for correctly describing God's characteristic self-preoccupation but being unable to explain why there is a world at all, which is how the scholastics could see God planting an "engine of frustration" in nature propelling humans toward a "theology of revelation," and ultimately a "theology of the cross," but because it forms part of man's fallen condition, whose end products are inevitably infected with sin (especially pride) and compromised by self-centeredness. Redemption for Luther is thus not incremental, but discontinuous. He would have nothing to say to a Greek philosopher or someone standing totally outside the Christian tradition. Rather than first accepting that there is a God, and then coming to believe that Jesus is his son, for Luther we first learn who God is through Jesus, and specifically through the cross. See WA, 5, pp. 163, 176.

[16] See WA 1, pp. 362–365; 39 II, pp. 26–27. A "theology of glory" is the disqualifying sin of scholasticism. See WA 1, pp. 224–28; 39 II, p. 13. See Denis Janz, *Luther on Thomas Aquinas: The Angelic Doctor in the Thought of the Reformer*, Stuttgart, Franz Steiner, 1989, pp. 11–81.

CHAPTER 5

Duns Scotus and the Rehabilitation of Self-Love

I t has been claimed that the Catholic Church has never made its accommodation with the European Enlightenment of the eighteenth century. Preoccupied with preventing a victory of Islam in the West, the Church practiced a defensive appeasement before the growing theory of French rationalism and practice of absolute monarchy, an appeasement which culminated in the suppression of the Jesuits in 1773. As a consequence, the Church reeled before the earthquake of the French Revolution, and scrambled during the Napoleonic and Restoration periods to retrieve as many of her prerogatives and possessions as possible. Stung into a permanent defensive posture and preoccupied with practical matters relating to her very survival, she had little time or energy to devote to purely theoretical concerns. Except for a few concessions relating to the rights of labor to organize, concessions extorted from her by the prospect of worldwide revolution, the Church's main policy toward the "modern" was to condemn it, or what she knew of it, disguising her retreat to safety by protecting herself behind not Augustinian but "daringly" Thomistic ramparts. While churchmen interacted fruitfully with intellectual currents from Plato, Aristotle, the Renaissance, to the early modern period, the political turmoil of the period, it has been claimed, kept the Church from reaching an accommodation with the Enlightenment mentality, and this gap or lacuna unfortunately has persisted to the present day.

Without wishing to enter into a discussion of the myriad developments in Church affairs during the period called the "Enlightenment," in this article I would like to profer the name of Duns Scotus, the sometimes reviled Franciscan philosopher and theologian who lived around the year 1300, as someone who may have anticipated some of the concerns of the Enlightenment, at least in its psychology, and proposed bold ways to meet them—in the form of innovative ways of viewing traditional Church doctrines that would make them acceptable to the Enlightenment, while instructing and correcting this emerging naturalistic and secular mentality. For concerns about the nature of love and desire, their proper object and proportional intensity lie at the heart of the deepest dispute between Greek philosophy and Christian doctrine, as well as between Christianity and the Enlightenment. Leibniz, for one, was profoundly influenced by Duns Scotus in the theology he put forward to reconcile Catholics and Protestants.

The Greek Psychology of Love

Beneath the appeal from tradition or authority to reason as the arbiter of allegiances and justifier of institutions, a major objection by the Enlightenment to Christianity was its psychology, specifically its psychology of loving. For the Enlightenment as for the Greeks, love should be proportional to its object. Love relates to the good the way knowledge relates to truth. Of two good objects, we should (and normally do) love the greater good more. This is only right; anything else would be wrong. For the Greeks, love is close to being a sign of imperfection, for love causes us to "move" toward the object we love, and we move toward what we lack. Love is thus a symptom and measure of our incompleteness. The Christian suggestion, somewhat adumbrated in Plotinus though in deterministic guise, is that there might be another kind of love based on completeness, over-fullness, and generosity; the Greeks, however, did not consider seriously a "love" or friendship in which both sides did not get *something* from the relationship. The recognition or acknowledgment which a superior receives, even while he or she is being generous, makes such a relation between unequals acceptable, and in a way establishes the "equality" at which all friendship aims.[1] It may seem strange to us that the Greeks would break down and thus analyze a relation as amorphous and mysterious as friendship; in response they might say that we are simply unreflective and unrealistic.

This psychology of love created problems for the Greeks when they came to explain the relation between God and man, or God and the world. Why is there a world at all? God is all sufficient; he needs nothing. As Aristotle described him, he is "thought thinking itself." He is his own best company, so why does he need anything else? What can anything else give him that he cannot get better from himself? Plato had used a comparison between God and the sun in the *Republic*, suggesting that the highest form, the "Form of the Good," is responsible not only for the light that allows us to see and understand the world, but also for there *being* a world at all; however, he did not develop this simile.[2] It is responsible for the notion that the good naturally overspills or diffuses itself, an idea which Plotinus developed five centuries later in his theory of "emanations" or spontaneous and necessary outbursts from the "One" through "Mind" to "Soul" and finally to "Matter." However, Plotinus in a sense overshoots the mark by making this series a *necessary* development within God's nature, something he could not help engaging in, and thus something predetermined and impersonal. There is also a potential contradiction, because in a sense the world is not really distinct from God, since it is a necessary offshoot of the divine nature; and yet, being in motion, for a Greek the world is emphatically *not* divine.

The Greeks could not explain the existence of the world; strictly speaking, God should exist alone in his splendid isolation. The influence of Parmenides indicated that it is better to be unmoving rather than moving, and creation is a form of "motion" or change. What could God be getting out of it? Christian thinkers suggested a form of perfection higher than substance, that is, higher than being complete, independent, invulnerable, unmoving, needing nothing; but when they came to explain the relationships into which God might be tempted to enter in virtue of his perfection as a *person*, they had to grapple with the conventions of proper relationship the Greeks had presented. Friendship is based on love, but it is not for that reason irrational. For the Greeks, love is never blind. What attracts God to creating one kind of being rather than another? For that matter, why create at all?

Plotinus himself had suggested a solution that Christian thinkers would later exploit. In knowing Himself, God simultaneously knows all that follows as a consequence from His nature.[3] This makes the production of the world a necessary emanation from the divine essence; as a correction or further refinement, however, God could be said to know how He could be imitated and would appear from every possible "outside" perspective. Thus, knowing other beings would not necessarily "distract" God from knowing Himself, or cause him to "dip down" to their level (since, for a Greek, in knowledge knower and object known become one. Knowledge thus has a metaphysical effect on the knower, causing the knower to rise or fall to the object he or she is contemplating). In knowing himself, God would simultaneously know all other possible objects as well; it is not an "either/or" situation, but rather "both/and." In wishing to share his goodness with another being, God would naturally be attracted to that being who would be maximally able to receive, comprehend, and appreciate this gift—thus giving back to God the acknowledgment, respect, and praise that according to the Greek conventions of friendship are due to the superior in any relationship. Thus, creation can be "explained," in the sense at least of no longer giving scandal to the Greek conventions. There is a natural tendency of the Good to diffuse or share itself, and this can all take place along personal lines which respect the Greek convention of God's necessary self-preoccupation and reciprocity between unequals.

The Enlightenment

A basic impulse within the eighteenth century Enlightenment rejected the Augustinian (through Calvin) form of Christianity, with its stress on original sin, a consequent fallen human nature, and the outsized or disproportional love God supposedly lavished on wretched sinners (whose chief sin was pride), in favor of a secular approach which announced natural human goodness and unashamedly proclaimed the universality and propriety of self-love, notably as the foundation for all relationships, even the so-called generous or altruistic ones. It thus rejected the Augustinian view of this world as a "vale of tears" through which we must pass as a consequence of the sin of our first parents, in constant "fear and trembling" lest we succumb again. It refused to equate self-interest, enlightened or otherwise, with selfishness; the latter is indeed a fault, but suppression of the former is not desirable, if indeed it is even possible. The two have often been conflated in a manipulative evangelistic strategy to frighten or bully people into accepting Christianity by trying to make them ashamed of what is not only natural but good.

God, it was said, is not the stern and awe-inspiring final judge used by priests to reinforce their own position but the distant heavenly watchmaker of the Deists or the benign nonsectarian force hidden behind the Masonic brotherhood of world religions in Mozart's *Magic Flute*, or with a more skeptical attitude toward purported revelation in Lessing's *Nathan the Wise*. One can view in Hobbes an early phase of the Enlightenment as a kind of secularized Calvinism, seeing human nature as unreformable, so one throws up one's hands at the impossible task and merely tries to engineer what one cannot correct. Thus Adam Smith's *Wealth of Nations* takes self-interest as a universal and irreversible human tendency which we do better to harness and direct rather than chastise or attempt to repress. In a later, Rousseauistic phase however, the Enlightenment views human nature as positively good; Mandeville occupies a halfway position when he purports to discern "public virtues" lurking behind "private vices" in *A Fable of the Bees*. From Rousseau to Goethe, from Voltaire and Diderot to Gibbon and Hume, further to Lessing and Kant,[4] the Enlightenment consists of an overturning of the Augustinian interpretation of Christianity, a rejection of the primacy of original sin, a celebration of the goodness of human life and of natural social existence—and in particular an affirmation of the primacy and unavoidability of self-love.

If the Enlightenment left something out, it was the necessity, for proper human development, of a "conversion experience" if self-interest is not to develop indeed into selfishness; that is, one has to recognize one's capacity, and even strong tendency, to misdevelopment and step in to correct and realign this process. Compared to the other animals, Aristotle would say, man comes into the world only half-baked or half finished. He has to step in and complete the process himself, paradoxically, if his "natural" development and fulfillment are to be achieved. The Enlightenment countered one exaggeration (the Calvinist) with another equal exaggeration or omission. In this essay, however, I would merely like to point out a possible accommodation which was presented well before the Enlightenment between what looks at this juncture to be irreconcilably opposite positions.

On the question of social relationships, Aristotle presents a remarkably sophisticated analysis of the interplay between egotism and altruism in the various types of friendship. Self-love is indeed not the same thing as selfishness, and he would agree with the Enlightenment theorists that the first obligation of the "great man" or fully developed virtuous individual is to love himself. Thus this type of person is sensitive to slights or insults, especially coming from members of his own class, because he expects them (but not the common people) correctly to perceive his excellence and outstanding features.[5] The only difference is that for Aristotle such self-love should occur only after a long period of ethical preparation and training, during which one has fashioned him or herself into an object worthy to be loved. Of itself, human nature, like matter, is neither good nor bad; it has the potential to go either way. It all depends on what formation we give it. The Enlightenment theorists, less sensitive to the time factor or perhaps taking for granted an ethical formation through Christianity which had become cultural and almost universal, tended to think that human goodness was innate and automatic.

The subtlety and insight of Aristotle's thought comes out especially in his analysis of the friendship between two good men, or one based on character, which is not common because "good men are rare." What has to be explained is the intensity of the love of one good man toward such a friend, which can go up to giving one's life, and how such feeling can be based on natural sources. How can egotism pass so naturally and completely into altruism? What is at work here psychologically? Basically Aristotle says that the ethical sensitivity of the one friend is "deceived" by the resemblance of the other person's character to his or her own. Such resemblance is first of all flattering; it reinforces my belief that my choices were not irrational or idiosyncratic. I was responding to a real value, which this other person has seen as well. Their choice, which mirrors mine and has now become habitual, ratifies mine; it makes me feel that I am not alone in the good I think I see. Thus I hold this person in esteem. But as a consequence of this, whatever feeling I have toward myself unavoidably spills over and becomes directed toward my friend as well. When I see this person, I think I am seeing myself. Indeed, such a friend becomes "another self." My ethical or value perception is "deceived" by the resemblance so that what I feel toward myself, I spontaneously feel toward my friend as well.[6] Thus, I might be ready to die for such a friend, since in a sense I am defending "myself"; I can be said to "live on" through my friend. Thus, from purely "egocentric" impulses, the most noble "altruistic" action can be generated; there is no fundamental or necessary opposition.

As a second point, much of both the Greek and modern Enlightenment objection to the divine "condescension" in loving fallen humanity to the point of the oblation, suffering, and death of his Son, on the grounds that such a love is out of scale, extravagant, or out of proportion to its object, and probably owes its origin more to wishful thinking and self-flattery on our part, can be deflected on the theoretical plane by saying that God sees us *as we could be*; he sees us as He intended us to be, as imitations of Himself and theoretical possibilities in His mind "before" He made us—and thus before "original sin." It was this that initially attracted and still legitimately holds His interest. That is, this is a worthy and deserving object for such love; in a sense, God loves us *toward* this goal as our final cause, our true or best selves, no matter how far our actual selves may have strayed or currently fall short of this. This is probably the best interpretation to be put on the faith/works controversy, and the assertion that "grace" comes first; it is not merited. Thus this claim of an astounding and gratuitous divine love for a fallen humanity need not necessarily constitute a violation of the Greek (and Enlightenment) stipulation that love should be proportional to its object.

Duns Scotus

We have seen that Christian thinkers early discovered significant resources within the classical tradition to forge an accommodation between the potential egotism/altruism opposition and to respond to the claim that a divine love for humanity must be dismissed as a fantasy which blithely ignores the uncrossable chasm separating the two, both aspects of the Greek and Enlightenment psychology of love which the Christian "good news," especially in its Augustinian expression, seemed to contradict. As we saw in the previous article, Duns Scotus went even further and proposed what may be the ultimate synthesis of the Christian announcement of God's unexpected and astounding action with the Greek convention of proportionate love. If Augustine is revered for reconciling Christian doctrine with Platonic philosophy, and Thomas Aquinas for reconciling Christian doctrine with Aristotle, perhaps Duns Scotus should be celebrated in our own day for forging a reconciliation between Christian doctrine and the Enlightenment values which increasingly are all that bind the modern world together.

The reason for creation, that is, the reason there is anything besides God, or a world at all, had long been clarified or rescued from absurdity by the notion that there could be a form of "motion" not based on need or lack, but rather on completeness, over-fullness, and generosity, and that a complete being would be most attracted to sharing its goodness with a creature best able to comprehend and appreciate the gift it is receiving. This seemed to fit well with the biblical witness from *Genesis*, where the animals appear to be made for, and to be subordinated to, man, and also with Greek conventions concerning a proper relationship between unequals. However, the motive for the Incarnation reposed and exacerbated the problem, and this led Duns Scotus to introduce a further refinement into this theory, one which has the triple effect of basing philosophy more radically upon theology, simplifying the traditional two-beat syncopation of salvation history, and solving the potential opposition between egotism and altruism in a way that reconciles the biblical witness with the Greek convention of relationship in a deeper and more satisfying way. It is a breathtaking and bold innovation, one which introduces an unprecedented unity into the relationship between philosophy and theology and also surprisingly satisfies the Enlightenment sensibility by insisting upon the legitimate self-interest of God, thus overcoming the objection to what seemed an inappropriate *kenosis* or self-emptying, an unacceptable self-abasement by God in the Augustinian/Calvinistic depiction, producing a more satisfying synthesis between faith and reason, and thereby a more powerful rhetoric or apologetic for Christianity for today's Enlightenment or "post-Enlightenment" audience.

The unitary approach abolishes the two-beat syncopation of the traditional (scriptural) approach to salvation history, and makes God look less surprised and dismayed by the appearance of sin among men. On the contrary, he foresaw and is able to exploit this development to occasion a revelation of the extent of his love for himself which he wishes to open up and share with a creature worthy and able to appreciate it. Christ both *discloses* the Father's love, and is also the perfect *response* to that love.[7] Further, this interpretation is in surprising accord with the Greek canons of perfection, where the greater is properly taken up with the greater. It makes the divine *kenosis* or "condescension" toward fallen humankind no longer the scandal or stumbling block, the violation of proper canons of perfection or the psychology of loving, a mythological indulgence in self-flattery, self-pity, or wishful thinking, it had appeared before to a Greek (as St. Paul discovered when he preached to the philosophers on the Areopagus) or to the modern Enlightenment sensibility. On the contrary and paradoxically, it for the first time allowed the completion of the Greek project to develop a "scientific" or rational account for the world's existence, in the face of the Greek failure to produce such. The Greek problem or impediment is removed, not by *denying* the Greek doctrine of God's proper involvement with Himself, his satisfying knowledge and love for Himself, but rather by stressing, *intensifying*, and reinterpreting this. Surprisingly, this makes the production of a world not only possible; it seems almost to imply it.

Philosophy culminates in Theology, with the Greek conventions of divine perfection respected at the same time as they are revised in an imaginative way. Not only the Greek project but the Christian project is brought to completion at the same stroke. In a sense, the Western enterprise is now complete. A final synthesis between Christian doctrine and Greek philosophy—and with it a response to the deepest objection posed by the Enlightenment—has been forged.

It is a long way from Duns Scotus to the Enlightenment—almost five hundred years. But did Duns Scotus anticipate its concerns for freedom and an unsentimental testing and probing of the deepest Christian mysteries by naturalistic criteria? If he did, then in the incompletely achieved project to "inculturate" Christianity with the modern Enlightenment mentality is Duns Scotus a neglected but providentially still available guide, perhaps even an apostle or "patron saint" for our time?

Notes

[1] See Aristotle, *Nicomachean Ethics*, 1158b25; 1136b1–5; hereafter "NE."

[2] See Plato, *The Republic*, Bk. 6, 508.

[3] The One of course cannot know itself, since this would bring division; it knows itself at the second level, Mind. But from there on, Plotinus makes this suggestion: "What we know as Nature is a Soul, offspring of a yet earlier Soul of more powerful life; it possesses in its repose, a vision of itself; it has no tendency upward nor downward, but is at peace, steadfast, in its own Essence; in this immutability accompanied by what may be called Self-Consciousness, it possesses a knowledge of the realm of subsequent things perceived in virtue of that understanding and consciousness." *Enneads*, 3.8.4 (MacKenna trans.).

[4] Kant had a silhouette of Rousseau hanging in his rooms, the only thinker he so honored. Kant's case is complicated, in that he underwent a reversal in order to give the moral law some opposition and to make its victory in conscience not automatic in true "freedom." See Emil L. Fackenheim, "Kant and Radical Evil," in *The University of Toronto Quarterly*, July 1954, pp. 339–353.

[5] NE 1124a5–15.

[6] NE 1166a30–35.

[7] For a good discussion of this, see Eric Doyle, *Duns Scotus and the Place of Christ*, Clergy Review, Sept.–Oct.–Nov. 1972.

CHAPTER 6

Lawrence of Brindisi and the Completion of the Project of the West

The most novel and serious attacks upon religion in the twentieth century have centered not on the traditional arguments for the existence of God but on the psychological motivations and effects which acceptance of the "god hypothesis," and specifically of its Christian expression, might have for the devotee. In the wake of Nietzsche and Freud specifically, these criticisms have tended to bracket investigation into the accuracy or truthfulness of religious doctrine, which is charitably held to be impossible to determine, to view religion instead as a compensation mechanism when dealing with experiences of marginality, powerlessness, inferiority, and hopelessness—as a way of turning the tables upon the master or dominant class, displacing them from their positions of power in an apocalyptic reversal, dismissing them in the end to the marginality and insignificance from which the devotee first suffered. In this optic the gospels appear as a kind of first century Semitic *samizdat*, an underground and covert spoof of the powers that be, an understandable, if not especially constructive, channeling of the devotee's *réssentiment*, anger, and will to power into an imaginary or pretend victory, insulting and caricaturing in secret the master class whose yoke they cannot—and dare not attempt to—throw off. Religion is ultimately a pathetic gesture, an impotent substitute and make-believe triumph by a class that cannot achieve this in practice, and thus a further measure of their abject and miserable condition.

The Judeo-Christian scriptures certainly offer rich resources for such an interpretation. One need not list all the passages—ranging from the fifteenth chapter of *Exodus* where the Israelites rejoice over the Egyptian army becoming mired in the Red Sea, making fun of pharaoh going down together with "his chariots and charioteers," to the numerous places in the gospels where Jesus gives an illustration or parable expressing "the last shall be first, and the first last," to recognize the powerful tow or attraction which this theme plays throughout the canonical texts. Ironically, what Christian theologians have held up through the ages as a strength or power of the gospel message is here turned upon its head, or into a liability. Traditionally Christian apologists have stressed the discrepancy or gap between God's merciful love manifested in the passion and death of his Son, when contrasted with the objective merits of sinful humanity—that is, the lavish, excessive, disproportionate character of God's outpouring of love when measured against the desserts of fallen mankind, as a way of inducing not only repentance for sin, but also acceptance of Christian doctrine *tout court.*

Such a device caused suspicion and unease from the beginning. St Paul preaching on the Areopagus was doing fine, getting a respectful hearing as long as he talked about the unknown god whom the Athenians already worshiped, in whom we "live and move and have our being." As soon as he started talking about the death and resurrection of Jesus, however, they invited him to speak to them again another day, which was a polite way of fobbing him off entirely. Not only would this appear a step back toward mythology, which the Greeks already had too much of and which the "philosophers" were trying to leave behind in favor of a "scientific" discourse which would be the same at all times and in all cultures, but it raised the question of *why* a god-man would have to suffer and die for humanity.

For the Greeks, the gods were properly taken up with themselves. Mankind was too far below their level for them to take an interest in anything that went on here. It seems to be a bit of recurrent tribal self-delusion or self-flattering wishful thinking for a group to think that a god (or a god-man) could seriously care about what happens to them or take an interest in helping them. To say that he "died" for us only compounds the error, or distracts us from the main issue by heightening it into melodrama. We start asking the wrong question; not "*Could* he have died for us?" but "Why did he *have* to die for us?" Further, it shamelessly exploits our emotions to force assent by arousing embarrassment and guilt over a topic which should be the subject initially of a purely disinterested, objective deliberation. For the Greeks, love should be proportional to its object; and although sharing nothing of the Christian notion of "original sin," they did concur that the distance between ourselves and the gods was simply too great, they would not and did not "come down" to our level or mix themselves with our affairs. Such is the stuff of entertaining and sometimes edifying mythology, but not of a serious account of the real.

Tertullian and Augustine in the West followed St. Paul in Romans by stressing atonement for Adam's sin as the chief motivation for the

Incarnation. After all, if Adam had never sinned, there would have been no need for a "messiah" to come. Augustine did allow, however, that this "original sin" was in a way a *"felix culpa"* or "happy fault," in that it opened for us a fate that was higher than our initial condition in the garden of Eden. When asked the same question, the Eastern Fathers tended to follow St. John and suggest that God became man so that man could become God—not literally God of course, but could participate as far as possible in the divine life. This may resemble the question of whether the glass is half empty or half full, since presumably our share in Adam's sin initially poses an obstacle to our deeper participation in God's life, and must be removed if we are to share more fully; however, it makes an important difference in rhetorical technique and the eventual psychological motive of the ephebe which one the proselytizer emphasizes.

Eastern theology shows an enduring influence of Neo-Platonism, with a tendency to subordinationism in Origen, Arius, and Eutyches, that is, denying the full humanity of Jesus while still refusing to place him equal to the Father. Western theology preserves a more powerful sense of the transcendence of God and of Jesus' equality with him, but with a correspondingly stronger sense of sin not just as our ontological condition as creatures but as a practical reality that widens the gap between God's merciful love and our merits, so psychological manipulation through the emotions of embarrassment, guilt, and shame is a stronger possibility, as is also an "exclusionist" model of the Church as the elect or "saved," over against a world that cannot be saved, in contrast to an "inclusionist" model, which incorporates a recognition of human weakness and the possibility, indeed the necessity, of forgiveness and reconciliation *within* the Church. While the Eastern Church may have the more noble or healthy psychology of conversion, perhaps it is a fair comment that few of us, at least when we come into the Church, have the mentality of Greek philosophers. But for those of us who do, good reasons are still there.

This stress on the gap between God's outsized love and our lowly merits continued through the Middle Ages, gradually being corrected until the Reformation, when unfortunately the West took a giant step backward, and this discrepancy became institutionalized as the official confession of the Protestant Churches. Thereafter not only was this gap not crossed over or reconciled, it was exploited for evangelistic, polemical, or ideological purposes. "Amazing grace, how sweet the sound" may have been balm to the repentant sinner, but it was less

aromatic to the classical Greek as well as to the emerging Enlightenment mentality, which began with a secularized version of Calvinistic
Christianity in Hobbes' sense of an inherently self-seeking and violent
human nature, but gradually converted to Rousseau's kinder reading,
and decided, with the Duke de la Rochefoucauld, Mandeville, and
Adam Smith that self-interest should be harnessed rather than chastised
or reformed. The modern world has ceased to feel guilty about self-
interest, and thus paradoxically rejoins the classical Greek mentality
which holds that love should be proportional to its object, that it is
wrong to love an object above or below its merits, and is unapologetic
about seeking its own fulfillment by finding and acquiring the best
objects around.

God is right to be preoccupied with the highest or the best. After
all, we are—why shouldn't he? We are in general unmoved by the
special pleading involved by stressing the outsized love God showered
upon a sinful humanity; along with this, we are suspicious about appeals
to emotions of embarrassment, guilt, and shame at having been the
occasion of such a divine sacrifice and humiliation. These smack of
manipulation or appeals to our less rational nature, and if we choose to
stay Christian nonetheless, we do so for other reasons. We fast and
purify ourselves, but to enter more deeply into the divine life, not out of
guilt. The doctrine of original sin is equivalent to the need for conversion, which we can grant is experientially true apart from one's
position on Christ.[1] But this must ultimately be compatible with the
philosophic truth that love should be proportional to its object, on pain
of falling into an inconsistent or schizophrenic world. The two can no
longer be kept apart. In short, there has been a rehabilitation of (critical)
self-love as a classical virtue in the contemporary world, and this is
largely the result, not of instruction by the Christian authorities but just
the opposite, from an underground uprising and rebellion by an
Enlightenment mentality which has kept the peace and gone along with
a (largely Protestant) expression of Christianity which stresses this gap,
one which we, however, no longer accept or deeply honor.

In such a conflicted climate it is perhaps not out of place to mention
the name of Lawrence of Brindisi, a Capuchin Franciscan who lived on
the cusp of the seventeenth century, who accepted the Scotean revolution of trying to reconcile the traditional Christian doctrine of the gap
between God's outpouring of love and our sinful condition with the
Greek principle that love should be proportional to its object, by boldly
announcing that God is justly and properly occupied with himself, and

after that with the best that creation has to offer; and extended this Scotist doctrine by adding and reconciling to Christ's nature as the perfect creature his office as the redeemer of humankind.

The Development Up to Lawrence

Both the Eastern and Western churches accepted the same creeds, but they were subjected to different historical and cultural influences, and different emphases were placed upon them. The trinitarian and christological doctrines were hammered out in the East against the background of an all-embracing Neo-Platonic thought world, already apparent, or at least susceptible to being read into, the prologue and other parts of John's gospel. Monasticism developed in the East, and the monks exercised considerable theological influence; in general they opted for a high christology, emphasizing the divinity of Christ, or the cosmic view of Christ as the mind or *Logos* of the Father, from whom all things flow and to whom they return. Speculation stayed fairly close to the scriptural drama, with the devil fishing for the souls of men to drag them down to death, but instead being caught himself on the "imperishable hook" of Christ. The full human nature of Christ, apart from sin, was finally, and sometimes grudgingly, granted on the principle that "what is not taken on, cannot be saved," and later speculation opened up the connections between the various faculties in Christ, for example, between his divine and human will. A parallel exploration of the relations between body and spirit, or the inter-workings and potentially problematic relation between grace and human free will, was not forthcoming in the East. It would have seemed a foregone conclusion and irrelevant to the obvious process of sanctification and mystical union practiced by the ascetics and other holy people. What is actual must be possible.

In the Roman West the interest in law, the cold, sober light of day on practical affairs in contrast to mystical union, and the interest in allocating responsibility with a finer distinction shifted attention to what had been left undone by the pioneering work of the East. The cosmological speculations of John Scotus Erigena, similar to what had been generated in the East, had no resonance and left no lasting effects on developments in the western Mediterranean basin, reeling under the influence of the barbarian invasions and trying desperately to preserve what it could of its Roman heritage. The traditional Roman interest in law, the disorder of the times, a residual feeling of cultural inferiority with regard to the East, and the fact that its two most influential theologians, Tertullian and Augustine, had passed through a licentious youth, combined to produce a greater emphasis on overcoming personal sin than scaling mystical heights. Two elements in Augustine, his doctrine of original sin and his almost rabid anti-Pelagianism, marked the West for over a thousand years, and were only gradually corrected by the complementary doctrines of the goodness of creation and the Greek notion that love should be proportional to its object—both in God and man.

Augustine is known as the "doctor of grace," but he could equally well be known as the "doctor of original sin." The two doctrines go together in his thinking, and are further tied to his anti-Pelagianism. Pelagius was a lay ascetic from Britain, and took it for granted, as did everyone embarked on what medieval spiritual writers would later call the "ladder of perfection," that God does not so much desire that the sinner die in his sins, but extends our life so that we may repent. Every monk, in particular, presumes that with effort we can make progress in the spiritual life, for God's grace is normally available in every case but the most serious, and even then there is no sin that cannot be forgiven. Pelagius went too far, however, in affirming the perfectibility of man; he asserted that a man could be without sin. The reality of sin means rather that, to come to maturity, every person must go through a conversion experience, that is, acknowledge from experience his or her own capacity for sin. Pelagius' position provoked Augustine into an equally exaggerated counter-position.

Augustine's own experience as virtually an addict to sin and his complete hopelessness of overcoming his sin by his own efforts led him to stress the primacy of God's grace both for initiating our conversion and for sustaining us at every step along the path. Of course, Pelagius would have said, but this does not take away the possibility and indeed the necessity of human freedom. Augustine in his rigorism would hear nothing of it, and the issue was not properly resolved, or even joined, during their lifetimes.[2] The danger in such a position of collapsing human freedom into a divine determinism was apparently not brought home to Augustine; it was left to the "predestination" of the Protestant reformers for this possibility to become explicit. More broadly, the understanding of grace as a mechanistic force rather than an empowering invitation, as is proper between persons, spoiled the discussion by skewing the relation between grace and free will into an inverse rather than a direct proportion, thereby leading speculation on this issue down a dead end from which it has only recently recovered.

When asked about God's motive for the Incarnation, Augustine following St. Paul said it was to make up for Adam's sin. If Adam had never sinned, there would have been no need for a savior. The apogee of the atonement theory was reached under Anselm around the year 900, when using a banking metaphor, Anselm said that through the fall of our first parents mankind had incurred an "infinite debt" against God. Since no creature could pay off an infinite debt, God himself had to make good on what was owed against him, or see all creation carried off by the devil. There was a difficulty with this theory recognized as early as Augustine, because our state after Christ is better than was our state in the garden of Eden; Adam's sin then becomes a *"felix culpa,"* and it seems incongruous when not downright improper to make our greatest felicity depend upon the act for which we feel greatest shame and regret. Also, as a side issue, it seems to make God look surprised and unintelligent at not foreseeing the use some of his creatures would make of their free will, so he has to scramble and develop a "Plan B" when Adam and Eve spoil his first plan of creation.

Speculation was gradually drawn to these issues as the Middle Ages progressed; it centered on the question, "If Adam had never sinned, would the Incarnation still have taken place?" Most early thinkers followed Augustine in answering "No," that Christ came to atone for Adam's sin. Support gradually waxed for the other side. Thomas Aquinas stays balanced on the fence as far as reason is concerned, as he was on the question of the eternity of the world. God *could* have made it either way; scripture (or in this case the creed, *"propter nos homines et propter nostram salutem"*) decides the issue in favor of Augustine. However, in his final production, the Lenten homilies he delivered in Naples shortly before he died on his way to the second council of Lyons, Thomas developed a more nuanced view. In his commentary on the creed, Thomas declared that Adam's sin is the cause of Christ's *Passion*, but not specifically of the *Incarnation*, and he quotes approvingly the Greek maxim that God became man so that man might become God.[3] In other words, God might have become man even if Adam had never sinned.

It required the subtle doctor, Duns Scotus, however, to declare this openly and unreservedly. It forms part of his overall metaphysic in which he recasts the entire unfolding of Trinitarian theology in a way that was as revolutionary as was Augustine's treatment of the same topic in his *De Trinitate* over what the Greek Fathers had produced. Most noticeably there is finally a reconciliation between Christian faith, with its traditional doctrine of the discrepancy between God's lavish, even disproportionate display of love in the passion and death of his Son and the merits of fallen humanity, with the Greek principle that love should be proportional to its object. Previous efforts in Christian Neo-Platonism, for example, Bonaventure, had limited themselves to saying that God's love is proportional because He sees us as he made or intended us, *before* our sin; his love is thus not excessive, or he loves us *toward* our final, converted, or true self. But Scotus plunges in boldly to attack the central issue.

First of all, God is justly and properly preoccupied with himself. Self-love is not wrong, nor is it the same as selfishness; indeed, the two are almost opposed. God's knowledge of himself and the love between himself and this knowledge generates the Trinity; but such is the power or intensity of the divine goodness that this love cannot stop there or be contained within the godhead. God wishes to share his love or goodness with a creature qualified to appreciate it and reflect back to God the acknowledgment and glory which is his due. As the third Eucharistic prayer expresses the point of creation and of all salvation history:

From age to age you gather a people to yourself,
so that from east to west
a perfect offering may be made
to the glory of your name.

This is not a "disinterested love," which is willing or even eager to stay anonymous, if only the good of the beloved is achieved; this is the love of the God of the Old Testament, a God who is jealous and easily piqued into sorrow or anger. It is the love of the Greek *megalopsyché*, the "great souled" individual who has a high regard for himself and insists that others, especially those qualified to appreciate and measure his greatness, show a similar response. So it is not any creature that God will produce; on the contrary, it is the highest being that creation is capable of, the one most able to appreciate, acknowledge, and deliver back to God the praise that is his due. For Scotus this being is not simply humanity, an impression the account in *Genesis* could arouse, but rather the human nature of Christ, which is higher than humanity in general in that it is suited to be united with the Godhead. To get Christ, God of course had to make humanity; but this theory moves humanity a bit off center as the apple of God's eye. Rather it was Christ who was

God's first intention from all eternity. The Incarnation was God's intention even before the creation; it was not a second "Plan B" that God had to resort to when Adam and Eve upset his first plan. Indeed, since God is able to extract good even from evil, he was able to exploit the apparent failure of our first parents, to occasion an even greater or more powerful display of his goodness than would perhaps have been possible without it.

From Scotus to Lawrence

Lawrence of Brindisi was born in 1559 and died in 1619. From 1575 he was a Capuchin Franciscan friar. He was beatified in 1783, canonized in 1881, and declared a doctor of the Universal Church in 1959. Burdened almost continually with leadership positions within the Franciscan order, he nevertheless distinguished himself as a master of languages, diplomat, and brilliant controversialist, disputing with Protestants throughout Germany, Austria, and Bohemia, and winning back many areas for Catholicism. His chief contribution to theology consists of showing how Scotus' doctrine of Christ as the perfect creature is extended and complemented by Christ's role as the redeemer of humankind.

Although God gives mankind freedom, his will cannot be frustrated. God foresaw the misuse our first parents would make of their gift of freedom, but he included this in the economy of his primary intention, in the vocation to which he called the perfect creature Christ, in such a way that God's own goodness, and this creature's perfection, would be all the more manifest. Adam's sin was responsible not directly for the Incarnation, but for the Passion, a terrible tragedy and humiliation when isolated from its wider context within the circle of God's appropriate self-love, but an ingenious example of "intellectual judo," using a blow or apparent setback at the hands of the enemy to one's own advantage. Specifically in this case man's misuse of his freedom allowed God not only to bring forth the perfect creature Christ which he would have done anyway, but also through him to display a love out of proportion to what we could have imagined (but still proportional to what we could be), and thus to spread the revelation of the intensity of his goodness to the widest possible audience capable of appreciating it, thereby to bring about their conversion and return them to a deeper share in his internal life. The two-beat syncopation of the biblical narrative is replaced, or rather deepened and simplified, with the presentation of a single continuously unfolding intention which unifies the nature of Christ as perfect creature with his role as redeemer of humankind in such a way that the two descriptions reinforce and solidify one another. Weaving his defense out of scriptural allusions, Lawrence writes:

> God is love, and all his operations proceed from love. Once he wills to manifest that goodness by sharing his love outside himself, the Incarnation becomes the supreme manifestation of his goodness and love and glory. So Christ was intended before all other creatures and for his own sake. For him all things were created and to him all things must be subject, and God loves all creatures in and because of Christ. Christ is the first born of every creature, and the whole of humanity as well as the created world finds its foundation and meaning in him. Moreover, this would have been the case even if Adam had not sinned.[4]

Because this union of roles constitutes the final step in the reconciliation between the Greek and Christian world views, between Athens and Jerusalem, Duns Scotus and Lawrence of Brindisi may justly be said to have brought the project of the West to completion.

Notes

[1] For example, Plotinus has a strong doctrine of conversion, but obviously no doctrine of Christ as necessary for this, or even of God as being able to help us in this, because his self-preoccupying perfection forbids him from giving any aid whatsoever.

[2] Interestingly, the Protestant Peter Brown adopts a "Catholic" defense of Augustine against the "icy Puritanism" of the Pelagians; he does, however, concede that Pelagianism was a system of ideas (occasioned primarily by the activity of his disciple Caelestius in North Africa) in the mind of *Augustine*, and not in the mind of Pelagius. See his *Augustine of Hippo*, Faber & Faber, London, 1967, p. 345.

[3] See *The Greatest Prayers: Commentaries on the Our Father, the Hail Mary, and the Apostles Creed by St. Thomas Aquinas*, trans. by L. Shapcote, Burns, Oates, & Washbourne, London, 1937, pp. 54, 56; see also *Summa Theologiae*, III, Q. 1, art. 3.

[4] Cited from *St. Lawrence of Brindisi, Doctor of the Universal Church*, Capuchin Educational Conference, Washington, D.C. (no page given). For a further account of the relations between Scotus and Lawrence, see B. de Margerie, S.J., *Christ for the World*, Franciscan Herald Press, Chicago, 1973, pp. 4–14.

PART II

CHAPTER 7

Space in Leibniz and Whitehead

One noteworthy feature of modern relativity physics is the shift it involves away from a Newtonian conception of space and time as fixed and independent axes toward what might be called a "Leibnizean" reduction of space and time to a subjective, phenomenal status. Whitehead's philosophy of actual entities in process is deliberately intended to be in tune with the results of recent scientific research, and it is not surprising to find this shift reflected in the analysis Whitehead gives of space, or, as he calls it, the "extensive continuum."

His doctrine of space is not the only, or even the most prominent, Leibnizean aspect of Whitehead's philosophy. Whitehead's "actual entities" bear a marked resemblance to Leibniz's "monads." Both are considered the ultimate foundations of all that is real; neither philosopher will tolerate a free-floating property or relation not tied down to one of the basic substances.[1] For both men these basic ontological units are organic, capable of development, and enjoy, even at the lowest levels, a perspective upon the world as a whole. For neither philosopher is God an exception to the basic categorical scheme; God differs from other entities essentially by the character of the perception he enjoys on the cosmos. Both men posit a realm of "possible essences" or "eternal objects" which contribute the types of definiteness which may appear in the world of process and are the means by which other aspects of the world are grasped and unified by each monadic entity. For both men God plays an essential role in regulating the monad's response to his world through an adjustment in his perceptions. For both men, further, the ultimate principle of the world is a mysterious agency whose actions are not inherently rational; space (and time) is enlisted by both to serve as a principle of restraint upon the unpredictable actions of this divine agency.

Although Leibniz recoiled before Spinoza's deterministic account of the emanation of the world from God, he was not himself notably successful in rendering God's choice of this particular world either a freer or a more rational act. For Spinoza God is the *causa sui*, the unique substance which "is in itself and is conceived through itself"; if he is free, it is only in the sense that he "exists from the necessity of his own nature alone, and is determined to action by himself alone"—a description which makes God's self-genesis and the creation of the world both an unpredictably spontaneous and a totally determined act, irrational in the sense of grounded only in the inflexible nature of God, and yet inevitable given God's essence as necessarily including existence.[2] In opposition to this view, Leibniz attempted to locate a properly free act separating God's existence from the creation of the world. Everything in the universe is the way it is for a sufficient reason. God chose to elect into existence this particular set of compossible essences from the realm of all possible essences because this set was most congruent with his free choice to will the best. But what determined God to will the best? And more basically, what about this set warrants calling it the "best"?

To answer these questions, Leibniz seems to have taken his cue from the principle Descartes had used strategically in the third *Meditation* to break out of solipsism: "my ideas may be considered all on the same level as aspects of my mind, but they may also be ranked in a hierarchy depending upon the degree of reality they 'objectively' or 'representationally' contain." Descartes has in mind here as the highest idea that of God, which then comes to demand a cause proportional to its objective reality. With Leibniz, however, this singular qualitatively preeminent idea is transformed into a *system* of compossible essences which differs from other such systems only by the greater number of distinct essences brought into mutual interrelation. The qualitative preeminence of Descartes' "objective reality" in an idea is flattened out by Leibniz into its quantitative constitution.[3] The locution "best" is explicated by means of the twin principles of plenitude and continuity. God's choice is not free but becomes tied to the outcome of the calculus of essences. The "infinite" analysis that would be necessary to understand the interconnections between the essences insures only that a human mind will never be able to see this choice as determined, not that the choice is not in fact determined. Indeed, this divine decision insures not even that the "best" possible universe will be realized in any sense that is directly relevant to human needs or aspirations, but only that the greatest amount of "being" will be realized, each distinct essence being considered as of the same metaphysical "weight" as every other. God's "antecedent" nature wills each essence for itself; it supplies to each its *conatus* or drive to existence. Fortunately, God's striving must submit to the laws of logic; only a set of *compossible* essences can be actualized. The potential incompatibilities are smoothed out; the power of the *conatus* is harnessed to bring into being one variegated but still coherent world. The drive to existence, first at the level of essence, then further to the status of full existence, has a compelling, uncritical, basically inexplicable and irrational hold over God's energy. It operates with essences on an individual, virtually indiscriminate basis. In his earliest moment and most basic impulse, God would bring into being *all* essence. A chaos would result, a world of contradiction and essentual mutual frustration among monads.

The locution "best possible world" is thus with Leibniz only a roundabout way of expressing that God is *not* free to bring into being *any* set of essences but is subject to logic in his choice. God is subject first to the general requirement of compatibility among elected essences; then, once he has acquiesced to the outcome of the "strife of essences," this set itself exercises a further restraint upon God's activity. But how do we know that this interesting speculation is true? What evidence does Leibniz offer to assure us of the consistency and coherence of our world? Leibniz's clever innovation, which Kant will later follow, is to play upon the evident phenomenal immersion of all perceptions in space and time, together with the apparent unity and coherence of the latter, to argue for the deeper coherence of the logical ordering.

Space for Leibniz is the order of coexisting things, time the order of successive things. As such, space and time are real but not in the sense of being independent substances as Newton believed; rather they are relative and phenomenal. In detaching and absolutizing these relations, we introduce a subjective and (to the extent these relations are taken as independent) a distorting element into our ideas of space and time; nevertheless, there is a real, basically logical order structuring the interrelations between monads, so even the abstract ideas we form have an objective reference. They are subjective ideas, but well-founded on objective reality, in the sense that the limitation they place on what can become real for us is derived from and is ultimately grounded in the logical relationship which must exist between essences elected into existence. The possibility of a radical disharmony in our lived experience is thereby precluded.

Space is ontologically of intermediate status, a pale simulacrum which, however, is a valid phenomenal representation of the basic logical order that must obtain among the phenomenal appearances. It is insubstantial, like a ghost, but nonetheless valid, informative, and efficacious as a principle; it derives all its ontological strength from the underlying logical order whose coherence it communicates. As the order of persuasion is often the reverse of the order of ontological dependence, however, it is the phenomenal unity and coherence of space which is taken by Leibniz as a sign for the deeper submission of God's will to a particular set of logical categories and, more deeply still, to the limitation to logical compossibility in the first place. The *fact* of space and time is read as an empirical indication that God does not bring into being all possible (and therefore incompatible) essences, although this is his natural tendency. The basic logical demand for compatibility, and the more specific set of essences God agrees to elect into existence, act as a series of obstacles which direct his basically irrational impetus toward being into channels where it can do us no harm, or more precisely, where it can do us the least harm possible.

Just as space has both a subjective and an objective reference for Leibniz, the "extensive continuum" is given two independent developments by Whitehead. There is a "realistic" or metaphysical treatment wherein space is described as the "outermost society" or most general set of relations which bind and, in Leibnizean fashion, are grounded in actual entities:

> The physical relations, the geometrical relations of measurement, the dimensional relations, and the various grades of extensive relations, involved in the physical and geometrical theory of nature, are derivative from a series of societies of increasing width of prevalence, the more special societies being included in the wider societies.[4]

But Whitehead has also given an epistemological description of space as seen from the perspective of its appearance to the individual actual entity. The "extensive continuum," as a relatively clear and distinct appreciation of our environment as a *present* (and not just as a past) forms an aspect of, and arises for the first time with, the mode of awareness known as "presentational immediacy."[5] Presentational immediacy itself arises as a development out of the received or implanted datum of "causal efficacy"; to invoke T.S. Elliott, it is causal efficacy "spread out against the sky." An essential ingredient in the development of presentational immediacy out of causal efficacy, however, is the "subjective form" of the individual entity, which is in turn supervised in its operation by God's own "subjective aim." The extensive continuum, then, in its epistemological aspect as the outermost horizon of the clear mode of awareness of presentational immediacy, is a joint product of the raw datum of causal efficacy and of God's modification of our subjective form.

God is decisively implicated in the advance to a more discriminating appreciation of the world involved in the concrescence constituting each actual entity. The basis for the "valuing" conferred upon each concrescence is a function of God's own initial (timeless) concrescence, in which the termini of his own prehensions are the unchanging eternal objects. God's own constitution (in his primordial nature) consists of a structuring of the eternal objects in a hierarchy of values which thenceforward becomes regulatory for the time-bound concrescences of other actual entities.[6]

It is apparently not God's own decision which properly determines the initial and decisive structuring of eternal objects, but the conditions for maximal intensity of experience, which is God's chief aim. God for Whitehead is not the truly ultimate agency in his philosophy, but only the first modification of the formless but dynamic center called more properly "creativity." Creativity for Whitehead is a basic drive, not to existence, as with Leibniz, but to higher intensities of experience. "God" is the name for the fusion of this basic creative force with the first, timeless valuation.

> Creativity is without a character of its own in exactly the same sense in which the Aristotelian "matter" is without a character of its own. It is that ultimate notion of the highest generality at the base of actuality. It cannot be characterized, because all characters are more special than itself. But creativity is always found under conditions, and described as conditioned. The non-temporal act of all inclusive unfettered valuation [i.e., God] is at once a creature of creativity and a condition for creativity.[7]

In practice, the limitations placed upon the operations of this force by the conditions for maximal intensity of experience come to much the same as they had with Leibniz in the attempt to achieve the maximum of variety among monads compatible with unity. Generally speaking, an increase in discriminating sensitivity is achieved by the ingression of a greater number of eternal objects into our experience, and is accompanied by a heightened intensity in our final satisfaction:

As stated, God's tendency is primarily toward intensity of experience; from the divine point of view, it is of only incidental importance that this goal is furthered by "balance" or coherence.

Intelligibility is not an integral element in God's intention but is only a necessary condition and accompaniment if higher plateaus of enjoyment are to be reached. In his initial fixing of the eternal objects, God is bound by logical canons which legislate the conditions for such heightened experience. Unity is a means to this increased satisfaction, not an end in itself or a feature directly intended by God. To this point, Whitehead's precautions against the potential for disorder in creativity (although weak) resemble those of Leibniz against the "antecedent" nature of God; but Whitehead introduces a further check upon his primary agency's activities which Leibniz does not have.

We have stated that God is directly involved in the elevation and clarification of causal efficacy into presentational immediacy as this takes place in the concrescence of the actual entity with the help of its subjective form. The extensive continuum for Whitehead is not just a reflection of God's ordering of the eternal objects, as space had been for Leibniz, but is an outgrowth and clarification of the implanted datum of causal efficacy, and is thus limited by the elasticity with which this darker force is receptive to the full sweep of God's creative thrust. A further limitation is thereby introduced to the forms space, or the extensive continuum, can assume, by the limits to the ductility of this rough medium of which it is a part. Causal efficacy, as the foundation of all phenomena in the mode of presentational immediacy (and with it of the extensive continuum), thus acts as a check and restraint upon what God can launch into experience, beyond and independent of that imposed by the set of eternal objects which regulate intensity of experience. This is a check which Leibniz, with his "windowless" monads, did not have. The extensive continuum is dependent ontologically on causal efficacy; it is simply the clearest distillation and most sensitive reading of the latter. But rhetorically the undeniable reality of space and the raw force connecting entities function for Whitehead as a further assurance, beyond the conditions of logical unity, that an otherwise uncontrollable creative agency will indeed be directed along acceptable lines.[9]

In Plato's *Timaeus* the divine artisan looks to the changeless forms as models for his product, but he is limited in his ability to introduce these forms by the medium he finds at hand. With Leibniz and Whitehead the divine artisan remains the essential but now questionable motor behind world history. Leibniz has this power limited only by the logical forms (and by his subsequent choice therefrom). Whitehead throws a further rope over this fundamental dynamism by invoking the medium with which this deity must work, a medium which has certain limitations to its potential malleability. With Leibniz, Whitehead appears to want to exploit the apparent unity of space and time, their ubiquity as the media of experience, as an indication of the deeper integrity of God's cosmic plan. The hardly dubitable realities of space, time, and gravity are enlisted to serve as experiential referents for a metaphysical coherence lying indiscernibly deeper; they are used to cast a rein over the potentially unlimited and uncontrollable activity of the deity which both have identified as the center and dynamo of the cosmos.

For both men, space and time are used in a strategically suasive capacity in keeping at arm's length the possibility of a discordant, chaotic world, a real alternative given their descriptions of the primordial reality as an irresistible drive toward existence and experience; later philosophers, such as Schopenhauer, Nietzsche, and Sartre, will maintain this description of the fulminating center of reality while dispensing with the screen of logical or esthetic categories that both men used to keep such divine sparks from flying out to disturb our experience. This precaution is a measure of the optimism both Leibniz and Whitehead share and of their desire to have their systems reflect the confidence of their outlook; yet it also indicates the care they take to plant a restraint at the same time as they avail themselves of a powerful but unnerving genie as the center of their systems. Both men are led to thematize space in the particular way they do by a problem they have laid for themselves in their doctrine of God. Both men maintain a division in God's nature; God's intelligence remains foreign to his most basic essence, which is reduced univocally to force or power. Logical or esthetic coherence remains at best an ectoskeleton or set of organs which, however vital, remain outside the pulsating center of divine activity, and whose impulses they are barely able to restrain.

One can agree with Leibniz's insistence that there can be no unattached properties of space and time as Newton had posited without embracing his view of space as a surface reflection (and thoughtfully arranged guarantee) of the logical coherence of God's plan for the cosmos. Whitehead, one suspects, was led to this view through the less commendable motive of wanting to appear in step with the most recent trends in physical theory. We may avoid the systematic embarrassment of having space a "thing" which paradoxically contains other things without itself being contained within something of wider scope, by moving away from space as a "thing-like" substance to the conception of space as a principle or essential component in any object of our experience. This would accord with Leibniz's insight into space's derivative status without requiring that we see space as a false abstraction or shade of logical order. Space may be a positive element or principle in its own right, apart from a logical element. It can never exist by itself as a "thing," however, but always in conjunction with an opposite, logical component. Such a shift in our conception of space would also resolve its puzzling status as an isolated substance which can then only be related to the other full (and unique) substantial entity, God, by way of an identity—either as the "sensorium" or body of God as for Newton; an infinite physical mode or manifestation of God as for Spinoza; or again as a hardening but pellucid surface which serves symbolic notice of the deeper, successful activity of the Transcendental Unity of Apperception in its project to unify the full manifold of possible experience, as with Kant.

Once space is viewed not as a substance in its own right but as a correlative principle, as outlined above, the way is left open to accord to this principle the other functions presented by the non-logical aspects of our experience—such experiences as resistance, the potential for disorder, and of distinction between objects otherwise similar. The basically Aristotelian direction to this solution need not here be drawn out to completeness; its relevance for us lies in the continuity of such a solution with the basic direction taken by both Leibniz and Whitehead before they were detoured by the decision to enlist space to handle the problem of divine irrationality in their systems. This problem, though certainly a vital one, lies too deep for a philosophic analysis of space alone to handle; further, such a mobilization of space for purposes foreign to its natural interest threatens to distract attention from the truly important issues involving space, of which a properly conducted philosophical analysis should serve to heighten our awareness.

Notes

[1] This is in fact the basis of Leibniz's criticism of Newton's conception of space. Actually, whereas Leibniz's monads are by nature immortal, Whitehead's actual entities are constantly "perishing" or have a life span of only one concrescence. As "drops of experience," they might better be compared with one in the sequence of ideas or perceptions upon the world Leibniz's monads enjoy and which, in summation, constitute the essence of each monad.

[2] Spinoza, *Ethics Demonstrated According to the Geometrical Order*, White tr., I, Definitions; as reprinted in *Spinoza Selections*, ed. J. Wild, Scribner, NY, 1930, with "his" substituted for "its" with regard to freedom.

[3] See A.O. Lovejoy, *The Great Chain of Being: A Study of the History of an Idea*, Harper & Row, NY, 1960, ch. V, "Plenitude and Sufficient Reason in Leibniz and Spinoza," esp. p. 177.

[4] A.N. Whitehead, *Process and Reality*, Harper & Row., NY, 1960, p. 141; see also p. 96. Hereafter "PR."

[5] "In our perception of the contemporary world via presentational immediacy, nexus of actual entities are objectified for the percipient under the perspective of their character of extensive continuity." PR 119; see also 188.

[6] "The primordial created fact is the unconditioned conceptual valuation of the entire multiplicity of eternal objects. This is the 'primordial nature' of God." PR 46 "He is the unconditioned actuality of conceptual feeling at the base of things; so that, by reason of this primordial actuality, there is order in the relevance of eternal objects to the process of creation." PR 52 "By reason of this complete valuation, the objectification of God in each derivate actual entity results in a graduation of the relevance of eternal objects to the concrescent phases of that derivate occasion." PR 46.

[7] PR 46.

[8] PR 424.

[9] That the extensive continuum does indeed function for Whitehead as an epistemological guarantee against disorder is indicated by the following: "Extension, apart from its spatialization and temporalization, is that general scheme of relationships providing the capacity that many objects can be welded into the real unity of one experience." PR 105 "The extensive continuum is that general relational element in experience whereby the actual entities experienced, and that unit experience itself, are united in the solidarity of one common world." PR 112

CHAPTER 8

Time in Locke and Kant

In this paper I would like to discuss the re-emergence of the theme of time in the Kantian "critical" philosophy after a period of relative neglect during the scholastic and rationalist periods. The fundamental role which time plays in Kant's solution to the problem of the successful application of the *a priori* categories to experience, the problem Hume had raised with specific reference to the category of causality, is generally recognized, and to this extent one can speak of a re-emergence and indeed of a "triumph" of time in Kant's philosophy in the epistemological order. The dominance of the epistemological problem has tended to cast into shadow, however, a subtle and in some ways more substantive role which time takes on in the Kantian system, a role which I shall call for contrast the "metaphysical" role of time. It is toward the elucidation of the latter that I would like to progress in this paper. I have chosen to compare Kant with Locke because the re-emergence of time can be illustrated by a comparison of Locke's and Kant's doctrines on the idea of substance and because Locke anticipates, in his criticism of substance, the essentials of Hume's criticism of the category of cause, by pointing out the decisive discrepancy between the purported universal scope of the *a priori* idea and the more modest empirical origin of this idea. It was Hume's account of this discrepancy which, if we are to believe him, was the proximate cause in rousing Kant from his dogmatic slumbers in the Leibnizean-Wolffian system.

I have chosen Locke's *Essay* because Locke therein anticipates much of Hume's later critique and because Locke treats there the traditional idea of substance. Kant also discusses the idea of substance and does so with specific reference to time. The comparison of the two promises an insight into the skeptical attack on knowledge during this period and into the nature of Kant's response. Unlike his discussion of causality, Kant's treatment of substance shows a separation between an unknown, noumenal object and its phenomenal representation. Should we restrict ourselves to Kant's defense of the idea of causality and, for example, compare Hume with Kant, the temptation would be strong to suspect that Kant identifies time, as the form of representations, with the source of these representations, that he dissolves the hard "pellet" of substance into the sequence of ideas of cause and effect. This, as I hope to show, would be an inadequate and simplistic account of the way Kant, in his deepest thinking, relates time to the source of phenomena and representations.

I

Locke was concerned, as he himself tells us, to set down in his *Essay Concerning Human Understanding,*[1] the views and common assumptions of an educated English gentleman of about the year 1700. He attacks enthusiasm in all its forms and is against the theory of inborn ideas; but apart from these topics the *Essay*, composed of pieces written at various times and set together finally around 1690, displays far less evidence of a systematic viewpoint or unity of purpose than does, for instance, Kant's first *Critique*. Locke seems in fact a bit surprised, and a bit embarrassed, when toward the end of the *Essay* he is forced to report how meager, according to his canons, the scope of human knowledge turns out to be. Indeed, to save mathematical knowledge, Locke is forced to the extreme tactic of abandoning the definition of knowledge he gives in Chapter One of Book IV as "the perception of the agreement or disagreement of two ideas" (vol. 2, p. 133).

Locke begins his *Essay* by describing his purposes there in good modern or Cartesian fashion as the project to examine the faculty of knowledge which, as the tool or medium of access to the real world, rarely itself comes under inspection:

> The understanding, like the eye, while it makes us see and perceive all other things, takes no notice of itself; and it requires art and pains to set it at a distance, and make it its own object. (p. 5)

> I shall imagine I have not wholly misemployed myself in the thoughts I shall have on this occasion, if, in this historical, plain method, I can give any account of the ways whereby our understandings come to attain those notions of things we have, and can set down any measures of the certainty of our knowledge, or the grounds of those persuasions which are to be found amongst men. (p.5)

Locke proceeds to elaborate a metaphysics which recognizes two sorts of objects. There are empirical objects without and a self within. We are not directly acquainted with either of them directly, however, but have access to these objects only through the sensations they produce in us. For both Kant and Locke, the understanding is not able to produce sensations itself. External objects produce in us "sensations," while the simple ideas of "reflection" reveal the internal operations of the mind. Sensation and reflection are responsible for all our simple ideas; or as Locke expresses it, these two sources supply us with "all the materials of thinking." Elsewhere Locke calls perception "the inlet of knowledge."

The ideas of sensation and reflection are not only simple, they are also *clear* ideas. Or as Locke writes:

> There is nothing can be plainer to a man than the clear and distinct perceptions he has of these simple ideas. (p. 90)

This characteristic of clarity is important, in that Locke will later criticize the idea of substance as being confused or obscure. The characteristic of clarity is, in fact, used as an easily detectable tracing element which can be followed through the various operations of the mind and used to separate those complex ideas that begin from these clear simple ideas from those which do not. It is worthy of note that Locke here joins hands (for a brief moment) with the continental rationalists in finding in clarity and distinctness the hallmark of trustworthy ideas.

Because the ideas the mind has of its operations play a large role in both Locke's and Kant's particular philosophic achievements, it is worthwhile here to see what Locke says about the ideas of reflection. This "other fountain," he writes:

> is the perception of the operations of our own minds within us, as it is employed about the ideas it has got; which operations when the soul comes to reflect on and consider, do furnish the understanding with another set of ideas which could not be had from things without; and such are perception, thinking, doubting, believing, reasoning, knowing, willing, and all the different actings of our own minds; which we, being conscious of, and observing in ourselves, do from these receive into our understandings as distinct ideas, as we do from bodies affecting our senses. (p. 78)

It is clear that it is only because the mind has such simple ideas of reflection that a critical project such as Locke's, a project to examine by the "historical, plain method" the origin and certainty of human knowledge, to separate the reliable from the unreliable amongst our mental furnishings, can first be considered possible. Further, it is by the fact of having such simple and clear ideas of *reflection* that the project of a critical investigation which aspires to become a critical science or well-founded knowledge according to Locke's canons, also first becomes feasible. The simple ideas of reflection thus accomplish two ends. They give the inquirer initial access to the operations of his own mind, access which he would not have were he restricted in knowledge to the ideas of sensation. Second, as *clear*, simple ideas, the ideas of reflection measure up to Locke's technical standards for valid knowledge, and thus make a critical and decisive knowledge based on this investigation possible. The same requirement will drive Kant to speak of *perceptions* as well as conceptions of space and time, to allow his own critical investigation to conform to his own (different) paradigm of valid knowledge. The postulate of such perceptions also helps Kant save a segment of human knowledge (mathematics) which, we shall see, Locke is eventually forced to abandon to the skeptic.

Locke writes further:

> But as the mind is wholly passive in the reception of all its simple ideas, so it exerts several acts of its own, whereby out of its simple ideas, as the materials and foundations of the rest, the other are formed. (p. 130)

These "other" are the complex ideas, and among the more interesting from our point of view are the complex ideas of substances. Locke writes:

> The ideas of substances are such combinations of simple ideas as are taken to represent distinct particular things subsistent by themselves, in which the supposed or confused idea of substance, such as it is, is always the first and chief. (p. 131)

Locke gives his classic critique of the genesis, or pedigree, of the idea of substance in Chapter Twenty-Three of Book II:

> The mind being, as I have declared, furnished with a great number of the simple ideas conveyed in by the senses, as they are found in exterior things, or by reflection on its own operations, takes notice, also, that a certain number of these simple ideas go constantly together; which being presumed to belong to one thing, and words being united to common apprehensions, and made use of for quick dispatch, are called, so united in one subject, by one name; which, by

inadvertency, we are apt afterward to talk of and consider as one simple idea, which indeed is a complication of many ideas together; because, as I have said, not imagining how these simple ideas can subsist by themselves, we accustom ourselves to suppose some substratum wherein they do subsist, and from which they do result: which therefore we call substance. (p. 244)

Locke is using two ideas of substance: the one (indicated in the first quotation) refers to the traditional idea of substance as an independently subsisting object; the second, which we might call the modern or empirical idea of substance, is that of a constant conjunction of certain sense qualities, or the "substrate," physical or mental, which acts to bind these sensations together. Unlike Leibniz, who united the two ideas, Locke here separates them. Leibniz had, in effect, solved the problem of defining the mysterious dynamism of his monad by stating that the essence of the monad is given by the rule for its development, a rule which specifies an essence existing as a possibility in the mind of God. The mysterious inner nature of a substance thus renders itself explicit in the articulate sequence of its successive phases; this nature is captured within the rational confines of the clear sequence of the stages of its development. The dark or elusive notion of independent existence is translated into a clear systematic equivalent. The mysterious nature of substance is projected onto the temporal plane of its actions and dispositions; the successive manifestations are summed up and labeled the essence of the substance. Leibniz converts without loss of content, so he thinks, the traditional idea of substance into the modern.

Locke is equally intolerant of this unwieldy remnant of the traditional idea of substance, but he is clumsier in his handling of it. Rather than proclaiming the identity of the two ideas, Locke maintains a rigid separation; he impugns the one as confused and obscure, while commending the other for its clarity and distinctness. In the genesis of the idea of substance, none of the clarity in the original set of ideas has been lost, but a new confused idea has been added above (or just under) the original set; the original ideas are not less bright, but Locke finds them joined by a rude, even surly newcomer.

Both Locke and Leibniz suffer from a repressive antipathy to the darker element in the traditional idea of substance, the part which resists expression through a sequence of sense qualities. One way of appreciating Kant's achievement is, in fact, to recognize Kant's determination, like Locke, to maintain a strict separation between the darker element of substance and the clearer half without, like Locke, minimizing the positive character of the former. Like Leibniz, Kant finds a way to relate the two parts of the idea, though in a more sophisticated fashion than Leibniz's simple identification. The key to this relation is given by Kant in the idea of time.

Locke, as we have said, opts to defend only the modern idea of substance, that of a constant conjunction of sensations. He writes:

> We come to have the ideas of particular sorts of substances, by collecting such combinations of simple ideas as are by experience and observation of men's senses taken notice of to exist together, and are therefore supposed to flow from the particular internal constitution or unknown essence of that substance. Thus we come to have the ideas of a man, horse, gold, water, etc., of which substances, whether any one has any other clear ideas, farther than of certain simple ideas coexisting together, I appeal to every one's own experience. (p. 245)

Locke concedes, however, that:

> our complex ideas of substance, besides all these simple ideas they are made up of, have always the confused idea of something to which they belong, and in which they subsist. (p. 246)

Given this understanding of the origin and nature of the idea of substance, it is no wonder that Locke anticipates Hume in his skeptical conclusions with regard to the extent of human knowledge. These conclusions come in Chapters Three and Four of Book IV of the *Essay*. Locke begins with the general warning to the reader that "our knowledge is much narrower even than our ideas," and proceeds to expand this statement by applying it to each type of idea taken in turn. The disturbing fact which quickly emerges is that not only are the mind's cloudy or confused ideas suspicious, but even the complex ideas built entirely from clear and distinct simple ideas result in a knowledge that is only probable. Locke is forced to admit, specifically, that our knowledge as to the "agreement or disagreement of our ideas in coexistence" is

> very short, though in this consists the greatest and most material part of our knowledge concerning substances. For our ideas of the species of substance are as I have showed, nothing but certain collections of simple ideas united in one subject, and so coexisting together. (vol. 2, p. 149; see also p. 168)

Here we have the initial expression of what became a traditional embarrassment for modern empiricism: its inability to account for the cohesive element in our experience, to give anything more than a psychological account of the cords which bind experience together. Locke's embarrassment is even more acute when he turns to discuss the ideas fundamental to mathematics and natural science. Locke is forced to concede that mathematical conceptions are complex constructions of the human mind, but he cannot justify them as a science on his own canons of valid knowledge. Locke is unable to point out the sensations or simple ideas from which the ideas of mathematics are built up, either as empirical sensations or ideas of reflection from the mind's own workings. In fact, Locke is forced to the desperate tactic of completely redefining knowledge. The validity of the knowledge given by a certain idea can only be questioned when that idea is supposed to be a copy of something else, either of an external object or another idea: then only may the possibility of a nonconformity between idea and original arise. But these complex ideas basic to science and mathematics are not intended, Locke now asserts, as copies of anything that comes to us either from the empirical world or through ideas of reflection. As free creations of the human mind, they are archetypes unto themselves and cannot fail to conform to their own structure:

> For that which is not designed to represent anything but itself, can never be capable of wrong representation, nor mislead us from the true apprehension of anything by its dislikeness to it; and such, excepting those of substances, are all our complex ideas: which the mind by its free choice puts together without considering any connection they have in nature. And hence it is, that in all these sorts the ideas themselves are considered as the archetypes, and things not otherwise regarded but as they are conformable to them. So that we cannot but be infallibly certain, that all our knowledge we attain concerning these ideas is real, and reaches things themselves; because in all our thoughts, reasonings, and discourses of this kind, we intend things no farther than as they are conformable to our ideas. So that in these we cannot miss of a certain and undoubted reality. (vol. 2, p. 168)

We must be wary of seeing in the above quotation an incipient "idealistic turn" in Locke, a turn which was properly accomplished only with Kant and the later Idealists. Locke does anticipate Kant in adapting his definition of knowledge to the special case of mathematical science, and raising this formula to a general description of all valid knowledge.

But the machinery underlying the effectiveness of our ideas is too scanty, the general effectiveness of our ideas in the empirical world too scattered and irregular on this account to satisfy any of the later German thinkers. In reality Locke is merely backing into a skeptical position on the issue of our knowledge of the empirical world. Knowledge is limited to the realm of ideas; how far the empirical world as a whole conforms to these ideas, we can never know with certainty. Kant, who developed his critical philosophy at least in part as a response to such a skeptical position, would find that Locke has failed to explain why the scientific laws discovered in experience cannot fail to conform to the *a priori* and more general ideas the mind uses in organizing experience, ideas illustrated for Kant in geometry and what he calls the "pure" part of natural science.

The real damage to the idea of substance has been done by the description of it as a substratum which somehow binds together discrete sensations, a description which erodes our confidence in this mysterious binding mechanism, and which strikes deeper than the Humean point about the "shortness" of our knowledge as to which sensations are bound up with which others. The essence of Locke's criticism of substance is that, to the extent this idea is confused or obscure, it could not have been built up from simple ideas produced either by objects in the empirical world or by the operations of the mind. The idea must then be a product of the mind's own spontaneity.

The route one would have to take, if one accepted Locke's general description of our epistemological situation but wanted to resist his skeptical conclusions, is clear: since the mind apparently chooses to "suppose" or to "imagine" a substratum whenever it sees a regular conjunction of simple ideas, one could list this "supposing" or "imagining" as a natural (if perhaps unpredictable or indiscriminate) operation of the mind, along with willing, believing, doubting, etc., to which we have access by our "ideas of reflection," and then "criticize" this operation of the mind, that is, distinguish those occasions on which it can contribute legitimately to knowledge from those occasions on which it does not. Kant's project can in fact be described without too much distortion as the attempt to go beyond Locke, while accepting Locke's assumptions as to the two sources of our perceived ideas, by performing such a transcendental critique of the spontaneous activity of the mind, its production of "pure" ideas, distinguishing under which conditions these ideas may be used to produce knowledge from those on which they may not. Only once does Locke come close to considering this option—in fact, he puts his hand on the very device Kant will use as a criterion to distinguish the correct from the incorrect applications of the *a priori* ideas to experience. In Chapter Seven of Book II, Locke writes that besides the ideas of power, unity, and existence, as ideas "which convey themselves into the mind by all the ways of sensation and reflection,"

> there is another idea, which though suggested by our sense, yet is more constantly offered us by what passes in our minds; and that is the idea of succession. For if we look immediately into ourselves, and reflect on what is observable there, we shall find our ideas always, while we are awake or have any thought, passing in time, one going and another coming without intermission. (p. 101)

Succession is not just a relation between two (or more) ideas for Locke; it is an idea in itself, one more idea, a clear and simple idea produced in our mind when it turns its gaze inward upon its own operations. Further, it is an idea with content: when Locke looks within himself, the idea produced indicates a "compact" or "tight" relationship between ideas. There is no "intermission" or empty space between the ideas which pass there. Further, the ideas apparently go by one by one single file; there is no "ingression" of one idea into another, while the first is still "before" the viewer. The succession is specified as happening *in time*; time is the locus where the parade of ideas takes place, the medium in which the ideas are "packed" or imbedded. This may seem a minimal content for the idea of "succession," and humble beginnings for a philosophical system.[2] Still, there clearly lies here, if in implicit form, Kant's doctrine of time as the form of inner sense; Locke picks up the idea and examines it curiously, but puts it down again, undeveloped.

It is not hard to see why Locke put the idea down. It is certain that in Locke's mind, and in the minds of his readers, this statement would naturally be interpreted as a denial of Descartes' claim that, upon intro-spective analysis, I may discover an unchanging "Ego" within. Locke's claim was a daring statement against this context, and it is unlikely that Locke's readers saw any but its destructive consequences. It was Kant's breakthrough to see in this apparently critical or negative claim the basis for a new beginning for philosophy. It was Kant's peculiar genius to be able to use the tools and arguments of the skeptic to provide a tran-scendental justification for knowledge. Kant will accept the apparent dissolution of the unity of the knowing subject implicit in this description of the results of introspective analysis; in the fashion inaugurated by Descartes, however, Kant will enlist the strength of this apparently skeptical thrust to defeat a fully skeptical conclusion—to separate what he takes to be essential and valid from what is invalid and dispensable in our traditional knowledge, and to save the former from the onslaught of skepticism. At the basis of Kant's solution is the role played by time in relating the intellect to the object of knowledge, that is, the epistemological relation between knower and object known; but more basically the role played by time in the other direction, in relating the mysterious essence of substance as the source of the necessary succession of sensations to the manifold or conjunction of clear representations themselves, a role which can more accurately be described as the "metaphysical" role of time.

II

Kant was first led to introduce the theme of time through his efforts to meet the crisis in epistemology implicit in Locke's writings. Kant accepts, roughly speaking, Locke's postulate of two objects which produce simple ideas, a "self" within and empirical objects without, with one difference. Kant adds a third object between these initial two, an object closer to being "within" than "without," closer to being an object of "reflective" than of sensitive knowledge, to use Locke's terms, and yet an object which still refers to empirical experience, so from "perceptions" of this third object we may gain knowledge about the empirical world (and the laws which hold good of it). Like the object of Locke's ideas of reflection, the object of this third type of knowledge shares the ambivalent characteristics of being both an object and an operation of the mind, partaking of the natures of both substance and function.

As an object, this third structure between the two Lockean objects is able to produce perceptions, and thus provides the requisite basis for valid knowledge or science. This is essential to Kant because of his distinctive, if anti-Lockean, paradigm for valid knowledge. As we have shown, Locke is ultimately forced to abandon his own paradigm in the case of mathematical ideas. Kant defends the claims of knowledge against the attacks of skeptical empiricism by pointing to a new object which mathematics and the "pure" parts of natural science are a knowledge of—an object which, because it refers to experience or the conditions of experience, explains the necessary conformity of empirical laws with these *a priori* ideas. Thus the very project of a "critical" philosophy is more ambitious with Kant than it is with Locke; not only will this project uncover a basis for distinguishing between legitimate and illegitimate uses of the mind's ideas, as it does for Locke, but critical philosophy will also, for Kant, discover an entirely new land not represented on the Lockean cartography; in doing so it will provide a solid foundation for our "uncritical" (or at least pre-critical) knowledge of the empirical world through natural science. Kant's *Critique* is thus no longer "critical" in the sense of Locke's *Essay*, but conforms to the precedent of Descartes' *Meditations* in being a response to the critical doubt of a skeptical adversary.[3]

With Kant as with Descartes, the project of critical philosophy is to find for natural science, which forms the trunk of Descartes' "tree of knowledge," a sure foundation in the roots of philosophy. The difference is that, whereas Descartes hoped that metaphysics would provide this basis, Kant now turns to a transcendental criticism, which aspires to become a transcendental science, to anchor his defense. Kant subscribes to the Lockean notion that all knowledge must be based on perception; he differs from Locke only in holding that perceptions without concepts are not yet valid knowledge. For Locke, sensations are clear and distinct, and constitute knowledge by themselves; sensations in fact constitute the norm and standard against which all "higher" types of knowledge (complex ideas) are to be judged. For Kant, on the other hand, perception is only one of two essential stems to knowledge. It must be joined with concepts. Only when thought and perception work together is real knowledge produced. A transcendental criticism which aspires to become a transcendental *knowledge* must then join perceptions of some sort with its (pure) concepts. Although Kant is in some ways a more rigid empiricist than Locke (in insisting consistently on an empirical or "given" component to all valid knowledge—even mathematics), he nevertheless maintains that sensations without concepts are blind.

The problem which Kant treats in the *Critique of Pure Reason*[4] is that of how the two stems of knowledge, *a priori* or "pure" ideas, and the "given" component for experience, are brought together, or, expressed in Kant's vocabulary, the problem of how synthetic *a priori* judgments are possible. The problem of these *a priori* judgments appears to stand in some relation to the problem which Locke had taken up, that of substance. Kant's initial description of his investigation runs as follows:

> In synthetical judgments *a priori*, . . . (i)f I want to go beyond the concept A in order to find another concept B connected with it, where is there anything on which I may rest and through which a synthesis might become possible? . . . What is here the unknown X, on which the understanding may rest in order to find beyond the concept A a foreign predicate B, which nevertheless is believed to be connected with it? It cannot be experience, because the proposition . . . represents a second predicate as added to the subject not only with greater generality than experience can ever supply, but also with a character of necessity, and therefore purely *a priori*, and based on concepts. All our speculative knowledge *a priori* aims at and rests on such synthetical, i.e., expanding propositions. . . . (A9/B13)

Kant directs the inquiry into the justification for synthetic *a priori* judgments in the direction of the search for an "unknown X, on which the understanding may rest" when it discovers a synthetic but necessary connection between two ideas. Kant reopens the investigation into the notion of substance which Locke had concluded a hundred years earlier by discrediting the idea of an "unknown X" and rendering the necessary union of such ideas a mystery. Kant appears to be searching for some other way of handling the traditional notion of independent existence than by simply jettisoning the unwieldy element as excess baggage. The fact that Kant, in the passage just quoted, specifically characterizes the support he will need for the understanding as "universal" is an indication that he can no longer be satisfied with a basis that comes from a particular locus in experience. The project to explore the nature of substance thus leads Kant directly to the project to uncover the universal basis for synthetic *a priori* judgments.

Like Locke, Kant has made one particular type of knowledge, in this case mathematical science, the paradigm around which he shapes his general description of all valid knowledge. Kant distinguishes a "pure" or *a priori* part of natural science, a part which consists not only in ideas like cause and effect but also in the mathematical theories used in these sciences. Kant differs from Locke in holding that these universal *a priori* ideas, which proceed entirely from the mind, *do* give us real knowledge of the empirical world; he thus has a higher estimate of the extent and validity of human knowledge than does Locke. Further, Kant did not fall back on Locke's ploy of saving the reality of this "pure" part of knowledge by finally denying that these *a priori* ideas are designed to match any other reality. All valid knowledge must, as stated, result from the synthesis of both perception and conception.

Space and time are not only *a priori* concepts for Kant, they are also perceptions, "pure" perceptions which fertilize our *a priori* ideas and together with them produce real science, real knowledge. This transcendental science has as objects, specifically, the forms of perception, space as the form of outer sense, time as the form of inner sense. Further, because of the peculiar nature of these objects, knowledge of our *a priori* faculties is also decisive for our "empirical" experience, which cannot be received except in accord with these *a priori* forms. That, in essence, is the way space, but more basically time, constitutes Kant's response to the skeptical challenge from Locke. Kant writes:

> The only possible intuition for us is sensuous; the thought of any object, therefore, by means of a pure concept of the understanding, can with us become knowledge only, if it is referred to objects of the senses. Sensuous intuition is either pure (space and time), or empirical, i.e., if it is an intuition of that which is represented in space and time, through sensation as immediately real. By means of pure intuition we can gain knowledge *a priori* of things as phenomena (in mathematics), but only so far as their form is concerned. (B 147)

The relation between the *a priori* laws and the empirical laws, as well as the direction of the further course of Kant's investigations into the nature of substance, is indicated by the well-known passage which occurs at the end of the "Analogies of Experience." Kant writes:

> By nature (in the empirical sense of the word) we mean the coherence of phenomena in their existence, according to necessary rules, that is, laws. There are therefore certain laws, and they exist *a priori*, which themselves make nature possible, while the empirical laws exist and are discovered through experience, but in accordance with those original laws which first render experience possible. Our analogies therefore represent the unity of nature in the coherence of all phenomena, under certain exponents, which express the relation of time (as comprehending all existence) to the unity of apperception, which apperception can only take place in the synthesis according to rules. The three analogies, therefore, simply say, that all phenomena exist in one nature, and must so exist because, without such unity *a priori* no unity of experience, and therefore no determination of objects in experience, would be possible. (A 216/B 263)

There are several important points here. First, there is the aforementioned broadening of the object of investigation from substance to "nature" as a whole, with "nature" redefined so as to render it synonymous with experience as unified by time. Second, there is the ambivalent use made of the phrase "unity of apperception"; this unity of apperception is new and seems to function in this paragraph as an already proved or acknowledged fact, when in actuality it is just this unity of the experiencing Ego which has been threatened by the downfall of the category of substance and which Kant is attempting to rescue. A fuller discussion of each of these topics should deepen our understanding of what happens to the traditional notion of substance in Kant's handling.

It is clear that the category of substance in the traditional sense is no longer a large enough category to denote the true object of Kant's investigation. The unity of nature is identified with the coherence of all phenomena. The object under consideration has now been expanded beyond the principle of the necessary union of particular simple ideas in a certain sector of experience to become the condition of the unity of all possible phenomena. The question into the nature of substance has led to the question of the unity of nature as a whole, which must be satisfactorily resolved before the original question can be adequately answered. The meaning of Kant's earlier comment that the necessary support for the mind in making synthetic *a priori* judgments must be universal and thus not derived from any particular experience is here expanded and used to direct the inquiry to the consideration of the relation of time to the unity of apperception. This investigation offers promise for our inquiry about substance in that the unity of apperception, as the agency responsible for the necessary synthesis of distinct phenomena, bears some resemblance to substance as the mysterious principle which knits together in necessary union distinct simple ideas; and time, because it comprehends all existence (all that we can experience), promises to supply the designated universality.

"Nature" for Aristotle did not have the global reference it takes on in the modern period. Strictly used, it designated the "nature" of each individual substance, the inner dynamism responsible for propelling that substance through its distinctive motion toward a mature state which represented the fullest possible actualization of what that thing was potentially. The structure or regularity of nature thus rested, precariously perhaps, on the independently existing "activities" of all such "natural" substances, each attempting to imitate the regularity and order of the divine substances to the degree that its potentiality permitted. In substance the "form" was more the "nature" of the object than was the matter; the form served as a sort of visible but changeless element in the sense object, inspiring motion by a desire toward itself while standing itself apart from motion. It served as the ontological core of substance and simultaneously provided the stability upon which knowledge must rest, borrowing its own stability from the absolutely unmoved mover, which was the dynamic center of the Aristotelian cosmos. Kant here recasts "nature" to mean the unity or coherence of all phenomena, the latter drawn together at one level by empirical laws which may be discovered through scientific investigation *in* experience, but more deeply by certain general laws which may be discovered *a priori* as necessary patterns to which all further structures in nature must conform, and which first make nature as experienced, or the "unity of experience," possible.

Kant mentions here a word he borrows from Leibniz: apperception. Leibniz had believed, like Descartes, that each monad has a direct perception of itself (in fact, *only* of itself), which may be, however, either clear or confused. Since each monad is structured to act in perfect harmony with every other monad in the universe, a monad's clear perception of itself, through "apperception," would constitute at the same time a knowledge of the careers of all other monads, their past histories and future activities. With Locke's "reflective knowledge" and Kant's "inner sense," however, the monad no longer permits such a direct vision of its naked self. The Ego slips behind the screen of its own activities, which are now, in principle at least, distinct from the actor or "self"; the repertoire of willing, believing, doubting, etc., now forms the full scenario and exhaustive content of inner perception—and a decisive barrier to any further knowledge of the self. The apperception or Ego joins Locke's "confused" idea of substance (and Kant's "unknown X") behind a curtain of internal representations. However, the cord is not totally cut between the self and its world of representations. The unity or coherence of sense intuitions is still a matter of vital concern for Kant; indeed, in the wake of Hume's pressing emphasis on the possibility of a radical dissolution, it has become a matter of considerable urgency. The self or hidden Ego will be pressed into assuming the job left vacant by substance, to effect single-handedly the unity of its own experience, like a drive blade in a gear box communicating motion across the medium of time through the rotating unity of its own action. Kant clearly understands that the dissolution of the concept of substance entails the dissolution of the "world" experienced by this subject, and thus of the experiencing Ego itself; but he looks for a new source of unity in the "unity of apperception."

What I mean is that, as my representations . . . they must be in accordance with that condition, under which alone they can stand together in one common self-consciousness, because otherwise they would not all belong to me . . . In other words, it is only because I am able to comprehend the manifold of representations in one consciousness, that I call them altogether my representations, for otherwise I should have as manifold and various a self as I have representations of which I am conscious. The synthetical unity of the manifold of intuitions as given *a priori* is therefore the ground also of the identity of that apperception itself which precedes *a priori* all definite thought. Connection, however, does never lie in the objects, and cannot be borrowed from them by perception, and thus be taken into the understanding, but it is always an act of the understanding, which itself is nothing but a faculty of connecting *a priori*, and of bringing the manifold of given representations under the unity of apperception, which is, in fact, the highest principle of all human knowledge. (B 133/134)

The unity or coherence of inner representations, like the "unity of apperception," remains for Kant an act of faith as well as a directive for practical reason, a presupposition which can paradoxically be constituted or demonstrated by discovering the empirical laws which bind experience together, as Newton has done, or by discovering *it's a priori* laws, which project Kant is pursuing. Kant is in effect saying: "We stand *in medias res*; our empirical experience is neither totally segmented, nor yet completely unified. We should respond to this discrepancy by attempting to close the gap, to effect a full unification of experience until no representation stands unassimilated to the others, a unification, further, which we already know exists, *must* exist, if we are able to experience at all." The owl of Minerva flies only at dusk; philosophy waits until the specific empirical laws which order experience have been discovered before it sets about its distinctive (Kantian) activity. What a *critique* of reason can do, among other things, is to show how reason, in its "pure" or spontaneous activity, *must* be successful in applying it's *a priori* categories to the manifold of representations, or to show how experience is constituted and made possible, as "nature," at its deepest level by these categories.

But with all this effort, the "Ego" or "Apperception" remains invisible; it remains a posit of practical faith behind all our philosophic, scientific, and cultural activities, as well as a *project* to be carried out and established by these very same activities. Leibniz never bothers to refer to the *unity* of apperception; for him it is a foregone conclusion as well as a theoretical axiom. In the post-Humean world, however, Kant must specifically refer to the "unity" of the apperception he is positing. But, in admitting that the philosophizing individual finds himself, as he begins to philosophize "critically," midway between an irredeemably disparate and fully organized experience, Kant introduces an ambivalence into the expression "unity of apperception": this expression refers in one direction to the unified Ego as a presumed fact, the rotating center of all our activities, without whose dynamism none of our specific projects could hope to meet with success; but at the same time it is a symbol for the *telos* and last stage of our collective enterprise, the terminal point of history, the point at which the *already established* kingdom of reason's reign will be brought to full expression and clarity.

Kant's use of the "unity of apperception" might be described, in his own words, as "regulative" rather than "constitutive"; it is directive of our projects as both posit and product, but never itself encountered in either inner or outer experience. The unity of apperception is at once the Alpha and the Omega of history—therein, in fact, lies its difficulty. Kant feels free to use it in both senses. As a consequence, he sometimes speaks as though we were working to establish what is and must be the source of our energies, that without which our activities cannot possibly succeed. The unity of apperception peeps coyly from behind the curtain of representations; as a goad for our endeavors, it is tantalizingly deposited on the horizon, just out of reach. The very tenuity of its grasp upon (empirical or phenomenal) reality is used to provoke us to greater efforts to secure its ultimate victory on all fronts, cultural, scientific, philosophic, even political. At other times its existence is invoked and alluded to to assure us that all of these enterprises which are nourished by our support and soak up our energies must ultimately meet with "success"—have already done so, in fact, and are known to have done so as a reliable fact. The unity of apperception serves both as something in the process of being constituted and something already completed; it constitutes perhaps the classic example of the risky theoretical technique of exploiting a substance that is at the same time a function, in fact, its *own* function; here it is specifically a function constituting itself as a substance in world history, with man's help, and which is, at the same time, the perduring source of man's energies in this endeavor. It is a transcendental bootstrap whose cosmic performance consists in pulling itself up to itself. Aristotle's unmoved mover is stable and active at the same time also; but in inspiring motion by attraction, its transcendent existence is not implicated in the world processes to the point where its distinctive identity would be bound up with the outcome of the processes it inspires.

In his redefinition of nature, Kant has described the "analogies of experience" as "certain exponents, which express the relation of time (as comprehending all existence) to the unity of apperception." The unity of apperception, though an equivalent expression for the "unity of experience," remains always just out of range of human experience. Time, however, *is* a part of our experience, both "inner" and "outer," and can serve, perhaps, by its own successful encompassing of everything that can become real for us, as a visible first product and symbolic representative for its deeper but unseen source, the unity of apperception. That, at least, is the service Kant seeks to extract from time.

In the "Transcendental Aesthetic" there is a passage that reminds us of Locke's one reference to time as the experience of succession. Kant writes:

> The internal sense by means of which the mind perceives itself or its internal state, does not give an intuition of the soul itself, as an object, but it is nevertheless a fixed form under which alone an intuition of its internal state is possible, so that whatever belongs to its internal determinations must be represented in relations of time. (A 22/B 36)

Time is thus the form of inner sense. Kant is able through this view to assimilate the loss of the unity of the subject, as this dissolution is affirmed by Locke and later by Hume, and yet use this apparently negative result to defeat a fully skeptical position. In this form of "intellectual judo," Kant is able to successfully enlist the skeptical doctrine to carry out a positive function within his own philosophy. Kant's decisive discovery was that this principle of dissolution has a structure of its own, a minimal structure, to be sure, but one which nevertheless is sufficient to save what, in Kant's estimate, is worth saving of the traditional cargo of human knowledge. This minimal structure is supplied by time as the form of inner sense. Kant writes:

> If then we consider that the receptivity of the subject, its capacity of being affected by objects, must necessarily precede all intuition of objects, we shall understand how the form of all phenomena may be given before all real perceptions, may be, in fact, *a priori* in the soul, and may, as a pure intuition, by which all objects must be determined, contain, prior to all experience, principles regulating their relations. (A 26/B 42)

Time, like the analogies of experience which it determines, may itself be taken as a general representation of the successful synthesizing activity of the transcendental unity of apperception. Kant is very much aware of the need for such a representation; since the mind does not create its own perceptions, an alternative state of affairs to the order and unity of experience is conceivable:

> If every single representation stood by itself, as if isolated and separated from the others, nothing like what we call knowledge could ever arise, because knowledge forms a whole of representations connected and compared with each other. This is a general remark which must never be forgotten in all that follows. (A 97/B 169)

The introduction of the theme of time is used by Kant, however, to rule out this possibility:

> Whatever the origin of our representations may be, . . . as modifications of the mind they must always belong to the internal sense, and all our knowledge must therefore finally be subject to the formal condition of that internal sense, namely time, in which they are all arranged, joined, and brought into certain relations to each other. (A 99)

The single remaining step in Kant's defense of knowledge is to show that the basic concepts of experience, the *a priori* categories of the mind, can be represented through a serial ordering of intuitions in time as the form of inner sense. This involves a redefinition of the notion of "concept," which reduces it from being a distinct representation in its own right (although the traditional vocabulary is often retained) to being simply a synthesizing function of other representations. This step has already been anticipated; by forbidding us direct access to the empirical object without or the human soul within, Kant has restricted knowledge to the screen of ideas which these sources (hypothetically) produce in consciousness. The demonstration that our *a priori* ideas can (in fact, *must*) be serially represented demands a transcendental critique of the origin of these ideas.

In the "Transcendental Analytic" the traditional understanding of an idea as a match or copy of an object is abandoned; an idea is no longer to be thought of as mirroring something else but as a process or function organizing *other* ideas according to certain patterns. The unity supplied to our knowledge by the underlying substratum for Locke is here clearly replaced by the unity of subsumption under a higher concept. The source of unity no longer comes from a mysterious something "below" but from a mysterious something "above" the ideas. Nor is even this notion of a higher concept strictly necessary to grasp the activity of the understanding. Indeed, the idea of a concept or a faculty as in any sense a "thing" distinct from the ordering function it introduces into ideas "below" it is pointedly abandoned. The unifying idea is subsumed *into* the unified stream of ideas that is taken to be its result. The substantive nature of a "higher concept" is no longer something distinct from what it binds together; it is dissolved into the successful completion of its appointed task.

This description of the understanding's role in judgment allows Kant to explain the activity of judgment as one of unifying a series of ideas under a higher idea or a rule; in other words, it allows Kant to convert the task of knowing an empirical object into the task of successfully ordering a series of discrete ideas into a unity. This is the essential transformation which, once accomplished, allows Kant to explain, through the interposition of time, the successful application of the *a priori* synthetic concepts to experience. More deeply, this explanation transforms the source of the unity in knowledge, for experience and ultimately for "nature" as a whole, from the traditional notion of individual substance or substratum—even of the "I know not what" variety—lying *below* sense representations, to the "concept," the "understanding," ultimately to the "unity of apperception" operating *above* the representations. Of these last three, the one remains as hypothetical for Kant as the other. All three are removed from the status of a distinct or palpable "thing." It is time that is the first visible form this newly based ordering takes, the first (and only) sign we have of its existence and of its success.

Kant has saddled himself with a problem: accepting the Lockean epistemology has committed him to individual, qualitatively homogeneous and distinct intuitions as the sole contribution from the outside world, which the apperception must run over and put together in some unified way. We are allowed no more encompassing types of perceptions to suggest if or how these intuitions might be (validly or truly) put together. But a second point carries Kant beyond Locke and constitutes his problem: Locke's "simple" ideas are not yet valid cognition for Kant, although they are necessary. Until they are "unified," "related and compared," "arranged, joined, and brought into certain relations to each other," individual representations do not yet constitute valid cognitional coin. It is not until these representations are "run over and held together," rendered "coherent," first in a relatively weak way by time (which simply establishes a sequential ordering among them, renders them "denumerable"), then in stronger ways by the various *a priori* ideas, that they come to constitute genuine knowledge.

The problem here is that the terms "unified" and "incoherent," when one is talking about atomistic sensations, are not clearly defined. In the Lockean epistemology, the principle of non-contradiction applies only to single, individual sensations (which are admitted or presumed to be homogeneous); but there is no clear meaning attached to the description of two *successive* intuitions as "incoherent" or "contradictory." For contradiction, one must have two different (or opposed) properties asserted of the same *thing*; but in the sequence of successive representations which constitutes the object of Locke's and Kant's investigations, as soon as one has to do with a different (or "opposed") trait, one also has to do with a different object. With the demise of substance as the basic measure of objective reality (and as the one category which tolerates and will support contradictory predicates), the fundamental increment of existence reduces to the individual sensation. A different trait or quality *is* a different object, is its *own* object in fact. Consequently, contradiction or incoherency between two *different* intuitions is ruled out.

Consider, for example, the question: "Is the intuition 'red' compatible or incompatible with the intuition 'large'?" How could two intuitions be opposed to each other, or "not-able-to-be-unified"? What would it be like to have the manifold of representations "incoherent"? Various possible meanings come to mind: the reduction of the scope of perception to a single intuition, the fixation on a single representation or Santayanan "Essence," leading perhaps to a "solipsism of the present moment"; but even if this experience is repeated successively with distinct representations, such a sequence of experiences is not necessarily "incoherent." Time as the form of all representations rules out a crowding into one moment of many distinct intuitions; this latter might possibly qualify as a Kantian "intellectual intuition," one free from the limiting conditions of sequential attention; but again it is not clear that such an experience would be appropriately characterized as incoherent. From logic, the term "contradiction" as applied to a sequence must apparently refer to two intuitions of the order "red" and "non-red" (or some other color, say "green"). But with the unit of reality (or object of attention) reduced from the independent substance to the atomistic sensation, there is no opposition or "contradiction" involved between these two. There is not even any contradiction involved in having this particular sequence of "opposed" sensations unified by one and the same idea, such as "object" or "event." We might say, for instance, that one and the same object had undergone a development, had changed its color, which is a common enough observation and comment. The terms "unified" and "incoherent," "foreign" and "related" are regularly applied to the successive intuitions of the manifold by almost all of the prominent thinkers of this period; the great battle between English "empiricists" and continental "rationalists" is fought over an issue whose fundamental meaning is not clarified; this conceptual failure threatens to undermine the import of the entire dispute.

Leibniz, for example, holds that all our representations are "related" or "unified." At the phenomenal level he is willing to admit a division into two types of truth: "truths of fact," which appear as contingent connections between empirical intuitions (as in Newtonian science), and "truths of reason," which are groups of ideas which are said to be "connected" or "related," in the sense that one idea can be deduced from the other.[5] If we were perspicacious enough, however, Leibniz maintains that we could perceive the infinitely subtle rational connections which do in fact cement the most (apparently) random and unrelated ideas in "truths of fact," a vision which only God enjoys, and which, if we could ever attain to it (since monads are distinguished chiefly by the scope and clarity of their perceptions), would suffice to make us equal to God.

Hume stresses the opposing view that, try as he might, he can see no *rational* tie connecting the events brought together by even the most simple and obvious empirical generalizations. He challenges his readers to uncover for him any *rational* ground behind the apparently arbitrary shapes scientific laws take. A radically eccentric seat to the power of nature seems as much suggested by the data as its opposite. For Hume, the intuitions which arrange themselves discretely in the temporal succession remain unalterably independent, stubbornly autonomous, unrelated and "foreign" to each other, to use Kant's expression.

Kant is committed to both, to the empiricist severing of a *deductive* connection between successive ideas in the manifold, but still to the rationalist conviction of an ultimate "unity" behind the manifold (whatever that now means). His situation is no better or worse for these claims, but, more to the point, the words themselves have less meaning with him than they have with either Leibniz or Hume. Once one has ruled out a deductive connection, the one claim seems equally as unwarranted or out of place as the other. It seems simply a case of a "category mistake" to apply the terms "unified" or its opposite to the sequence of atomistic intuitions. The proper context for applying such terms does not appear to be present. How would the sequence of representations appear if it were unified? How would this differ from its appearance if it were *not* unified? Sensations or intuitions are not "compatible" or "incompatible," "related" or "unrelated"; they are simply *there*, arranged in a group, or, after the imposition of time, strung out in a line. There would be no more problem in unifying the most "disparate" bunch of discrete sensations than there would be in scooping up a handful of brilliantly tinted gems and arranging them in a row—nor would the result be any more or less "unified." The terms "unified" and "related," although heavily used and figuring prominently in the controversy which divided empiricists from rationalists, are in fact not well defined in the context of Lockean intuitions. In short, the entire controversy seems to have revolved around the applicability or non-applicability of certain categories to a situation where they are equally unwarranted and out of place.

We have seen that Kant's unity of apperception has tended to take over the traditional role of substance as the "unknown X" upon which the mind can rest when it joins necessarily two "foreign" ideas. Time mediates, for Kant, between the manifold of representations and the unity of apperception. Kant does not, like Leibniz, attempt to reduce the traditional idea of substance completely to the modern; rather, he maintains a suspense and distance between the two. Similarly, he does not try to reduce the unity of apperception completely to time. In the first analogy of experience, entitled "the principle of the permanence of substance," Kant takes up the relation of time to the general notion of substance. His treatment of this relation indicates that time and substance, though intimately related, are yet connected in a more subtle way than Leibniz's simple identification. Kant writes:

> Our apprehension of the manifold of phenomena is always successive, and therefore always changing. By it alone therefore we can never determine whether the manifold, as an object of experience, is coexistent or successive, unless there is something in it which exists always, that is, something constant and permanent, while change and succession are nothing but so many kinds (*modi*) of time in which the permanent exists. Relations of time are therefore possible in the permanent only (coexistence and succession being the only relations of time) so that the permanent is the substratum of the empirical

representation of time itself, and in it alone all determination of time is possible. (A 183/B 226)

Here substance, as the permanent, is identified as the "substratum of the empirical representation of time itself." A first relation of time to the permanent is here suggested. Time is related to the permanent in a way analogous to the way phenomena are related to the "unknown X" of substance which produces them in consciousness. Further, the determination of an object of experience is seen as a reflection or representation of the permanent through the medium of time. Kant writes further:

> Without something permanent therefore no relation of time is possible. Time by itself, however, cannot be perceived, and it is therefore the permanent in phenomena that forms the substratum for all determinations of time, and at the same time the condition of the possibility of all synthetical unity of perceptions, that is, of experience; while with regard to that permanent all existence and all change in time can only be taken as a mode of existence of what is permanent. In all phenomena therefore the permanent is the object itself, that is, the substance (phenomenon), while all that changes or can change belongs only to the mode in which substance or substances exist, therefore to their determinations. (A 184/B 227)

We come back here to the ambivalent characterization of time within the Kantian philosophy: time has properties of both an object and a function. Time is a function in that through time is achieved a first synthesis of all possible phenomena. The permanent is here specified as the changeless substance, a sort of underlying nebulous presence, which expresses itself through the changing phenomena. Through such formulae, faintly reminiscent of Spinoza, Kant clearly does not allow the opposition between the permanent and time to collapse; he does not identify time with the permanent, as his view occasionally suggests; yet time is a unity of sorts and is related in an important way to the posit of the deeper unity of apperception. Kant does not dismiss the darker element, here called the permanent, in the traditional idea of substance, as Locke had done, nor does he empty the permanent completely into its phenomenal equivalent, as Leibniz had done, or into time. Kant's achievement in the first *Critique* with regard to the problem of substance consists of drawing a cover over this dark center of synthesis while yet maintaining its existence and insisting on its necessity for the possibility of experience. Kant thus admits with Locke that this segment of the idea of substance is dark and beyond our knowledge, yet he brings this dark half back to the position of respect from which Locke had dismissed it. A suspense is maintained, in Kant's considered view, between the two halves of the traditional idea of substance, a suspense which makes his view more adequate to the traditional notion than the explanations of Locke or Leibniz. Nevertheless, there is with Kant a decisive change in the understanding of the source of the unity behind substance.

An indication of this comes in the clarification of the relation of time to substance given in the deduction of the categories, where Kant discusses the three syntheses of knowledge: apprehension, reproduction, and conception. There Kant writes:

> In order to change this manifold into a unity of intuition (as, for instance, in the representation of space), it is necessary first to run through the manifold and then to hold it together. It is this act which I call the synthesis of apprehension. (A 99)

It is clear that time, as expressing the coherence of all phenomena, is a representation of this unity; time does not create it, just as it is the function of the understanding not to produce representations but to unify them. It is the peculiar function of the transcendental unity of apperception, whose similarity to the idea of substance we have noted, to, as Kant says, "run through" and "hold together" the data of experience. This unity of apperception is further explained in the third synthesis of knowledge, that of conception. There Kant writes:

> No knowledge can take place in us, no conjunction or unity of one kind of knowledge with another, without that unity of consciousness which precedes all data of intuition, and without reference to which no representation of objects is possible . . . As that unity must be considered as *a priori* necessary (because, without it, our knowledge would be without an object), we may conclude that the relation to a transcendental object, that is, the objective reality of our empirical knowledge, rests on a transcendental law, that all phenomena, if they are to give us objects, must be subject to rules *a priori* of a synthetical unity of these objects, by which rules alone their mutual relation in an empirical intuition becomes possible. (A 108/110)

Here the unity of an object of experience is explained as a reflection of the unifying action of the transcendental unity of apperception; the object itself may then be taken as a correlate, a symbolic representative, a sort of ontological satellite revolving around the unity of apperception, basking in and throwing back the light of its mother planet. The form of time, in its status as both an object and a function, may also be taken as a representation of the unity of this apperception. First as a peculiar third type of object which can produce perceptions, it may be associated with a distinct rule of its own synthesis, as Kant himself asserts. Then time would reflect the unity of apperception by virtue of the latter's nature as the faculty which synthesizes phenomena according to rules. Further, as the form of inner sense (a function), time expresses the coherence of all phenomena which it organizes, and may thus be taken as a direct representation of the successful synthesizing activity of the unity of apperception. Thus time's true relation to substance is most adequately expressed by saying that time is a symbol or representation of the success of the project of the transcendental unity of apperception to construct an ordered "nature" through the unification of phenomena according to rules.[6] Time becomes the only visible symbol for the success of this function, when all the other "revolving satellites"—the common objects of our experience—are reduced in the Lockean epistemology to a congeries of discrete, atomistic sensations.

Aristotle was able to "see" in the individual, concrete "thing," as its deepest nature, a "form" which was motionless itself and yet paradoxically the active principle, moving the composite individual by attraction. The form thus tended to stand aloof from the motion which characterizes temporal existence, almost like a Platonic Form, and is, in fact, at one point characterized by Aristotle as an "unnatural" (that is, non-moving) cause of natural activity. Where Plato saw a sharp cleavage between the moving and the unmoving realms, Aristotle saw a gradual shading, starting from the unaltering brilliance of perfection, moving through the regular motion of the celestial substances, ending with the less regular motion of the sub-lunar beings. The form present in sensible substance was a representative from another, higher realm, a visible delegate from the unmoved mover who also moved things by a desire for itself, while itself remaining absolutely still.

Form was truly a "gift from the gods" for Aristotle, a furnishing from a divine household which some Prometheus had stolen and brought back to earth. Aristotle's "god" is more powerful or at least more generous than Kant's "unity of apperception"; his gift is the gift of unity itself rather than the promise of the gift to come. Aristotle has "read" time differently than Plato, but it was the spontaneous perception of form acting through time and temporal processes which prompted Aristotle's "softer" reading. This symbol is lost on Kant, vaporized in the parched wasteland of Locke's epistemological reduction. Time is all that is left. But the unity that time symbolizes is of a decidedly weaker sort than that which would have been achieved had the common objects of ordinary experience been able to stand (or been left standing) by a perception not persuaded to diminish its own panoramic or comprehensive vision. The unity of time is compatible with far greater "disunity" or disparity between successive sensations than would have been allowed by the objects themselves.

Kant's philosophy is a second response, after Descartes' *cogito*, to the skeptical challenge to traditional knowledge which distinguishes the modern movement in philosophy.[7] The undeniable factual existence of time, indeed, its alarming consequences for the unity of the subject, is converted by Kant into a surprisingly sure basis for philosophy, through the discovery of a minimal structure contained in the idea of time, a structure which nevertheless is strong enough to save what Kant considers valid in human knowledge. The re-emergence of time into Western philosophy thus formed part of both the attack by and also the response to the skeptical challenge: in the form of inner sense and the *a priori* knowledge built upon it, Kant hoped to have uncovered a firm basis for empirical knowledge, a basis which the "Evil Genie" of Descartes would never be able to snatch from us. The undeniable reality of time in the epistemological order, pressed by Hume, is converted by Kant into a symbol for the metaphysical success of the unity of apperception in its project to synthesize all phenomena according to rules, a role traditionally held by the notion of substance. Time serves Kant both as an object and as a function: its undeniable "objective" reality is appreciated as empirical evidence for the success of its organizing function and the activity of the deeper unity of apperception — whose own unity rises or falls with the unity of the world it attempts to integrate. Time serves for Kant, as the "Ego" has served for Descartes, as an empirical discovery that solves an epistemological problem, a discovery which makes possible a return, in systematic fashion, to deeper, metaphysical issues.

There is, then, a sense in which one can speak of a metaphysical as well as an epistemological triumph of time in Kant's system. Time is seen as a visible symbol for the successful activity of the transcendental unity of apperception, which has taken over the traditional role of substance as the source or unifying element in our perceptions and whose reign may be described in metaphysical as well as epistemological terms. This recasting or novel analysis of the traditional concept of substance as, at its base, identical with the transcendental subject, an assimilation or sucking "upward" of substance into the subject rather than an absorption "downward" into a lower substratum, is fully carried out in German philosophy only after Kant, most particularly with Hegel; still Kant has certainly laid the groundwork for any such future step.

However, the characterization of both the manifold of experience and this new foundation for experience as "unified" rather than "non-unified" is based on a totally empty distinction, a use and fabricated opposition between terms which show themselves in this context to be equally inapplicable and, once applied, without significant difference in content. Careful examination reveals that the terms "unified" and "non-unified," when applied to the same segment of the Kantian manifold of experience, indicate not a single difference between the manifolds thus qualified. By the principle of the identity of indiscernibles, a distinction without a difference is equivalent to no difference at all. The distinction crumbles and vanishes; the dispute is reduced to nothing.

The danger, however, is that, once the manifold has been (illegitimately) qualified by one group as "unified," it can with equal justice be described by the other as "non-unified." By emphasizing the "ultimate unity" of sense experience, Kant leaves himself vulnerable to others who see the "foreignness" between successive intuitions as stronger or more radical than Kant himself, on other occasion, is willing to admit. Most of the important figures in later Western philosophy work within the tradition opened up by Kant, but almost all of them opt for a vocabulary of opposition and contradiction to describe the spectacle of phenomenal appearances. This interpretation is not as unfaithful to Kant's philosophy as it might at first seem: the deepest theoretical roots of Kant's philosophy in fact point to a noumenal reality which can only appear and be described from our perspective as irrational.

Kant has reintroduced the theme of time into Western philosophy and used this theme strategically much as Aristotle did, to release the pressure resulting from having contradictory attributes apply to the sense world, a contradiction as intolerable as it is undeniable. The psychological strain produced by this admission prompted Plato to dismiss the sense world as less than fully real; he redirected attention to a transcendent realm of true objects which would display the stability and freedom from contradiction worthy of full reality. Aristotle used tactically the very motion which embarrassed Plato, embracing it as the solution to the problem it seemed to create: contradictory attributes do indeed characterize the sense world, but never at the same time. Motion is in fact the passage from one trait to its opposite, e.g., from not-red to red. It is one and the same object which supports these changes, changes which involve opposites in the mitigated sense of being passages from potency or privation to actuality. Through it all, it is the formal element in substance which shines through the shifting qualities, inspiring the motion of the object as a whole toward itself, while itself remaining unmoved. This "softer" reading of the motion which characterizes the sense world supplies a locus for the unity and stability of knowledge *within* the sense world (in substance) and resolves the tension which could otherwise have driven such a this-worldly philosopher as Aristotle, loath as he was to posit a surrogate reality beyond the sense world, to a ringing indictment (similar to Nietzsche's, perhaps) of this one reality as irrational and contradictory.

For Kant, as for Plato and Leibniz, time and the sense world are less than fully real. Further, this diminished ontological status carries with it the stigma of contradiction. As with Aristotle, however, the apparent contradiction of the phenomenal order is mitigated, is seen to be not "fully" contradictory. With Leibniz, Kant is convinced of the "ultimate unity" of the manifold of experience (as well as of the "foreignness" of distinct perceptions which Hume has noticed). What, finally, does this "unity" amount to? The mitigation of the contradiction of the phenomenal order is achieved by Kant in a markedly different fashion than it had been by Aristotle. Unlike Aristotle (also unlike Plato and Leibniz), who finds a saving logical order *in* or *behind* the shifting phenomenal appearances, Kant now embraces fully the apparent contradictions of the sense world. His way of saving this experience from the charge of contradiction is to find an even worse state "below" this one: phenomenal contradictions are saved from being "radical" by the strange technique of comparing them with a state of *simultaneous* or *immediate* contradiction, a state from which *time* protects us by demanding that our intuitions introduce themselves *sequentially*. This is the full extent of the "rescue" from contradiction and the "unity" which time imposes upon our experience.

As with Leibniz, time with Kant signifies a phenomenal order ultimately insubstantial but supposedly "well-founded," reflecting a deeper, a-temporal, logical structure which governs the order in which sense intuitions introduce themselves into our experience. However, where Leibniz would hold that, were we sufficiently perspicacious, we could see the logical ligatures which bind the apparently unrelated bits of our experience together, Kant has finally and decisively severed the umbilical cord which the rationalists maintained between experience and the underlying logical order. With the empiricists, Kant grants the definitive discreteness and insular unrelatedness of the intuitions which the understanding, through its concepts, holds together. It is an understandable exaggeration, but one completely in line with the tradition established by the empiricists and accepted by Kant himself, when Hegel and Schopenhauer will later denominate these successive intuitions as "opposed" and "contradictory." It is certainly as inappropriate to describe this sequence as "contradictory" as it is to term them "unrelated" and "foreign" (if anything more than "different" is meant); but if the one is to be allowed, why not the other? What defense does Kant have against such a reading, having committed in fact the same offense himself? Kant's "originality" (and ultimately his "solution") consist of applying *both* terms, "unified" and "foreign," to the stream of sense intuitions; but this is merely the statement of a problem, not a solution. Where for Leibniz the logical order which time reflects is that of a system of compossible essences coexisting in the mind of God, for Kant time is simply a floating symbol, a disembodied sign, as the rainbow in the sky was after the flood for Noah, reflecting the successful (though unseen) activity of the unity of apperception in its basic unifying activity, and a promise that the ever threatening "disunity" of the manifold of intuitions will never be a fact, but rather that its total organization and integration will finally crown human history.

Hegel is simply being a more consistent Kantian when, in his "dialectic," he reduces Kant's transcendental unity of apperception from a thing-like rule or faculty hovering *above* the parade of sense intuitions to but another expression for the guarantee that the various elements of experience, contradictory though they may seem when compared, introduce themselves single file into our experience, one at a time, do not transgress upon each other's domain, and thus avoid the bottleneck situation and congestion under which alone their opposition would become simultaneous and intolerable. Neither Kant nor Hegel rules out "mutual opposition" or "foreignness" between *successive* intuitions. The victory of time over contradiction, the structure which time successfully imposes upon experience, is on Kant's own admission a minimal one; if it were not, it would not be so easy to point out and demonstrate. Time rules out only contradiction at a moment, not contradiction between successive phases of world history, or in the constitution of the noumenal or transcendental subject, as Schopenhauer points out.[8]

Leibniz has pretended to deduce his entire philosophy, and every empirical truth about the world, from the principle of non-contradiction.[9] Kant has accepted the empiricist denial of any rational connection between successive empirical intuitions. Phenomenal experience is thus "contradictory," in the sense of being rationally unrelated and "foreign." But if the principle of non-contradiction no longer applies to the phenomenal world, Kant insists it still applies in the noumenal realm.[10] Schopenhauer's originality lies in denying the principle even at this level—and insisting that this follows on good Kantian principles. Schopenhauer's point thereby is simply that it does no good to posit a noumenal "unity" while granting a disparity between successive phenomenal intuitions, and claiming that the former somehow acts upon or "unifies" the latter. Such a unified noumenal agency is an empty posit, since it leaves the discrete phenomenal representations as it finds them, in their original and unrelieved "foreignness"; the only change is that they now are arranged side by side. Schopenhauer's deeper point is that the phenomenal order is all that we see of the noumenal; to accept a non-unified phenomenal order *is* to posit a non-unified noumenal source behind these appearances, if some deeper realm is thought to exist and to be the source of what we do experience. The one is a symbol for the other; they rise or fall together and must automatically take on each other's traits.

Kant uses time as a buffering rod to absorb the "opposition" between contradictory elements in experience which could otherwise, in direct contact or close proximity, quickly heat to a critical temperature and cause a psychological explosion. The "victory" of time for Kant thus depends as much on time's ability to keep certain intuitions apart as on its ability to group intuitions together, in a "unity." In fact, it is the unusual and distinctive feature of the "unity" which time imposes that makes it interesting, given Kant's problem, as a theoretical device: the temporal reticulum contains "compartments" for its constituent members, compartments which can be imagined as separated by watertight doorways when the "incompatibility" between neighbors renders such an arrangement desirable or necessary. The "unity" time achieves does not disturb or compromise the stubborn independence and discreteness of the successive intuitions; whatever "disunity" existed between such intuitions is fully preserved after time's imposition. In asserting the sequential unity imposed by time, Kant has been careful not to commit himself to the logical relation maintained by Leibniz.

As mentioned, Aristotle "softens" the impact of change upon reality by seeing the opposition mediated by time or movement as essentially one from privation to actuality in one and the same subject, or substance. For Locke, substance has ceased to be anything which changes at all; and for Kant and the later German thinkers, it is the transcendental subject which supplies the unity behind the movement of experience. But this latter unity is a posit, the only tangible sign of which is time. Further, the type of unity time imposes upon our experience is a minimal or vestigial one when compared with what Aristotle saw to be the distinctive motion characteristic of substance. Kant is careful to gauge the unity of the transcendental subject by the unity of the manifold of experience organized by time. This careful proportioning of the invisible element to the visible, another application of the principle Hume had used in his *Dialogues Concerning Natural Religion* to undermine the traditional notion of God, Kant here puts forward as his revolutionary discovery, the discovery that this principle can be used constructively as well as destructively, to call attention to a previously overlooked aspect of our temporal experience, an aspect which is yet enough to save us from "radical" contradiction and a "fully" skeptical point of view. Yet this "solution" rules out only a total, unrelieved contradiction—a contradiction which Kant concedes is not even a possibility for us (as creatures) in the first place. And in fact the unity which time achieves in the phenomenal order is totally compatible with a radically "contradictory" content to different segments of our experience, a situation which would be the phenomenal equivalent of a basic or noumenal contradiction. The net effect that the "unity" of time has is to render the experience of contradiction sequential rather than immediate or simultaneous. In effect, then, Kant withdraws or empties the impact of his "solution," since the only form that a (noumenal) contradiction could have for us is sequential, which his solution not only is powerless to prevent, but pushes us to accept.[11]

In the last analysis, change is potentially much more radical for Kant than it is for Aristotle. By gauging the unity of the transcendental subject by the unity imposed by time on the sense world, Kant leaves himself vulnerable to attack, and his system open to exploitation, from the quarter of those who read the opposition which exists between successive segments of experience much more radically than Kant himself does. By accepting the empiricist dismissal of the purported rational bonds between the elements of experience, and by yet maintaining the propriety of both kinds of language ("unified" and "foreign") to qualify the manifold of phenomenal experience, Kant leaves himself no defense against such an interpretation. Indeed, by redefining the concept of "concept" as a unifying function rather than a copy or match of an independently existing thing, Kant admits and propagates a view of the disparity existing between individual segments of experience before they are "run over and held together" by the transcendental subject—encouraging the dialectical interpretation of experience of Hegel, Schopenhauer, and Marx in which "conflict," "opposition," and "contradiction" figure as fundamental exegetical categories. In the final analysis, what Kant has wrenched from the grasp of the Evil Genie is at best the integrity and harmony of an atomistic slice of experience, a solipsism of the present moment, a present which grows "thick" at the risk of becoming infected with contradiction and irrational. It achieves integrity only as it approaches asymptotically the knife edge as a final limit, where content of any sort vanishes.

Kant's (and Hegel's) optimistic attitude seems to differ from Schopenhauer's viewpoint chiefly in the vocabulary one uses and the perspective one adopts upon a self-same reality: a world experience unfolding itself in alternating, conflicting stages, jack-knifing through history in a zigzag pattern of violent and random lurches. Kant's "solution" consists of seeing this world history (and human experience) as the moving transcript in which this fundamental contradiction is expressed and worked out clearly, in full articulation, by creatures who are limited, as language itself is, to saying one thing at a time, rather than in one simultaneous, garbled burst of words. Sequential contradiction is the only form that (metaphysical) contradiction could "take" for us.

The skeptics and empiricists have seen the contrast, the "opposition" between the various intuitions in the net of time; Kant calls attention to the reticulum which connects the interstices and seems to be saying: "It could be worse; at least their opposition is not simultaneous." The vision he is describing is able to be read in two different ways, with each interpreter calling attention to different aspects of what both sides admit to be present, as happens in the two ways of looking at an optical illusion. Interest in the dispute is weakened by the difficulty in knowing what "related" and "opposed" mean in the context of atomistic Lockean intuitions. But this much is certain: in that Kant accepts the empiricist dismissal of any rational connection between successive intuitions, his defense of an ultimate "unity" is puzzling, and his proclamation of a "solution" sounds hollow. How could experience be more contradictory for us than on his depiction? The brunt of his defense against Hume, in fact, is that experience could be no more contradictory than it already *is*. Experience could be worse only if we were purely intellectual beings, capable of intellectual intuitions, perhaps, able to experience many ideas at the same time, but not as the sensitive creatures that we are, limited by the form of inner and outer sense to a serial order in our experience—as Kant goes out of his way to insist we are. Traditionally sense has been interpreted as imposing limitations, hobbling our power to experience; but within the perspective of Kant's system, these limitations appear almost as a blessing. The "hell" he describes as, in fact, our common reality, is the only kind of hell *sensitive* creatures could have. Only higher creatures could suffer more exquisitely. "Unity" and "disunity" are equally inappropriate terms to apply to the manifold of intuitions; our "salvation" and rescue at Kant's hands looks suspiciously like our "damnation" at Schopenhauer's. The manifold of experience, when Kant's unity of apperception *succeeds*, looks not very different from the same manifold when the unity of apperception *fails*.[12]

Given the Lockean epistemology of atomistic intuitions, the belief that experience is "rational" can only take the form of a belief that there is a *deductive* connection between the isolated intuitions. As a result, when the discovery of the nonexistence of this (purported) rational connection is announced by the empiricists and accepted by Kant, the discrepancy between the results of the philosophic investigation and the appreciation of the world in common sense which philosophy should take as its point of departure and advance beyond rather than call into question, precipitates an outburst of disappointed expectation and leads us to burden the neutral intuitions, which are merely "different" or "distinct," with the much stronger epithets "foreign" and "opposed."

There is nothing now to keep us from radical pessimism and filing the maximal charge of "contradiction." But what else can be done? What other meaning can there be to "rational," in the context of discrete, isolated Lockean intuitions? Kant pleads for a wider understanding of "rational" by arguing for an "ultimate unity" behind the manifold of experience; but in the context of Lockean intuitions, which he has agreed at the outset to accept, his plea is meaningless. Kant had accepted the challenge to begin from imagined bits of epistemological data and to save the "unity" of a world that is not only "worlds removed" from such data, a world qualitatively different from such bits of homogeneous impressions, whose categorical richness and complexity resist expression in such a monosyllabic vocabulary, but to begin with a sequence of data to which the term "unity" (or "disunity") may not even be significantly applied. The project is hopeless to begin with.

The shift to a subjective explication of the concept of substance marks Kant's most basic break with the mainstream of previous Western thinking; it is perhaps best seen as an extreme ploy calculated to gain the upper hand in a desperate struggle with a totally rigorous form of skepticism—a ploy which, as we have seen, is by no means assured of success. It is difficult to know what lesson to retrieve from this endeavor, but a comparison with earlier philosophy should be at least possible, and possibly enlightening. Philosophy until shortly before the modern period had seen its distinctive activity as building upon other (successful) sciences, building upon certain realities that were accessible if not obvious to common intelligence and insight, realities which the skeptic sees himself in no way obliged to recognize. The radical nature of Kant's response, the major revision it entails for our normal, uncritical relation to the world, as well as its apparent theoretical difficulties, should perhaps give us pause as to the advisability not only about joining Locke or Kant in their partial skepticism, but even about taking up cudgels with such an opponent or in trying to force the skeptic from his covert with deductive coercion (which project Kant is also pursuing).

Perhaps, as in the proverbial contest between the Sun and the Wind, the best tack here is to attempt to induce the skeptic to relax his defenses against the suspected hostile or deceiving environment by flooding him in an atmosphere of expansive receptivity and sunny openness, rather than by attempting to blast these defenses (which also limit his vision) from him with argumentative vigor. Such a tack is, of course, by no means assured of success; the desire for a "guarantee" here, however, is itself a sign that we have not as yet extricated ourselves from this first (Kantian, or modern) way of dealing with the skeptic. The second response may be the most reasonable we can make to the situation. Past attempts to be rhetorically persuasive, to meet the skeptic on his own terms, to see things "his way" and still "talk him out of it" (as Kant has attempted with the "seeing through slits" of the Lockean epistemology) have led to such concessions that there is, in fact (as Kant should have seen and Schopenhauer later demonstrated), no "way out." The skeptical challenge, delivered and accepted by Descartes at the start of the modern period, should perhaps have been left unaccepted. Better to leave the Evil Genie, who is simply the ideal and metaphysically limiting correlate to the supreme skeptic, not indeed to a "philosophy" of which he is incapable, but to rule over the kingdom of nothingness which he creates for himself and attempts to lure others to enter as well.

Notes

[1] John Locke, *An Essay Concerning Human Understanding*, ed. J. Yolton, Dent & Sons, London. All references are to the two-volume Everyman's Library edition of 1965 published by Dutton in New York.

[2] Has Locke, we may ask, done anything more than rehearse the characteristics of a rational creature, a creature placed midway between the angels and the brute animals? If there were an "intermission" or spaces between our ideas, that would be equivalent, at such moments, to having no idea at all, to being an unthinking creature, which is what the inanimate objects of creation are. If, on the other hand, we were allowed to have ideas in a way *not* bound by the limitations of succession, if we could experience many different ideas simultaneously, what would then be the "specific difference" separating us from the angels, or indeed from the Almighty himself? Although there are, then, meaningful alternatives to the specific content Locke has infused into his idea of "succession," none seems appropriate to a creature of man's half-way status. The picture that emerges from this "phenomenology" of the mind's experience is that of an unbroken chain of ideas, some perhaps longer in extent or duration than others, which stretches with no gaps the full length of a man's existence. Locke delivers this picture casually, almost with a shrug, though he likely had skeptical (viz. Anti-Cartesian) intentions behind it. Kant will take up this account as a challenge and, without denying the dissolution of the static Cartesian Ego involved therein, will find in the connecting borders between the interstices, the saving feature in temporal succession that protects us, not indeed from the "hell" that may result from the reduction of the unity of substance and a world made up of substances to the atomistic discreteness of independent sensations, but at least from the greater hell that can be imagined if we had to experience these stubbornly discrete and unrelated sensations simultaneously.

Our creaturely status prevents us from experiencing different ideas at the same time. It thus keeps us from experiencing the divine pleasure that would result if these ideas were compatible, but also from the indescribable pain if they should not be. Admittedly, the terms "compatible" and "incompatible," when one is discussing univocal and independent sensations like "red" and "heavy," are not well defined. Nevertheless, it is incontestable that thinkers from this period played on such meanings in their attacks upon knowledge and in their defenses and "solutions" to such attacks. The point here for Kant is that our creaturely status functions as a buffer zone. It throws up a skein of limiting channels to mediate and soften the confrontation between cognition and reality. This skein functions as a barrier separating us from heaven, but also as a salvation protecting us from a worse kind of hell. Kant is only willing to accept the skeptical account (i.e., derived from Lockean atomistic epistemology) of the bases of our experience because he thinks this account can be turned against his skeptical antagonist. The importance of these extreme or limiting positions for a proper assessment of Kant's "solution" or defense of knowledge against Hume's attack, by dwelling on the type of "unity" or "organization" brought by time as the form of inner sense, will be brought out at the conclusion of this article.

[3] It is thus a reaction *within* Enlightenment thought to its own critical stance, while at the same time carrying forward its critical ambition.

[4] Immanuel Kant, *Critique of Pure Reason*, tr. Max Muller, Doubleday Anchor, NY, 1966.

[5] One could ask: What is the "principle of individuation" of an idea, in a crowd of others to which it is "related"? Does a deductive "connection" between two ideas compromise the distinctive identity of either? In such an interconnected network, where does one idea leave off and another begin?

[6] Time's relation to the unity of apperception is captured in the concluding lines of Goethe's *Faust:*

> Alles Vergängliche/Ist nur ein Gleichnis;
> Das Unzulängliche/Hier Wird's Ereignis;
> Das Unbeschreibliche/Hier ist's getan;
> Das Ewig-Weibliche/Zieht uns hinan.

Time is only a "Gleichnis" or likeness to the deeper reality of apperception, whose unity it reflects in its own order. Nevertheless, it serves as an effective promise and symbol for the ultimate victory of the principle of which it is only the harbinger. Time is, as it were, the first, small victory of apperception, but the promise of what is to come. Also, Goethe suggests that the coming era will inaugurate what was sought for but never experienced during the current era, implying (and accepting) the comparative disunity of the present state of affairs at the same time that it promises an imminent advance to a unified and satisfactory state.

[7] For a good account of the initial development and response to skepticism in the modern period, see Richard Popkin, *The History of Skepticism from Erasmus to Descartes*, Harper & Row, NY, 1968.

[8] In fact, Kant's limitation of the validity of the principle of sufficient reason requires that the noumenal world be thought of as not bound by this principle. In the field of ethics, where Kant thought that we attained a more penetrating vision in the nature of the noumenal subject than in the field of theoretic or scientific thought, Kant held, against the dominant Enlightenment opinion, that moral evil was a permanent and inextricable feature of human experience; just as the universal and necessary aspect of scientific laws, which was beyond the capacity of contingent sense experience to produce, demanded an *a priori*, apodictic element in the human subject as its source, so the radical nature of moral evil in human experience demanded the postulation of an equally radical capacity or bent toward evil at the very foundation of human nature for its adequate explanation. Thus in the ethical sphere as well as in the theoretic, the Kantian noumenal subject appears corrupt and irrational—almost diabolical. See Emil Fackenheim, "Kant and Radical Evil," *University of Toronto Quarterly*, No. 23, 1954, pp. 339–353.

[9] Leibniz prided himself on being able to deduce his entire system first from two, ultimately from one principle, the principle of non-contradiction. See A.O. Lovejoy, *The Great Chain of Being: A Study of the History of an Idea*, Harper & Row, NY, 1960, p. 175. Hegel maintains this rationalist (or rigorist) competition and, following Kant, with his "dialectical" method shows a form of "deduction" in which even the latter is dispensable.

[10] Accepting the radical "foreignness" between successive perceptions is equivalent to recognizing that the principle of non-contradiction no longer applies to phenomenal reality. In holding out nonetheless for an "ultimate unity" to phenomenal experience, Kant reflects his faith that the principle *still* applies to the noumenal object. Kant is better known for his demonstration of the applicability of the principle of causality (for Leibniz and Schopenhauer, the principle of sufficient reason) to the phenomenal order, and his denial of its applicability to the noumenal realm. The risk this doctrine runs of an irrationalist depiction of the noumenal source is mentioned in Endnote #8 above.

[11] See Endnote #2 above.

[12] To explain the point further: How would our experience differ if the faculty of apperception were to *fail* in its project to unify both itself and its world, rather than *succeed*, as Kant holds it does? Certainly we would be deprived of the "objects" which are scooped up and pounded together like snow balls by the Kantian categories, and thus of our visible symbols for the success of the unity of apperception in its self-defining project. But how would time *itself* change, or the discrete intuitions brought together by time (time itself being our only visible symbol or clue as to the nature of this unity)? We can see from this "*Denkexperiment*" how much more modest a claim *time* makes or achieves as a unification of experience than do any of the *categories*, which demand much stronger forms of interrelation and compatibility. The compartments between distinct intuitions may perhaps have to be made less watertight. Or perhaps the assumption of atomistic intuitions basic to the Lockean epistemology must be scrapped; at least a hypothesis about the psychological origins of an idea must not be allowed to prejudice at the outset its epistemological credibility.

CHAPTER 9

Madness, Satan, and Bloom's Antithetical Quester

Introduction

During the Cold War, we were caught in the conflict between two rival *romanticisms*, the one a liberation from the other. All romanticism carries forth a gnostic hatred for "Matter," and sells us a "salvation" by means of escape. To understand each species of *romanticism*, you must understand what it wants to escape from. For capitalism, "Matter" was the previous mercantilist system, with its rigid monopolistic structures generated by royal charters, and in general by governmental control. Capitalism provided a "liberation" by offering flexibility and a reward for individual intelligence, initiative, and hard work. Communism promised a "liberation" from the inequalities of wealth and opportunity generated by capitalism. Eventually in the economic sphere, of course, we worked our way back to a "natural law" position, just as we had in the political sphere, although we could not call it by that name. That is, just as in politics we follow a democratic policy of majority rule, but with a "bill of rights" limiting what the majority can do to any minority, so in the economic sphere all major countries today follow a capitalist policy, but with a socialistic "safety net" designed to catch those who "fall through the slats" of the capitalist system.[1] The precise mixture varies from country to country, as a function of its own traditions and present situation; and the "tinkering" goes on into our own day. But during the Cold War, one had to belong to, and use the rhetoric of, one or the other species of "romanticism"; everything else was a non-starter.

But what exactly is "romanticism?" Where did it come from? What does it mean? Why is it so powerful? In literature as in politics, it appears that today we are "all romantics," even if unconsciously. It provides the rhetoric of our self-fulfillment ethic and our entertainment. We are in a "romantic culture"; that phrase is a redundancy, for we can conceive no other. Like Monsieur Jourdan in Moliere's *Bourgeois Gentilhomme*, we have been *romantics* all our lives without even knowing it!

I

Jacques Derrida may well be the most obscure and enigmatic theorist on the literary scene today; but he is of the French mold, in an age where French philosophy has lost its fabled love of clarity above all else. Harold Bloom is the most provocative and controversial of our homegrown variety, and, although his style bristles with Kabbalistic, Freudian, and literary-critical jargon, a clear vision awaits the reader who perseveres in the study of the more than twelve major volumes Bloom has authored or contributed to, and who can bestow on them the attention and patience they richly merit. I personally hold that an *Auseinandersetzung*, or serious engagement with Bloom's work, may well be the most useful pedagogical device today for beginning one's study of the Romantic movement, because his is the most unorthodox, iconoclastic, or "antithetical" interpretation of our time—more so than the interpretations of René Wellek, Northrop Frye, M.H. Abrams, or Jacques Barzun—and yet it is powerfully argued; it also supplies a useful introduction to contemporary literary theory.

Bloom's central thesis, now well known, of the "anxiety of influence" as the key to appreciating the achievements of especially the Romantic poets, is considered debunking and reductionistic by some, itself perhaps an instance of Nietzschean *réssentiment*—a failed "strong" poet becomes instead a "strong" critic, as Bloom openly aspires to be, but in the process exacting revenge upon poets he could admire from afar but not equal or dominate; over whom he could not achieve "anteriority," as Bloom would put it. Even if this charge were true, it would be consistent with Bloom's own theory; all of us, as readers, go along for the "transumptive" ride, rising with the swell and surfing along the curve of the sublime reaction, when the novice poet is provoked into a powerful retaliation by the achievement of his intimidating precursor.

Bloom operates openly from a Gnostic base that justifies his interest in the sublime as constituting those few moments of transumptive strength where we attain whatever achievement and release are available to us from our condition here, not so much of error but of its—in a post-Nietzschean dispensation—less tolerable accompaniments, belatedness and weakness. Such moments of the sublime are the highest and most transforming experiences life has to offer; as the poet rises, expands, makes contact with and in some sense attains absoluteness, the reader accompanies and participates parasitically in the same experience.

However, I believe that Bloom has done us greater service than the defensive dismissal mentioned above suggests, that he has wiped away a lot of fog and cant that may itself have unattractive psychological origins, since, after all, we are still living and plying our respective trades in the artistic dispensation opened up during the post-Enlightenment period by the Romantic poets. The Romantic era never really ended; it is still going on; we are still in the "middle" of it, if there is any way of gauging how far along we may be in such an amorphous cultural phenomenon. "Modernism" and "postmodernism" are simply later phases, weaker ripples, more radical or desperate exertions within the self-same Romantic rebellion. We are still caught up in the competition inaugurated by Milton, Blake, Wordsworth, and Shelley, with our American writers Emerson, Whitman, and Wallace Stevens figuring as late entrants in the same tradition—in Bloom's language, which derives from Nietzsche through Yeats and Stevens, "antithetical questers" after the Romantic sublime. Bloom writes:

> Our [contemporary] poets were and are Romantic as poets used to be Christian, that is, whether they want to be or not.[2] . . . This mythic quester, who is defeated every day yet to victory is born, has become more than a literary tradition . . . So many nonliterary lives—British and American—in the nineteenth and twentieth centuries have wasted themselves in this erotic quest pattern of the Romantic solitary, that we can call this myth as grimly authentic as most we encounter.[3]

Since we are still in the competition, we may have a vested interest in "misreading" our ancestors, in keeping the official relationship with our imposing cultural antecedents as benign as possible; this disguise may be a tactical feint, concealing a long-term preparation for an eventual assault on what appears their otherwise impregnable position, to steal our own place in the sun, before we ourselves are displaced and blotted out in turn by our transumptive successors. In this case, Bloom has applied an astringent wash that has wiped away any such comforting blur from our vision; as a result, we are perhaps poised less tactically for an attack; but in compensation we may now appreciate our situation more soberly and accurately.

As Bloom argues in 1970 in the new introduction to his 1961 volume, *The Visionary Company*, Romanticism was, in its origins, an internalized, frustrated, and compensatory reaction, emanating from the tradition of Protestant dissent, the nonconformist vision that descended from the Left Wing of England's Puritan movement, in the wake of England's failed attempt to come up with anything corresponding to the French Revolution. In this historical perspective, Romanticism may appear a paper triumph, a pathetic and ultimately impotent gesture that lacked the will or the power to bring about anything truly significant or to make a real change; a substitute or declared victory that was finally indiscernibly different from defeat and emptiness. However, along the way a new kind of pleasure came upon the scene which became a serendipitous win for the movement—and henceforth the inescapable aim of all "strong" poets in the post-Enlightenment period—the pleasure of the Sublime, the sense of the rise and expansion of the inner self, of separation or estrangement from the earth or nature or history which had become unacceptable, of withdrawal and compensatory, even vengeful, satisfaction in a parallel dimension or along an alternative axis.

The Romantic movement may seem a species of "sour grapes"; psychologically, however, it is more serious. A victory brought about with such anxiety but at the same time achieved so cheaply, or which makes so little difference, is dangerous. For a Pelagian "salvation" achieved in the final analysis so simply, or a "victory" consisting essentially of violently heightened powers of consciousness when facing the self-same reality easily plunges, after its "manic" peak, into a depressive sequel; that is, it swings over psychologically toward its opposite—nothingness, emptiness, or the "abyss," as Walt Whitman called it, as its photographic negative and inescapable alter ego. The feebleness of this "victory" creates a characteristic insecurity and oscillation of mood in the resulting personality between exaltation and panic or despair, an instability that has its ultimate seat not in the personality itself, but in the vision that personality is contemplating, as when we view an optical illusion which has two valid, but opposite, interpretations. Our vision swings back and forth uncontrollably, and our emotions shift accordingly. Many of these poets did indeed wrestle with depression and madness. Poetry, like philosophy, appears to "leave things the way they are"; but never was this more the case, or more of a scandal, than during the Romantic movement.

Finally, as Bloom himself suggests, his analyses implicitly point to the emergence of a new model of aggressive and retaliatory human behavior as acceptable and even culturally rewarded, in areas ultimately far beyond Romantic poetry, which represents a clear swerve away from the attitude and posture encouraged by the Judeo-Christian scriptures, a change and difference which, because of the over-idealizing of the relationship between precursor and "ephebe," was little noted at the time and is not fully appreciated even today. We live in a "post-Christian" society, we are frequently told, but nobody seems to know, or at least is able to describe clearly, what exactly succeeded it, and how and why this change took place. It is not the least merit of Bloom's work that it puts us in a position to do so, and to gauge the price we have paid as our society has undergone this powerful, and largely underground, transformation.

II

Late in his volume *Poetry and Repression* (1976), Bloom writes:

The function of criticism at the present time, as I conceive it, is to find a middle way between the paths of demystification of meaning, and of recollection or restoration of meaning, or between limitation and representation. But the only aesthetic path between limitation and representation is substitution, and so all that criticism can hope to teach, whether to the common reader or to the poet, is a series of stronger modes of substitution. Substitution, in this sense, is a mode of creation through catastrophe. The vessels or fixed forms break in every act of reading or of writing, but *how* they break is to a considerable extent in the power of each reader and of each writer. Yet there are patterns in the breaking that resist the power, however strong, of any reader and of every writer. These patterns—evident as sequences of images, or of tropes, or of psychic defenses—are as definite as those of any dance, and as varied as there are various dances. But poets do not invent the dances they dance, and we *can tell* the dancer from the dance. The stronger poet not only performs the dance more skillfully than the weaker poet, but he modifies it as well and yet it does remain the same dance. I am afraid that there does tend to be one fairly definite dance pattern in post-Enlightenment poetry, which can be altered by strong substitution, but still it does remain the same dance.[4]

This "dance" Bloom lays out as a pattern of revision by which a strong poet "misreads" his precursor; his new poem is a commentary and even a rewriting, "inspired" by the old in the competitive sense that one athlete is said to "inspire" another to do better what the first has done well already. Artistic competition is different in that the first, by his performance, implicitly establishes the game, the goals, and the rules of the competition by the very fact of his achievement; the second shows how the same result, or "a" result, can be better achieved. As Paul Valéry writes in his *Letter about Mallarmé* which Bloom quotes with regard to Wallace Stevens:

> Whether in science or the arts, if we look for the source of an achievement, we can observe that *what a man does* either repeats or refutes *what someone else has done*—repeats it in other tones, refines or amplifies or simplifies it, loads or overloads it with meaning; or else rebuts, overturns, destroys and denies it, but thereby assumes it and has invisibly used it. Opposites are born from opposites.[5]

This kind of inspiration and competition has been part of the artistic enterprise from the beginning; it seems to be essential to art as an ongoing tradition. What is distinctive about the Romantic movement is that this natural psychic dynamic becomes exaggerated and lopsided. The sense of competition is heightened or radicalized; it becomes more ruthless and absolute. This is ironic, because the Romantic movement for many conjures up images of the soothing nature poetry, "the . . . waters, rolling from their mountain springs with a soft inland murmur" of which Wordsworth wrote. This is the canonical, "weak" misreading of such a poet, according to Bloom, and it conceals a Hobbesian "war of all against all" lying beneath the surface.

For Bloom, a poetic text is "a psychic battlefield upon which authentic forces struggle for the only victory worth winning, the divinating triumph over oblivion," or as Milton sang it:

> Attir'd with Stars, we shall for ever sit,
> Triumphing over Death, and Chance, and thee O time.[6]

And further on:

> Strong poetry is strong only by virtue of a kind of textual usurpation . . . a strong reading *is* the only poetic fact, the only revenge against time that endures, that is successful in canonizing one text as opposed to a rival text.

> There is no textual authority without an act of imposition, a declaration of property that is made figuratively rather than properly or literally . . . (P)oetry, when it aspires to strength, is necessarily a competitive mode, indeed an obsessive mode, because poetic strength involves a self representation that is reached only through trespass, through crossing a daemonic threshold.[7]

Bloom has his own theory on the psychic origins of "strong" artistic production; he differs from Freud in deriving the distinctive *agon* and energy not from the Oedipus Complex or the Primal History Scene of *Totem and Taboo*, but from what he calls "the most poetically primal of scenes, the Scene of Instruction, a six phased scene that strong poems must will to overcome, by repressing their own freedom into the patterns of a revisionary misinterpretation." Thomas Frosch summarizes these phases thus:

> A Primal Scene of Instruction [is] a model for the unavoidable imposition of influence. The Scene—really a complete play, or process—has six stages, through which the ephebe emerges: election (seizure by the precursor's power); covenant (a basic agreement of poetic vision between precursor and ephebe); the choice of a rival inspiration (e.g., Wordsworth's Nature vs. Milton's Muse); the self presentation of the ephebe as a new incarnation of the "Poetical Character"; the ephebe's interpretation of the precursor; and the ephebe's revision of the precursor. Each of these stages then becomes a level of interpretation in the reading of the ephebe's poem.[8]

The ephebe is "magnetized" through contact with the precursor's work; the latter exercises a fascination so powerful that he is "locked on" and drawn ineluctably into its field of influence. He takes on an orientation, an interest, and an activity determined by the attraction he finds in the artwork and in the precursor whose disciple he initially becomes. But, as in any pedagogic situation, there comes a time for the student to break free, to rebel, to find his own way, so as to realize his own vision and to produce his own distinctive works. This dynamic, true of all art, was heightened and exaggerated during the Romantic movement. The ephebe aspires to attain nothing less than direct, unmediated contact with the artistic source, and thence anteriority over his predecessor, thereby reversing their initial relation in the Scene of Instruction; the creative situation is laid out as a furious, all-out struggle for contact and control of the Absolute, with the vanquished being banished to derivative status. Bloom writes:

> A strong poet, for Vico or for us, . . . must divine or invent himself, and so attempt the impossibility of *originating himself*.[9] . . . we can define a strong poet as one who will not tolerate words that intervene between him and the Word, or precursors standing between him and the Muse.[10]

Metalepsis or transumption thus becomes a total, final act of taking up a poetic stance in relation to anteriority, particularly to the anteriority of poetic language, which means primarily the loved and feared poems of the precursors. Properly accomplished, this stance figuratively produces the illusion of having fathered one's own fathers, which is the greatest illusion, the one that Vico called "divination," or that we call "poetic immortality."[11]

As Bloom shows, each "transumptive" achievement by one Romantic poet creates a dilemma for the next; each suffers from a heightened sense of "belatedness," of coming "after the event," after the great artist has done apparently all there is to be done within the genre established. This requires greater and greater acts of "repression," in order to allow new experiences of the Sublime to be produced. Unable to outdo his predecessor in his own field, nothing is left for the daunted but not discouraged successor than implicitly to revise the rules of what is permissible, to alter significantly but covertly the very genre, so as to allow passage and acceptance for an alternative performance, thereby creating the opportunity for his own "transumptive" triumph, by which he secures "anteriority" over his predecessor, displacing him to the belatedness and marginality from which he himself suffered.

The persuasiveness and power of Bloom's interpretation come not so much from its theoretical substructure as from his reading of particular poems as "misprisions" and "revisions" of imposing precursors. To appreciate the force of this argument, there is no substitute for serious engagement with Bloom's work. Here only a rough sketch of his "map" of the Romantic movement can be offered: Milton as the severe precursor; Wordsworth as the "ephebe" who wrestles most successfully with his mentor, thereby bringing the movement to its high point and fulfillment, troping his precursor's biblical sublime into irrelevance through the images he plants of the inner self reaching toward immortality; and Tennyson, whose poetry shows characteristic strains of being "severely belated."

III

According to Bloom, the major precursor for the entire movement is the nonconformist Protestant John Milton; indeed, Romanticism may be defined as a humanization and naturalization of Milton's dissident and subversive apocalyptic. As mentioned earlier, and in opposition to C.S. Lewis, T.S. Eliot, and the "New Critics" of the American literary scene a half century ago, Bloom stresses the background of Protestant dissent behind almost all the figures inspired by what Hazlitt termed "the Spirit of the Age." This movement cannot be understood apart from the frustration of the left wing, nonconformist tradition after the dissolution of the Puritan commonwealth and the restoration of the Stuart monarchy in 1660. For Bloom, "there is no more important point to be made about English Romantic poetry than this one . . . (I)t is a displaced Protestantism, or a Protestantism astonishingly transformed by different kinds of humanism or naturalism"[12] The dominant character of English religious dissent was "its insistence on intellectual and spiritual independence, on the right of private judgment in questions of morality, on the inner light within each soul, by which alone Scripture was to be read—and most of all, on allowing no barrier or intermediary to come between a man and his God."[13] Milton's *Paradise Lost* is "the major Protestant poem in the language"; its dominant character is the Miltonic spirit:

> the autonomous soul seeking its own salvation outside of and beyond the hierarchy of grace.[14]

Bloom finds in Milton such a triumph of this English nonconformist temper that it "made him a church with one believer, a political party of one, even at last a nation unto himself."[15]

Bloom locates Milton's central concept in the Protestant doctrine of "Christian Liberty, which holds that it is the prerogative of every regenerated man under the New Law of the Gospel to be free of every ecclesiastical constraint."[16] The Stuart Restoration dashed the hopes for a continuation of the Puritan experiment; henceforth, it would have to be tried in America. Milton himself spent time in prison for his political sympathies. Thereafter he directed his energies inward, exploring the Paradise within as a substitute and compensation for the Paradise without, which had failed to materialize. These revolutionary energies fell dormant and moribund on the national scene until the Bastille fell in 1789 and fired again the imaginations of Blake, Hazlitt, Wordsworth, and Shelley. However, reactionary forces were again successful in quenching the revolutionary spirit and making sure that nothing happened in London akin to what had transpired in Paris; but again, politic's loss was poetry's gain.

As regards the "anxiety of influence" and the dynamics of the Primal Scene of Instruction, Bloom finds that "In English, Milton is the severe father of the Sublime mode,"[17] and that "(I)t is one of the great characteristics of the Romantic period that each major poet in turn sought to rival and surpass Milton, while also renewing his vision."[18] This involved secularizing and humanizing his representation of the never actually depicted Christian epic struggle between God and the fallen angels. Indeed, a naturalized version of this *agon* and emancipation became the (Gnostic) plot of all Romantic poetry; it is:

> the secular analogue to the . . . process by which Calvinist Protestantism became the radical dissent of the later eighteenth century. The immense hope of Blake and of the early Wordsworth, of Shelley and of Keats, was that poetry, by expressing the whole man, could either liberate him from his fallen condition or, more compellingly, make him see that condition as unnecessary, as an unimaginative fiction that the awakened spirit could slough off.[19]

Perhaps the most illuminating example of the development of the Romantic movement and of Bloom's thesis can be given by tracing the history of the image of the Divine Chariot, which Milton called the Chariot of Paternal Deity, as it is used by a succession of poets. The Hebrew decalogue forbade any image or representation of the divinity; mention could only be made of the "glory" of God (smoke or flame), God's voice, or of what Bloom, following the Kabbalah, calls the *Merkabah*, the "Covering Cherubs" which protected the tablets of the Law in the Ark of the Covenant. The prophet Ezekiel, for Bloom the first "revisionist" poet within the Hebrew tradition, daringly stretched this convention and broke with this restriction. In his first chapter, following Isaiah, he claims to have had a vision of God himself; unlike Isaiah, however, he goes on to describe this vision within the tradition of the covering cherubs, with a spectacular metalepsis of the moving throne of God, or of what he calls the "Wheels and their Work" (1:15–28).

Surprisingly, this heretical deviation was accepted into the Hebrew canon, which for Bloom means that henceforth it had to be "misread canonically," that is, against its clear intent, so as not to appear a violation of the law. In ch. 4:6 of his Apocalypse, St. John takes up and elaborates the description Ezekiel had given of the divine throne, now with a crucial "revision"—seated on the throne is a man, Christ, who is yet surrounded by Ezekiel's four-faced Cherubim:

> And before the throne there was a sea of glass like unto crystal: and in the midst of the throne, and round about the throne were four beasts full of eyes before and behind.

In Canto XXIX of his *Purgatorio*, Dante revises the image once more. Now it has become the Triumphal Chariot of the Church. Dante explicitly refers to both Ezekiel's chariot as well as to St. John's; but his chariot carries Beatrice, rather than an enthroned version of God. For Bloom, however, all this is merely preparation for the subversive and "transumptive" use Milton makes of this image in Book VI of *Paradise Lost*, where he depicts Christ riding the Chariot of Paternal Deity at the climax of the War in Heaven. For Bloom, Milton in no sense "fulfills" the type prepared for him by the earlier poets; rather he dashes and destroys their interpretations with a new trope that embeds itself in the reader's imagination and displaces all others:

> . . . *forth rush'd with whirlwind sound*
> *The Chariot of Paternal Deitie,*
> *Flashing thick flames, Wheele within Wheele, undrawn,*
> *It self instinct with Spirit, but convoyd*
> *By four Cherubic shapes, four Faces each*
> *Had wondrous, as with Starrs thir bodies all*
> *And Wings were set with Eyes, with Eyes the Wheels*
> *Of Beril, and careering Fires between;*
> *Over their heads a chrystal Firmament,*
> *Whereon a Saphir throne, inlaid with pure*
> *Amber, and colours of the showrie Arch.*
> *Hee in Celestial Panoplie all armd*
> *Of radiant Urim, work divinely wrought,*
> *Ascended, at his right hand Victorie.*

[VI, 749–62]

Milton's use of this image is clearly agonistic and competitive. In a violent revision of past uses, Christ is carrying Milton's own "tablets," that is, his own theological agenda. Indeed, the features of Christ tend to blur with those of Milton himself. Bloom writes:

> There is no biblical *figura* that Milton is fulfilling; he has mounted Christ in the Merkabah, made the throne world into a war machine, and sent Christ out to battle as a larger version of his own self-image as Puritan polemicist burning through the ranks of the bishops and the presbyters. If this is *figura*, then the Milton, who was Cromwell's Latin Secretary, is the only *figura* involved, which is to overturn the Christian notion entirely.[20]

> In his schemes of allusion in *Paradise Lost*, [Milton] replaced *figura* by transumption—not a fulfillment or even a reversed fulfillment of

tradition, but a true subversion of tradition that enforced Milton's own earliness while troping tradition into belatedness.[21]

The audacious, not to say blasphemous or heretical use Milton made of this image was picked up by Thomas Gray who, in his *The Progress of Poesy*, introduces Milton with a clear allusion to the image of the Christ of Book VI, line 771: "Hee on the wings of Cherub rode sublime."

The poet has indeed taken Christ's place in the chariot; as Bloom states:

Milton's major desire was to assert his own identity as poet-prophet, far surpassing Moses and Isaiah and the authors of the New Testament.[22]

Following suit, in the introductory quatrains to his own poem *Milton*, William Blake dares to place himself, as successor to Milton, ascending the same chariot:

Bring me my Bow of burning gold:
Bring me my Arrows of desire:
Bring me my Spear: O clouds unfold!
Bring me my Chariot of fire!

Bloom writes:

The emphasis is on "my," as Blake moves to be the Enthroned Poet riding the chariot that is at once drawn by, and constituted of, the Four Zoas, the "living creatures" of Ezekiel and Revelation.[23]

Similarly, in 1819 in *Prometheus Unbound*, Shelley appropriates this Miltonic chariot, and places on it, not the Paternal Deity, but a spirit of rebellion. (IV, 206–35).

However, it is to *Paradise Lost* and to the most interesting, developed, and dramatically successful character in that poem, Satan, that we must turn to find Milton's most enduring and powerful legacy to the Romantic movement. Milton's Satan is more ambiguous and sympathetic than the Satan of the Hebrew and Christian scriptures; for the first time, Satan becomes a fully rounded character, something more than the prosecuting attorney he is, for example, in the book of Job. Bloom recognizes that Satan is the central figure in *Paradise Lost*, and indeed, the reason for its fascination and influence on the modern mind:

Satan is vastly in excess of his utility in the narrative of Milton's epic. Scholars go on telling us that Satan is there for the myth, and for the poem, yet the reader's sublime always replies that the poem is there for Satan.[24]

Indeed, the Miltonic figure of Satan rears up as the father and source of the modern Sublime:

Satan is a great rhetorician, and nearly as strong a poet as Milton himself, but more important he is Milton's central way through to the Sublime. As such, Satan prophesies the post-Enlightenment crisis poem, which has become our modern Sublime.[25]

Satan is more than the central or most developed character in *Paradise Lost*; his fascination comes from the strong parallel between himself and the post-Enlightenment artistic quester, both in his condition and in his ambition. Satan's condition is described marvelously by Milton, playing upon the fundamental infantile fear of falling; for Satan's fall goes on interminably:

And in the lowest deep a lower deep
Still threatening to devour me opens wide
To which the hell I suffer seems a heaven.

It is the unspoken parallel with the Romantic poet that is responsible for his resonance with the modern imagination. Satan has the essential characteristics of a poet who feels himself thrown, in Gnostic fashion, out and down into a realm of error, shadow, and weakness. Bloom asserts that Satan is "the ironic representation or allegory of the post-Miltonic poet at her strongest"[26] This parallel includes not only the artist's condition, but also her ambition: "Satan, until the nasty surprise of learning that he owes his very existence to Christ, had been the glorious Lucifer, foremost among God's loyal flatterers. Down he comes, upon ceasing to be his father's favorite, and as he starts downward and outward he declares that he has fathered himself."[27]

Bloom can refer to "the equivocal heroism of Satan's questing onwards through Chaos to reach Eden,"[28] and on a Gnostic reading, Satan indeed becomes the hero of the poem. In a later incarnation, Goethe's *Faust*, beneath the Christian trappings this becomes clearer. The conventions of the traditional story are modified, and the Gnostic reinterpretation stands out more obviously. The grounds on which Faust falls are also the grounds for which he is eventually saved—perpetual striving—in an ending which hopelessly muddles and plays havoc with the point of the received story. Later Romantic poets catch the scent and show less inhibition in exploring the sublime possibilities to be produced by transferring Milton's description of Satan to the artist herself. As in the Gnostic theosophy, the creator god has done such a shoddy job that the artist must seek to overcome him and his world, to "father himself." Bloom in fact suggests that Milton's ambition as poet was the same as Satan's against the creator, so Milton also was speaking when Satan is made to say: "I know no time when I was not as now; I know none before me."

Thereafter the artistic progeny of Milton's Satan become legion and multiform; Bloom comments: "Keats' Hyperion is a touch closer to Milton's Satan than Keats would care for him to have been, since like Satan Hyperion is not so much a God in dread of losing his kingdom as he is a poet in dread of losing his poetic powers or mortal godhead. An obsession with divination, a fear of futurity, is the mark of Hyperion, of Satan, and of Blake's Urizen."[29]

For Bloom, Wordsworth is the most successful of the Romantic poets, but also for that reason the most problematic. This means that in his artistic *agon* with his strong precursor Milton, Wordsworth was the most successful in reversing their relation in the Scene of Instruction—more successful than Blake or Shelley, for example—but also that Wordsworth paid the important price, underwent the Romantic "turn," or suffered the characteristic Romantic distortion of "internalizing" his triumph, of developing his compensatory victory in an alternative dimension or along an internal axis. For Bloom, Wordsworth's is:

the poetry of the growing inner self. . . . In Wordsworth's supreme moments, as in Emerson's, things become transparent, and the inner self expands until it introjects not less than everything, space and time included.[30]

We find in *Tintern Abbey* and *The Prelude* already what became the characteristic, and never surpassed, Romantic plot of the interior artistic self developing under the stimulus of anxious contact with its strong precursor into a final consciousness and representation of its preternatural, divine powers. For Bloom, and against Geoffrey Hartmann, the tranquility and surface quiet of both these poems is deceptive; they are riddled with the "anxiety of influence," and that anxiety is from Milton.[31] Bloom writes:

It is the peculiar and extravagant greatness of Wordsworth that only he supplanted Milton as the tutelary genius of the Scene of Instruction, and it is the scandal of modern poetry that no one, not even Yeats or Stevens, in turn has supplanted Wordsworth.[32]

Still,

Internalization is at once the great Wordsworthian resource and the great Wordsworthian disaster, and it is never enough to praise Wordsworth for a process in which he was indeed, as Keats saw, the great poetic inventor and, as Keats also saw, the great poetic villain; indeed as much a hero-villain, I would say, as his true precursor, Milton's Satan.[33]

I suspect that *Tintern Abbey*, is *the* modern poem proper, and that in most good poems written in English since *Tintern Abbey* inescapably repeat, rewrite, or revise it. If there is something radically wrong with it, something radically self-deceptive, then this radical wrongness at last will not be seen as belonging to *Tintern Abbey* alone.[34]

Wordsworth was the first to be provoked by Milton's achievement to the only possible poetic scenario that could "trump" Milton's: a naturalization of the divine hierophany, with the trappings of the Christian epic thrown off completely, and the bare plot of the poet's emergence and triumph over his strong precursors taking the place of God's triumph over the fallen angels. Such is the "anxiety of influence," according to Bloom, that Wordsworth is pushed to the desperate strategy of securing his anteriority over his intimidating precursor and poetic immortality by claiming a direct influx from the divine. Bloom finds that *Tintern Abbey* is:

a very great visionary lie, not as much a myth of memory as it is a utilization of memory as a lie against time . . . [The poem] seems to turn upon the magnificent, primal poetic urge for *divination*, in the complex sense best defined by Vico, the poet's apotropaic concern for his own immortality.[35]

And in summary:

On an antithetical reading, *Tintern Abbey* is a Scene of Instruction in which the poet brings a Sublime response to a place or state of heightened demand, but the genius of the state counts for more than the genius of place, which means that Milton counts for more than nature does . . . It is Milton whose hidden presence in the poem makes the heightened demand that forces Wordsworth into the profoundly ambivalent defensive trope of memory. Renovation, or "tranquil restoration" as the text terms it, is only a mystification, a mask for the real concern of the poem. The Hermit is the synedoche for Milton's blindness toward anteriority. To see the writing or marking of nature is to see prophetically one's own absence or imaginative death. To see the "uncertain notice" of the Hermit's presence is to be disturbed into sublimity by way of repressing the mighty force of remembering Milton's sublimity, particularly in the Creation of *Paradise Lost*, Book VII, which haunts every Wordsworthian account of the subject and object worlds approaching one another again.[36]

All in all, Bloom sees Wordsworth as fairly successful in his *agon* with Milton, which means that his transumptive hyperboles, as both new and shocking, were successful at blotting out and displacing the Miltonic (Biblical) sublime. Later poets, suffering the burden of coming after both Milton and Wordsworth, were pushed to more strenuous acrobatics, stranger devices, and to more serious distortions. Shelley was too intimidated by Wordsworth to ever reverse their relationship in the Scene of Instruction. Later poets show more signs of strain as the sense of their own belatedness, of the demands made upon them, and of the difficulty of fulfilling these demands becomes more acute. Tennyson is a representative example.

In his major poems, Tennyson displays two apparently opposed attitudes: on the one hand, there are increased reservations and misgivings about the enterprise of the "Romantic Quester" as a whole as something too difficult, as perhaps a curse, a role which can never be carried out in a final or absolute fashion and which brings destruction to the poet and to all around him; it is a kind of Midas touch which the poet would, in his more candid and honest moments, give up. At the same time, and as if in compensation, there is an increased self-consciousness of himself as an artist or poet, and perhaps an over-confidence in the poetic estate as itself sufficient, as constituting enough distinction, no matter how the "competition" comes out; whatever happens, he "wins," and his superiority (at least over ordinary mortals) is secured. These apparently contradictory attitudes are comprehensible under the circumstances: the increased sense of belatedness and strain raises the "degree of difficulty" of executing a transumptive Sublime, leading the poet to rethink the whole affair, to perhaps consider the competition unfair, and to entertain the notion of abandoning it. Still, he has accepted the role, and rather than parade his anxieties, he chooses instead to parade his security, elevating his role and vocation as poet as itself enough of a distinction, enough of a "victory," to generate a sense of power and dominance, and on occasion to empower him to produce a sublime sequel after his initial insecurities.

In his poem *Mariana*, for example, Mariana is waiting for the arrival of her Romantic swain, which for Bloom is Tennyson waiting for transumptive success over his predecessors. Her fear, however, is that this swain will never come, and her practical, not too concealed solution is to cut her losses, to enjoy instead her present condition, ensconced in her romantic bower. However, this interjects a note of stasis, of narcissistic eroticism in place of the dynamic of competition and "heterosexual" fulfillment, as well as the hint of preference for a falling asleep in the arms of death to the trials of combat, with the possibility of defeat. Bloom comments:

> The poem is more deliciously unhealthy than all its Pre-Raphaelite and Decadent progeny were to be, and remains the finest example in the language of an embowered consciousness representing itself as being too happy in its unhappiness to want anything more.[37]

In *The Daughters of Hersperus*, similarly, the daughters sing; they establish their credentials as mystifiers; what more is needed? Any further competition should be called off, and is in fact blocked by their very success as enchantresses: "The pleasure they value so highly must be their pride as poets and as performers, as weavers of an enchantment so sinuous as to block all questers from fulfillment in an earthly paradise."[38] The poet exults in the display of his own artistic powers, which creates a compensating satisfaction, even if they be not up to securing anteriority over his Sublime precursors. Bloom comments:

> The end of the quest is to be not in the quester's merging in the identity of others, or of the poethood, but in the perpetual stasis of an earthly paradise preserved by enchantment from the single gratification it affords, and which would end it.[39]

In *Tithonus*, the eponymous hero, like Prospero in *The Tempest*, plays with the notion of giving up the poetic enterprise altogether:

> *... Let me go: take back thy gift:*
> *Why should a man desire in any way*
> *To vary from the kindly race of men,*
> *Or pass beyond the goal of ordinance*
> *Where all should pause, as is most meet for all?*

He recoils in a sublime metonymy based on the Wordsworthian glimmer and Keatsian eroticism, but Bloom comments:

> Aurora's tears are read by Tithonus as his own hysterical fear that his now noxious immortality cannot be withdrawn (which, on the level of Tennyson's own repressions, I would tend to interpret as his own evaded realization that he is doomed to go on seeking to be a strong poet, even though Hallam [his friend] is dead).[40]

In *The Holy Grail*, Percival's quest has the disturbing effect of destroying everything and everyone he encounters, even possibly the object of the quest:

> *Lo, if I find the Holy Grail itself*
> *and touch it, it will crumble to dust.*

Percival tells himself "This Quest is not for thee"; but Tennyson, like Percival, has taken a "vow" to be a strong poet, and this vow may not be broken, no matter what the human cost. Bloom unpacks Tennyson's resulting and scarcely hidden desire thus:

> Percival believes he is questing for the Holy Grail, but in reality he quests for Schopenhauer's quasi-Buddhistic Nirvana, where desire shall vanish, the individual self fade away, and quietude replace the strong poet's search for a stance and word of his own.[41]

Generalizing from the example of Tennyson, we may observe that the writers after Wordsworth, Shelley, and Keats show more signs of belatedness, and the natural strain of having to grapple with their increasingly strong precursors. Browning escaped anxiety by agreeing never to attack or break free from his precursor, Shelley, but thus also agreeing never to establish his own, distinct identity. He evaded the strain of combat, the "anxiety of influence," but at the cost of never developing the "antithetical" side to his personality. Moreover, his strongest poetry shows his residual misgivings about the wisdom of this strategy of choosing to remain in a hearty ignorance and permanent discipleship to his mentor.

Yeats goes to the other extreme, and it is clearly Yeats who has most strongly influenced Bloom's interpretations. It was Yeats who took the notion of the "antithetical" from Nietzsche and developed the Gnostic theosophy that lies at the base of the Romantic movement. If anything, Yeats so exaggerated the notion of the "antithetical" that he was a bit cowed by his composite "strong" precursor. *The Second*

Coming is commonly "misread" as urging a return to faith, as the sphinx "slouches toward Bethlehem"; however, Yeats was doing just the opposite, projecting transumptively the dawn of an "antithetical" age that would replace the twenty centuries of (weak, belated) Christianity which he felt were drawing to a close. The sphinx will triumph over the child in the manger, rather than kneel to become his disciple—and thus again reverse, this time transpersonally or culturally, the "scene of instruction," permitting Yeats and the "antithetical" to attain anteriority.

Conclusion

As is apparent from his quotations, Bloom is by no means an uncritical proponent or indifferent defender of the Romantic movement. Still, as a Gnostic, he would hold that it has been the primary source of the best moments of elevation, expansion, and release which have been and continue to be available to post-Enlightenment man, and he would give these up only with the greatest reluctance. His attitude seems to be like that of some toward the drugs and hallucinatory agents that have become widely available over the past decades: he recognizes that they often have pernicious side effects and negative consequences for society as a whole (the Romantic movement has supplied the operative myths by which contemporary culture understands itself and behaves); but the "kick" they give is so good, so much above or beyond our ordinary fare, that it's worth it. It is not even a question of learning to use them intelligently; as a society, we will always have to pay a certain price in terms of human casualties. But again, the cream or honey they offer is so much better than the ordinary gruel of our daily experience, that the "highs" they provide are worth the price we have to pay and will continue to have to pay for them.

Still, a social observer or intellectual historian may offer the comment with which I began this essay. On Bloom's own admission, the sublime effect, for both writer and reader, does not really consist of translation to another or better realm, but is achieved through a violently heightened power of language and consciousness with regard to the self-same reality. A "victory" which makes so little difference is dangerous, because after the transumptive, "manic" peak, the personality easily plunges into an apprehensive and depressive sequel, as the mind naturally seeks to explore alternative ways by which the same reality may be viewed, as part of its self-protective mechanism. There arises inevitably the oscillation between violently contrasting moods, against which the mind has no protection, as its vision of its situation swings unpredictably over to its opposite, that is, back to the Gnostic (or worse) interpretation of the same situation. When one adds to this the increased "degree of difficulty" in producing a sublime effect this late in the tradition, with a correlatively heightened and recurring anxiety about the adequacy of one's artistic powers, it is not surprising to read about the repeated bouts of depression and madness, as well as occasional tragedy, in the lives of such contemporary poets as James Berryman, Robert Lowell, Anne Sexton, and Sylvia Plath. On the contrary, these seem only too comprehensible, a consequence almost to be expected.

Notes

[1] See Francis Fukuyama, *The End of History and the Last* Man, Free Press, NY, 1992.
[2] Harold Bloom, *The Visionary Company: A Reading of English Romantic Poetry*, revised and enlarged ed., Cornell University Press, Ithaca, NY, 1971, p. 463; hereafter "VC."
[3] VC 464.
[4] Harold Bloom, *Poetry and Repression: Revisionism from Blake to Stevens*, Yale University Press, New Haven, CT, 1976, p. 270; hereafter "P&R."
[5] P&R 281.
[6] P&R 2.
[7] P&R 6.
[8] P&R 27.
[9] P&R 7.
[10] P&R 10.
[11] P&R 20.
[12] P&R xvii.
[13] P&R xviii.
[14] P&R xvii.
[15] P&R xix.
[16] P&R xix.
[17] P&R 21.
[18] VC xxiv.
[19] VC xxiv.
[20] P&R 91.
[21] P&R 96.
[22] P&R 112.
[23] P&R 92.
[24] P&R 111.
[25] P&R 23.
[26] P&R 101.
[27] Harold Bloom, *Ruin the Sacred Truths: Poetry and Belief from the Bible to the Present*, Harvard University Press, Cambridge, MA, 1991, p. 112; hereafter "RST."
[28] P&R 168.
[29] P&R 121.
[30] P&R 61.
[31] P&R 55–59.

[32] P&R 82.
[33] P&R 58.
[34] P&R 59.
[35] P&R 79–80.
[36] P&R 80–81.
[37] P&R 150.
[38] P&R 156.
[39] P&R 157.
[40] P&R 167.
[41] P&R 173.

CHAPTER 10

Pornography and the Culmination of Romanticism

Our age has sometimes been called a secular age, but this description is unsatisfactory because it identifies us by what we are not, instead of what we are. It would be more accurate and informative to describe our age as romantic. I am using "Romanticism" here to refer to the artistic and cultural movement that began in Europe in the early nineteenth century. While it ended formally around the end of the First World War, a strong claim could be made that what succeeded it—modernism, structuralism, postmodernism, and deconstruction—are so many branches sprung from the same trunk; that is, they extend and in various ways radicalize the self-same revolution begun by the Romantic movement, rather than representing an overthrow or repudiation of its basic tenets. Thus, the Romantic movement never really ended. The other movements mentioned are siblings from the same nest. The choice in our age is between different species of Romanticism; anything else is beyond the event horizon.

Although the first uses of the word were in England, Romanticism began seriously as a German reaction against French rationalist and neoclassical cultural hegemony, and spread from there back to England and then to France, and thence to the other European countries. It has left a permanent mark upon German culture, just as neoclassicism left a permanent imprint upon French culture. The difference between "classical" and "romantic" culture has been discussed at length by Jacques Barzun,[1] Irving Babbitt,[2] M.H. Abrams,[3] René Welleck,[4] and more controversially Harold Bloom.[5] They all have valuable things to say, and in what appears below I will draw on them all.

What does it mean to say that our culture is romantic? First of all, it means that the ultimate categories by which we understand our world and judge ourselves have come to be romantic categories. Our weaknesses, as a society, are romantic weaknesses, and our triumphs, such as they are, are romantic triumphs. These are the only standards which enjoy public recognition and universal support; the classical and religious categories of a previous age are practically banished to private discourse. Romanticism has subtly become the ideology behind our language of human rights, because it supplies the deepest "right" of all— the right to self-fulfillment and self-expression (the same thing), above everything else and at the expense of anyone. Romanticism is our *lingua franca*, our common vocabulary, the only language you can be sure everyone must recognize and respond to. They are the categories that appear in news broadcasts, political manifestos, book reviews, divorce proceedings, and entitlement hearings, not to mention textbooks in psychology and sociology—the statements that are meant to impress and be digestible by "everybody." In the theme park refugee camp we call the contemporary world, romantic categories represent the last, tenuous net we throw over reality by which we secure an experience that can in any sense be called "common," public, or universal. It is our last, weak bid for a "society" or "civilization" that is more than simply a heap of self-interested egos locked together in capitalist exchange, a thin gossamer web that keeps us, in some self-contradiction and thus not entirely successfully, from periodic outbursts of anarchy, whether individual, corporate, or national—which is simply the Romantic movement gone "too far"—since Romanticism by its nature undercuts social constraints to the individual's free expansion and thereby subversively encourages and reinforces anarchic energies. A "romantic" culture is, if not a contradiction in terms, at the least the description of a civilization always teetering on the brink of chaos, a society fundamentally opposed to itself and to the very idea of "society."

What are the romantic features of our culture? First of all, the cult of originality and creativity is a distinctively romantic allegiance. Aeschylus, Sophocles, and Euripides, among many lesser-known playwrights, quarried Homer for plots for their plays. While tinkering with the plot and character was encouraged in the yearly competitions, this was not done as an end in itself, but as an experiment to determine how more powerful or interesting dramatic effects might be produced. Originality was not rewarded for its own sake, if the resulting dramatic production fell flat. Indeed, in his *Poetics*, Aristotle seems to feel he is now at a point where all the interesting dramatic effects have been discovered, nothing new or noteworthy is to be expected, and he is thus in a position to describe the necessary means to secure what are for him the most interesting and powerful dramatic experiences—the comic and the tragic.

This takes us to a deeper point. Originality appears in the pre-Romantic discussion only as a concession to weakness, a sign of our embarrassment at our status as dependent substances; thus not able to carry on even the most excellent and pleasurable activities indefinitely (as the gods can), we are forced to fall back to a rhythm of alternation or exchange between our more excellent activities as our best means of approximating the timeless perfect activity of the independent or unconditioned substance, which everything in the universe is imitating, according to its status and structure. This need for "originality" or change, for variation and distraction, therefore, is a confession of weakness, not a profession of strength. It is nothing of which we are guilty, but is nonetheless a stigma, a sign of our less than godlike status. In a better world—or if we were gods—we would not need it. This evaluation is reversed under the Romantic dispensation. There precisely because we are gods, we must be endlessly original and creative.

A second or more substantive alteration occurs in the changed understanding of the vocation of art. This change concerns assumptions so deep they do not come up often for discussion; some people in fact assume that all such definitions of the nature of art "say the same thing" or at least are not contradictory. For the Romantic the plot of art is a movement from the inner to the outer. The inner is seeking a clearer expression of its true nature in an outer medium or penumbra that is at the beginning beset by obscurity, difficulty, and impediment. The only significant difference in types of Romantic art is whether this movement is successful. Like Hamlet, the romantic hero has "that within which passeth show" (Act I, Sc. ii). As a general characterization, the Romantic movement began in optimism and moved toward pessimism toward the end of the nineteenth century. There is no change at the "inner" or center; the change is all in the medium or expression, whether the subject attains its necessary and appropriate degree of clarity or glory. This movement is reflected in a title Lionel Trilling gave his last book, a study in the novel which was *Sincerity and Authenticity*.[6] Sincerity implies an accord between inner and outer, that the outer successfully or accurately portrays the true feelings of the inner. "Sincerity" becomes a category by which the romantic hero is judged, and by which he judges the world around him. As the dangers of deception and hypocrisy from the "outer" world become heightened, however, the demand on the hero, and on anyone who would be of "value," is commensurately raised from sincerity to "authenticity," which connotes a more radical, unsparing, and suspicious examination of any supposed accord.

In pre-Romantic art, by contrast, the movement is toward a greater conformity of the subject to the external world. The whole purpose of art is that the audience should change, either in the moral dimension (comedy) or in their theoretical or speculative orientation (tragedy). Art is the best device society has developed to minister to this deep-rooted need within its members, a periodic conversion in several dimensions, brought about in the least painful way. This contrast is brought out by opposing views toward a central convention of art—distortion. Pre-Romantic art immediately and automatically accepted the need for fiction or distortion, as a useful means to minister to this recurring human weakness. As Aristotle notes, even to mark a beginning, a middle, and an end is already to distort our experience, since short of birth and death our life knows no such absolute beginnings, middles, and ends.

The two most powerful pre-Romantic forms of drama, comedy and tragedy, deliberately engaged in further fictions: the comic hero is specifically constructed a bit below the average, while the tragic hero is a bit above. Such a distortion was found to be more successful in securing the uniquely powerful and satisfying comic and tragic effects. By contrast, the Romantic sensibility has to be opposed to fiction. It can then be described as an art which is paradoxically opposed to "art," in the direction of preferring the equivalent of photography. The embattled Romantic sensibility has given up fiction as a means of approaching the real because fiction is known ahead of time to be infected with error and obscurity, and the very goal of Romantic art is to overthrow error and obscurity in the expression of the center. For the less embattled or suspicious pre-Romantic sensibility, on the contrary, the only way to get to the deeper external realities on which our life depends, in both its practical and theoretical aspects, is through fiction, to give these experiences the increased weight and impact they need to have. Romantic art has a built-in suspicion of and bias against fiction because of its assumption of a barrier between inner and outer which must be breached if a higher expression of the inner is to come about.

This also explains why there is no opposition between romanticism and realism in the novel, but rather why the "realistic" novel—in the progressively different senses that "realism" has taken historically—is the logical culmination, the inevitable, necessary, and purest expression of the Romantic movement, just as an ultra-objective and non-distorting "photography" is the logical culmination of Romantic art. In Romantic art, there is at bottom little variety of mood or feeling; there is rather a remarkable continuity and consistency of affect, one of grim seriousness or no-nonsense earnestness. The prevailing attitude is one of aggrieved or injured merit. This is because the only real concern in Romantic art is whether the "inner" is on the way to achieving a finally satisfying expression in the outer. When that is achieved, then and only then will both artist and audience be allowed to relax. Romantic art has all the lightness of a space shuttle launch.[7]

There is no serious opposition, but rather a deep-seated if somewhat hidden accord, between Romanticism and the spirit of modern philosophy, as launched by Descartes; both are fundamentally involved in a furious struggle against deception. Both Romanticism and Cartesian philosophy are involved in a desperate project of escape from a condition of obscurity or self-estrangement by a subject who was meant, as E.M. Forster puts the purpose of the novel, to "see life steady and see it whole." Both view themselves as sweeping away clouds from a mind meant to know the truth pure and complete, by a being that does not need to grow and to be corrected periodically like every conditioned substance, but rather is owed from the beginning an unimpeded vision of Truth as its fundamental birthright. Its perfection should not consist in a rhythmic alternation of contrasting activities, reflecting its composite, conditioned ontological status, but in the single continuous activity proper to the simple, unconditioned substance. Thus this struggle for clarity of expression is viewed not as normal and inevitable, but as a surprise and fundamentally unjust. This accounts for the lack of humor or lightness, the tendency to principled self-righteousness and anger that is a surprising underlying tone of much Romantic art. Like D.H. Lawrence, the romantic hero wants to burn with a "hard, blue flame." This is a desperate, non-negotiable aspect to its program; after all, a first adequate appearance of its existence—a kind of "final judgment"—and not just an "improvement" is on the line.

The romantic hero is engaged in a fundamental revolt against the condition of being a creature or conditioned substance. Its program is rather the natural expectation of an unconditioned substance, of aristocracy finding itself born into poverty, shocked and enraged at finding itself initially cheated, its true nature denied or implicitly insulted, and resolved to do everything to redress this imbalance. In categories from the history of religions, both the artist and the audience or connoisseur who can take in and appreciate his message are now best understood as the traditional god of Gnosticism who discovers himself mysteriously, and through no fault of his own (but perhaps through the spite and machinations of another "evil" deity), "fallen" into matter, sullied with its grossness, his true nature covered and obscured by "appearances." The artist, however, now becomes the "genius" or, in effect, the "savior god," who brings a secret "logos" that accounts for our true nature and how we were imprisoned in this noxious nether zone.

Since knowledge brings about a union between knower and object known, once we know this "truth" we are magically and automatically delivered from this condition, transported to our proper position, and our rightful inheritance, now revealed in its pristine and untarnished glory, is restored. Pre-Romantic art also aims at an illumination of the subject, but an illumination leading to subsequent adjustment, conversion, or transformation as a response to an external reality now more clearly perceived. In Romantic art the only increased illumination is of the subject, since, as really unconditioned, the subject is ultimately the only thing that exists. That truth is part of the final, undistorted vision or Logos. This is a reversal of the movement from pre-Romantic art: it is now the outside world ("appearances") which changes; the subject remains the same. The mountain is now induced to move toward Mohammed.

A third change is that art now separates from both morality and metaphysics. This had taken place formally with Kant's "critical" philosophy, which appeared in the transition between the Enlightenment and Romantic periods. In it art proclaimed its independence and autonomy from all supposedly "higher" ends. From now on art, becomes an end in itself. Indeed, by default art now provides the only end for society—since science has banished final causality, and ethics similarly is "deontological," acting on an (otherworldly) duty, and not for any this worldly end, which would tarnish its purity. Indeed, it would not be a distortion to say (since Kant supposedly "destroyed" metaphysics) that art *becomes* metaphysics, as it describes most adequately the central movement within reality from inner to outer. Art further "swallows" or absorbs morality, since there is now no higher command or deeper obligation than to ally oneself with, or at least no longer to impede, this cosmic passage. This becomes the modern theology, the replacement to the traditional Judeo-Christian account of salvation history, since there is now no other way to achieve fulfillment or value in one's life.

There are important changes here. The Romantic view of art is more pessimistic about "saving" the world than is traditional Christianity, since "appearances," by definition, are obscuring the glory and true identity of the subject, and must then be dismissed or left definitively behind if this initial/final glory is to be revealed.

An unexpected and disappointing irony is that Romanticism is defenseless against pornography as a more successful escape, release, and revelation of the superior but hidden reality. Pornography becomes a legitimate alternative as a fulfillment of the subject because the everyday external world is no longer something to be dealt with or adapted to, but rather transcended, left behind, or replaced by a qualitatively different and supposedly "higher" experience. This is not to say that Romantic art deliberately prefers illusion over reality, but only that from our point of view, sunk in error, the supposed revelation of a "higher" reality will be indistinguishable from illusion, since we have no criteria in the external world by which to test or evaluate it. Instead, we are forced to fall back upon the power or intensity certain experiences generate within us or with which they are received, as the sole criteria by which we may rank one "revelation" as superior to another. On these criteria, pornography cannot be excluded from the competition. Expressed differently, if all supposed reality is dismissed as imperfect or an illusion, then pornography (like drugs) can present itself as a "higher illusion" or superior myth which provides a more powerful satisfaction than the alternatives.

This is a strange culmination to the program of emancipation whereby the individual courageously sought an unprecedented disclosure and his personal fulfillment, opposing the invisible ideal of his untrammeled right against the limitations imposed by society. The mountain heaved, and brought forth a mouse. The Romantic movement begins with a heroic act of Promethean defiance, and ends with the climax of the sublime.

Notes

[1] Jacques Barzun, *Classic, Romantic, and Modern*, Boston: Little, Brown & Co., 1961.
[2] Irving Babbitt, *Rousseau and Romanticism*, NY: Houghton Mifflin Co., 1928.
[3] M.H. Abrams, *The Mirror and the Lamp: Romantic Theory and the Critical Tradition*, NY: Oxford UP, 1971; *Natural Supernaturalism: Tradition and Revolution in Romantic Literature*, NY: W.W. Norton & Co., Inc., 1971.
[4] René Welleck with Austin Warren, *Theory of Literature*, NY: Harcourt Brace, 1949; *The Attack on Literature and Other Essays*, University of North Carolina Press, 1982.
[5] Harold Bloom, *The Anxiety of Influence, a Theory of Poetry*, NY: Oxford UP, 1971; *The Visionary Company, a Reading of English Romantic Poetry*, London: Faber & Faber, 1962; *A Map of Misreading*, NY: Oxford University Press, 1975.
[6] Lionel Trilling, *Sincerity and Authenticity*, Cambridge, MA: Harvard University Press, 1972.

[7] By classical standards, there are few novels which approach the tragic speculative interrogation—one thinks of *Moby Dick*—rather the classical effect the *genre* seems most suited to approximate is that of the epic. Alternatively, the novel may aim at the satisfaction of satire or melodrama in which the virtuous and vicious eventually get their just desserts, as in Dickens. Finally, for shorter novels, the *genre* may aim at the effect of growth or "conversion" discovered by classical comedy. Here again, in contrast to the "romantic" hero who grows only in the sense of rising to a clearer perception of his own "changeless" nature, the less than heroic protagonist is made to see the inappropriateness of his attitude or behavior toward the world in a series of painful, but not too serious, episodes, as in the novels of Jane Austen. The audience is implicitly invited to identify, through their similar occasional desire to rebel against social convention, with the less-than-average protagonist who is basically good but is experiencing an instability, or perhaps is as yet simply untried by social challenge; he is "encratic" or "weak willed," to use the phrase from Aristotle's *Nicomachean Ethics*. He is flirting with becoming a truly evil or vicious personality like the new "friends" he has made, if his actions harden into habits. In the course of the story, however, and before this can happen, he (and the audience through him) are allowed to see the likely consequences of these actions in the fates of the vicious personalities to which he has been exposed. He and we are thereby "scared straight" and reconfirmed upon the path of virtue from which he had been straying. Classic comic drama thus represents the least painful and most entertaining way to attend to the serious business of society's recurring moral correction and education. See my *Aristotle and his Modern Critics, the Use of Tragedy in the Nontragic Vision*, Scranton, PA: University of Scranton Press, 1992, pp. 54–73.

Walter Kaufmann claims that, due to its structure, the novel cannot attain the pure tragic effect, and that all so-called tragic novels are really epics strongly influenced by tragedy. See *Tragedy and Philosophy*, Princeton, NJ: Princeton University Press, 1992, p. 85

CHAPTER 11

The Terrible Fidelity of God to the Jews in Jesus; Fulfillment or Extinction?

In the *Acts of the Apostles*, Chapter Four, when Peter and John cure a crippled man at the Temple and begin preaching the resurrection of Jesus, the Temple authorities are vexed on two accounts: first, they are preaching that Jesus was raised from the dead, and second, they are preaching the doctrine of the resurrection of the body. While the first was certainly more prominent in the minds of Peter and John, the second was probably more central for the Temple authorities; Jesus was of almost incidental importance, and seems to have been considered by many of them a passing revolutionary or troublemaker. We are perhaps *too* familiar with the Christian "good news" that Jesus was raised from the dead and is therefore established as Lord and Messiah; it requires psychological effort on our part to achieve logical distance from this claim and to see what a unique fusion of two distinct and unrelated elements it represents.

Resurrection of the body is a Pharisaic doctrine that developed late in the history of Judaism, after the revolt of the Maccabees under the Selucids, in order to allow God to reward a good person whom death had taken away before this could occur. Of itself, it has nothing to do with messiahship. The Sadducees and Temple priesthood rejected this notion, restricting themselves to those doctrines mentioned in the first five books of the bible. The "messiah" was imagined according to the models of a "prophet like Moses" and a "king like David," and Jesus had obviously and spectacularly failed to live up to such expectations. As the authorities hoped, his movement was in danger of coming to an end. What averted this almost certain fate was the unique coming together of these two elements into a novel synthesis. With the claim of his "resurrection from the dead," Jesus was interpreted not according to the Mosaic or Davidic models, but according to someone like Job (although Job did not have to be raised from the dead), as a good man who had to bear extraordinary hardships which seemed to discredit his cause, but who was eventually vindicated by God.

So we have to ask, what is the exact meaning of the "good news" of the Christians? That the "general resurrection" has begun? That Jesus is the first to be raised of many brothers and sisters? But what difference does it make if the general resurrection starts sooner rather than later? This is not especially good news or grounds for excitement. Or is it that Jesus, as the Lord's anointed, has risen to the right hand of the Father? That is a different matter. The point is, with the Jesus event, "resurrection" was transformed and *altered* to become evidence and a vindication that Jesus *really was* the Lord's anointed. This is a dramatic alteration and expansion of its original function, which was merely to allow God to reward or punish a person after he had died.

In other words, the doctrine of the resurrection of the body came to the rescue when the claim for the messiahship of Jesus according to the conventional understanding had apparently failed. Thus two "outcast" or suspect ideas (from the point of view of priestly orthodoxy), although of independent and unrelated origin, complemented one another to produce a neat, if "Romantic" (in a sense to be explained below) theoretical package that granted plausibility and a new lease on life to a movement whose ideological "cellar" had fallen through and was in danger of extinction. After the debacle of the cross, the doctrine of the resurrection provided a new undergirding to the claim of an ultimate "victory" of Jesus, and also served handily to explain his disappearance (through the extension of the resurrection in the ascension). This is not to say that the resurrection did not occur, but that without this novel combination of these two distinct and unrelated ideas, it would not have been appreciated as it was in fact appreciated, and the Christian movement would almost certainly have come to an end.

Rabbi Leo Baeck has called Christianity a "Romantic" religion, in contrast to the more "classical" Judaism; in this he is thinking of parallels between Christianity and the Romantic movement which virtually created German literature, in contrast and opposition to the French neo-classical and Rationalist school.[1] It must be granted that Christianity can be called "Romantic" both in a popular sense, as putting perhaps excessive emphasis on the passion (which the gospels tend to minimize), but more importantly in a technical sense of proclaiming a "victory" which brings about no real change in the external or public world, that leaves everything exactly as it found them, thus a victory entirely of the inner realm; in this sense, it can appear a surrogate or "pretend" victory, a compensation precisely for a *failure* to bring about a real change or achieve a conventional victory.[2] For

Nietzsche, such a surrogate or "Romantic" victory is a sign of impotence, whose origin is the thwarted "Will to Power," and consequent resentment, hatred, and desire for revenge by a "slave" population which could not achieve mastery over a ruling class. It is to be pitied and dismissed as a sign of weakness, not of strength. The Romantic "victory" consists specifically of a strained or heightened awareness of elements in the situation which both sides recognize to be present, but which the "Romantic" party interprets as conveying more than the other party does, or than common sense normally allows—an element which they read as the "sublime" or an "epiphany" (to use Joycean language) of some deeper reality here coming to the surface and manifestation, and which serves as a substitute for the more usual "victory" one would hope for.

As a "victory," therefore, the resurrection could be called both spectacular and modest at the same time. It was spectacular in that, if Jesus could actually have pulled it off, it would have been the first time this happened (in this fashion) in recorded history. It was "modest" in that, as a victory, it left everything exactly as it was. It involved no political victory or change in the power relations in the Near East. Indeed, it seems the early Christian communities claimed they did not want to upset Roman rule. This victory was perhaps also "Romantic" in the sense that it could not be made without an act of faith. Switching this around, this victory was so modest that it went virtually ignored by the "enemies" it was supposedly prevailing over. It achieved very little, even if it could not be refuted. Perhaps so little note was taken of it precisely because all the main "spoils" apparently fell to the dominant party—the priestly class, scribes, and Sadducees. All this would change in 70 C.E. with the destruction of the Temple, but for the time being, this was the way things were. Since they got what they wanted, let the humiliated party have its little consolation and compensation. A Romantic "victory" is indiscernibly different from, and a synonym for, *defeat*. Let them therefore salvage a shred of their pride; if we demand total humiliation, they may come back twice as strong the next time.

So modest was this victory that it could appear "cheap," in the sense that a Jew who accepted Jesus as the messiah might well feel cheated. For what this claim really demands from us is that we accept that this—and only this—is the extent to which God is going to be faithful to the promises He made to the Jews through Abraham, Moses, David, and the prophets. This is all we can expect. If you have larger, deeper, or just different expectations, you are going to be disappointed.

Jesus did not look anything like the classical portrait of a messiah the Jews expected. No wonder many Jews would have felt underwhelmed. On the other hand, this claim forces us to ponder what is realistically possible with regard to these promises. Just out of enlightened self-interest and to reduce our psychological pain, we do well to gauge our expectations against the political, cultural, and historical possibilities, to trim the one with regard to the other, to save ourselves continued, on-going frustration, and to minimize our psychological wear and tear. Specifically, this means that the Jews are *not* going to be "as numerous as the stars in the sky or the grains of sand on the seashore"— at least not in the old, literal sense. Like an oracular puzzle, this promise may be a riddle that is susceptible to different interpretations. This means there will be no return to an independent monarchy under a "Davidic king"; such is not in the cards. That was a historical fluke, made possible by the temporary weakness of the major powers in Egypt and Babylon, and should not be considered Israel's normal condition. Perhaps it is still possible that "all the nations will be blessed in Israel" and "come streaming toward Jerusalem," but this brings Israel to the next question: What is its deepest desire; what does it really want?

One side question that emerges and may help in answering the larger question is why did so many Jews at that time—even those who had never known Jesus in the flesh—flock to his movement. Because it is clear now that many did, and kept on joining for several hundred years. The attraction seems to have been stronger among the hellenized Jews of the diaspora, the ones who had the least cultural and ideological investment in Jerusalem and the unique localization of cult in the Temple. While easy generalization is irresponsible, groups within the diaspora seem to have found the elaborate dietary and ritual laws otiose, exclusionary, and an impediment to easy commerce with their gentile colleagues; reciprocally, their claim to a privileged covenant with the unique God appeared, in the contemporary Greek philosophical world, too fantastic to be believed, and had the negative effect of making them appear backward, provincial, and uncouth. These hellenized Jews may have been ready to seize any pretext and opportunity to "renegotiate the covenant" in order to broker a more streamlined, cosmopolitan, and world-embracing version of Judaism.[3] The Jesus event would have fit this bill admirably; his claims to an authority equal to that of Moses or David, rather than being offensive, would have stood to his credit and made him more attractive; his disreputable ending was no definitive obstacle, since death at the hands of the Romans was an everyday occurrence in that part of the world. The claim to the resurrection would have "mapped" him onto Job as the vindicated righteous man, the "suffering servant" whom God had upheld, and also spectacularly sealed the new covenant which he forged the night before he died.

Just as we know now that many Jews who were forced to become Christians by the Inquisition preserved their Jewish identity and ritual for centuries secretly, so it is likely that many Jews in the first five centuries C.E. were also "new style" Jews, that is, Jews who believed in Jesus or accepted him as the messiah, both secretly and not so secretly. In those days the relations were reversed; Judaism was the established and powerful religion, and the movement of the Nazarene was the novel upstart. It was the Jews who sent out inquisitors like Saul to identify Jews who accepted Christ and turn them over for punishment. There was more freedom in the diaspora, and after the destruction of the Temple and the disappearance of the Temple priesthood, one could discuss the options more openly.

The prospects for a messiah on the political model were not promising. In a way, Jesus was lucky to die when he did. Over the centuries, the various contenders to be the Jewish messiah along the conventional model who lived longer were ultimately compromised by historic events. The Bar Kochba rebellion against the Romans was put down forcibly in 135 C.E., and the later movements of David Rubeni, Solomon Molcho, Lurya Levi, and Sabbatai Zevi ended badly. Any other form of "messiah" save that of Jesus could appear unrealistic. Perhaps only such a "sublimated" form of messiahship was susceptible of satisfaction. The other interpretations gradually began to appear as non-starters. To continue to wait for such a resolution was to set oneself up for perpetual frustration; the other kind of messiah was not going to arrive.

We are confronted here with the problem of the deepest desire within Israel: to be the chosen people of God, a nation set apart, or to be the means by which God comes to the nations. This is a problem because, as every spiritual master instructs us, one must be careful what one prays for, because one might just get it! There was a subdominant universalistic chord within "classical Judaism"; one famous example is that of Job sent to preach repentance to the Ninevites—a non-Jewish people—and being upset when they actually repent, and God does not punish them! In its classical expectation of a messiah who would be a "prophet like Moses" and a "king like David," Israel was cast into a state of perduring and inextricable frustration. What would such a "messiah" *look like* in our own day? What would he accomplish? What is there to go back to—or forward to? And yet as painful and untenable as this position is, it is not easy to move forward to an alternative, less conflicted position. For one thing, there is fear of the charge of disloyalty or betrayal—since the central obligation for every Jew is that of remaining faithful to the Mosaic covenant. But when this covenant has been co-opted by the Davidic strain, and that option is now bankrupt, it may not be irrational or disloyal to react as many hellenized Jews of the first five centuries C.E. did.

Another difficulty is that an old identity, grown no matter how painful, at least offers the assurance and security of familiarity. We can grow to love our chains. Such an identity can appear preferable to a distantly discerned new identity which is not familiar, which may appear indiscernibly different from the betrayal mentioned above, and, more pertinently, may involve giving up the secret gratifications, psychological compensations, "secondary gains," and perquisites which accompanied and partially reconciled us to our painful situation. Chief among these is the sense of specialness and superiority which paradoxically could be *strengthened* by one's sufferings. One says, "They wouldn't be doing this to me if I weren't different—and better. It is all based on envy." This naturally arouses a sense of spite and desire, even a preference, to *remain* apart and isolated, just to show them, and to show them that they can't have it. First of all, by this one ratifies and confirms one's specialness; further, as said, there are elements of revenge: "However much they hate me, they can't have what I have. I will dig in even deeper. I will go to my grave, if need be, rather than capitulate. I don't want to give them the satisfaction." Such can become the motivation for sticking to one's position, whatever one's views about God; such can be a complicated but common way of extracting psychological pleasure and gratification in the midst of pain, both physical and psychological.

Change here requires courage, the courage honestly to assess one's current situation and, if need be, to pull out and relay the deepest plank of one's soul and psychological identity—the plank that is the basis of one's pain but also, paradoxically and insidiously, that has become a basis of one's pleasure. In such a situation we must become our own physicians and our most severe critics. Paradoxically, that all nations might come "streaming toward Jerusalem" was what the Jews longed for. So what would they do if this actually happened? For in a way, this characterized the Jews who accepted Jesus; they gradually, as St. Paul did, tore down the lines between Jew and gentile. How would this affect their status as a "nation set apart?"

Stepping forward means giving up the consolations and anodynes which have sustained me, but also somewhat imprisoned me, within my painful situation and identity. It means the willingness to turn against what had previously appeared my best—perhaps my only—friends, both literally and figuratively. It means summoning the courage to forge a new identity, based on a novel, less passive, but perhaps more appropriate integration of the data. It is frightening; no wonder we remain crouched on the ledge, uncomfortable in our untenable situation, shifting our weight nervously from foot to foot, afraid to spring. Do we cling to our old identity, or do we accept our role in God's plan, whatever that plan may turn out to be? Are we clinging to our old identity for God's sake, or for our own sake? Perhaps the deepest question is, are we willing to put ourselves in the hands of a providential God the way Abraham did when he raised the knife against his own son and heir to the promise?

Notes

[1] See *Jewish Perspectives on Christianity*, F.A. Rothschild (ed.), Continuum Press, NY, 1996, p. 56.

[2] See Harold Bloom, *Poetry and Repression: Revisionism from Blake to Stevens*, Yale University Press, New Haven, CT, 1976, pp. vii, 10, 20.

[3] See Rodney Stark, *The Rise of Christianity: a Sociologist Reconsiders History*, Princeton University Press, Princeton, NJ, 1996, pp. 57–68.

.

CHAPTER 12

"Jesus Was Nothing But a Man": The Continuing Relevance of Nietzsche for Our Times

"In times when we are low, we ask ourselves
how could Jesus have been anything but a man?
Isn't it all a bit too fantastic?
Do we need that second-story superstructure anyway?
Aren't we just kidding ourselves?
He was like you or I, just shoved into different circumstances.
Poor fellow. But that's all there is to be said about it.
The rest is self-indulgence or wishful thinking.
Let's dismantle what we can no longer accept.
The human race has come into its adulthood;
with the Enlightenment, we have left all that behind.
We are here to fashion our future by ourselves.
Let's stop kidding ourselves—it makes the pain of our ultimate
letdown and frustration just that much more intense.

I f we are now able to face and consider this possibility, it is because this is the ridge along which the battle for the correct interpretation of Christianity in our day must be hammered out. Further, it is Nietzsche who has moved away the obstacles to allow us to consider this possibility clearly. The continuing relevance of Nietzsche is the reason why we may be said to live at the end of time or in the last days—because there are no other options. We have canvassed every possibility. Nietzsche had the sense that the culture of the West was approaching a secular *eschaton*, and perhaps an apocalypse. We shall live at a higher level of existence—or we may well exterminate ourselves. As Nietzsche wrote near the end of his life:

> For a long time now our whole civilization has been driving, with a tortured intensity growing from decade to decade, as if toward a catastrophe; restlessly, violently, tempestuously, like a mighty river

desiring the end of its journey, without pausing to reflect, indeed fearful of reflection . . . Where we live soon nobody will be able to exist.[1]

We have toned down or avoided the coarser, cruder, or simply more bizarre forms of psychological reduction which both Nietzsche and Freud produced, and which Nietzsche later repudiated as disclosing more about the "psychologist's" inability to live with greatness than about their purported subject. We are skeptical about a literal reading of the Oedipus complex, although we subscribe to a son's rebellion and testing of his father's settlement, his expectation that the father should have provided a finally adequate account of the world, or be judged to that extent inadequate. Still, it is also true that any kind of father is better than no father at all. If we are contradictory or inconsistent in our expectations, this is part of the "history of desire," or better, the "dialectic of desire" which structures all life, aiming not so much at perfection as at satisfaction. There is an oriental saying which goes, "A home without a father is like a house without a roof." We expect our father to provide the "roof" of our house psychologically and ideologically as well as physically; he is to provide the "dome," the "sacred canopy," the privileged area of intellectual as well as physical security. By accepting this, we should be able to grow and prosper. Or turning it around, we accept Bruce Lee when he said, "A father who does not overcome his personal demons leaves them for his children to face." Thus we have learned from Nietzsche and Freud, even if we do not follow them literally. This is the way that we acknowledge we face our fathers, and the way we expect Jesus faced His own Father.

This is the most natural of heresies, for Jesus was certainly a man. The burden of proof would have to be that he was anything else but. All the modern "lives of Christ," whether they be devout or debunking, approach Christ from his human side—from Ernest Renan to David Strauss to Albert Schweitzer to Nikos Katzantzakis to Shusaku Endo. Christ was certainly a man; therefore he was nothing but a man. This is the most natural and the most common of heresies, one which we almost have to pass through, sooner or later. It is the first and the last of heresies—the first one that occurs to us, and the last one we have to take seriously.

Jesus was nothing but a man; the whole thing was a pipedream, both for him and for us. It is a bit fantastic after all. What was it, then, about our situation that made us jump on board? It is as though in a drunken stupor or fit of enthusiasm we had emptied our bank account to invest everything in a hopeless prospect on the stock market, or cleaned out our savings to buy a lottery ticket. Was it our youth or naiveté? Our desire for a mentor or to please some authority figure? Was it something we were intimidated into believing ("Make them concentrate on the insignificant details, and they'll never ask you the tough questions")? Was it something we wanted or *needed* to believe—a version of a "secret companion" to our childhood who would stay by us when things went bad or all our other friends had deserted us? Was it my one, last safeguard against hopelessness and despair? What psychological job was it carrying out for us? All these processes are possible singly or jointly. In such a way a modern man queries himself.

We want it to be true—too much so; therefore it can't be true. It's the opposite of the traditional argument based on the attractiveness of this hypothesis; here it is turned on its head. It is too good. It is like Christmas—the jolly fat old man. We were disappointed then too. We won't let that disappointment happen again merely out of the need for self-protection against the psychological pain, the wear and tear. We hate the letdown, the embarrassment, the humiliation that follows the buildup and high expectations. We have been burned too often. We won't let it happen again.

Nietzsche forces us to probe the unconscious and perhaps unflattering motivations that may lie behind our most apparently noble, self-sacrificing, and pious actions. In *The Cheerful Science* he writes:

> Excelsior! You will never pray again, never adore again, never again rest in endless trust; you deny your self any stopping before ultimate wisdom, ultimate goodness, ultimate power, while unharnessing your thoughts; you have no perpetual guardian and friend for your seven solitudes; you live without a view of mountains with snow on their peaks and fire in their hearts; there is no avenger for you, no eventual improver; here is no reason anymore in what happens, no love in what will happen to you, no resting place is any longer to seek; you resist any ultimate peace, you want the eternal recurrence of war and peace. Man of renunciation, do you want to renounce all this? Who will give you the necessary strength? Nobody yet has this strength. There is a lake which one day refused to flow off and erected a dam where it had hitherto flowed off; ever since, this lake has been rising higher and higher. Perhaps that very renunciation will also send us the strength to bear the renunciation itself; perhaps man will rise ever higher when he once ceases to *flow out* into a god.[2]

And in *The Will to Power* is found this paragraph:

Type of my disciples. To those human beings in whom I have a stake I wish suffering, being forsaken, sickness, mal-treatment, humiliation —I wish that that profound self contempt, the torture of mistrust of oneself, and the misery of him who is overcome, not remain unknown to them; I have no pity for them because I wish them the only thing which can prove today whether one had worth or not—that one holds out.[3]

We have come to distrust ourselves too much—the power of our unconscious wishes to control and shape our view of reality. Therefore, if it feels good, it must be wrong. We have deceived ourselves too often, out of wishful thinking. When something good happens, or we get good news, we are always waiting "for the other shoe to fall." The cynical side of ourselves overcomes or ends up steering the hopeful side. We conclude by becoming a prisoner between our two selves. Our "ego" negotiates between our fantasy "libido" and our censor "superego" in the interest simply of survival, and we stay on the fence. We have been disappointed, and have disappointed ourselves, too often . . . We try to measure how much of an interest in this question comes from this irrational source. We try to identify and locate these forces within ourselves, and curb them. And then we wonder how much remains of Jesus.

We seek for some solid point on which to base our faith, as St. Paul seemed to give to the Corinthians when he said, "If Christ is not risen, your faith is in vain" (1 Cor 15:17). The resurrection then? Is that the one certain truth—the fixed Archimedean point from which I can move the entire world and fend off all attack? But when St. Paul got to Athens and began preaching to the philosophers at the Areopagus, they were attentive as long as he referred to their "unknown God—in whom we live and move and have our being." When he began speaking about Christ's dying and rising from the dead, however, they excused themselves politely and asked him to come back another day. In other words, they could not accept this thesis. They had too many stories like this of their own—basically nature cults for the fertility of the fields. This is too anthropomorphic, and the gods are properly preoccupied with themselves. It is too obviously based on wishful thinking; love must be proportional to its object, and we are too far below the gods' level for them to take notice of us. As Aristotle says, God and man cannot be friends.[4] If there is an answer, it must go deeper. But perhaps we have made some progress here; perhaps the real question at issue is the nature of God.

If we consider this question superficially, we see that it is really a thesis about our own woundedness—and about the consequent almost irresistible attractiveness of having Jesus be our messiah, our "Christ," the anointed one—and thus more than a man, whatever that might mean.

It is also an attack upon the logical proofs for God's existence, and the indications that God must be more than a substance, he must be a person.

But if we persist with it long enough, we see that ultimately it is a question about God's nature, and specifically his fidelity.

That is, both the resurrection and the belief that the "fullness of divinity" was pleased to dwell in Jesus are primarily theses about God Himself, and not about some second or "alien" nature that Jesus might have had, as if he were a human possessed by some other spirit. Has God been (or Is God now) faithful? This is simultaneously a highly personal and also a universal question, tied up with our own level of maturity, but also with a recognition of the possibilities Jesus has opened up for behavior in the world. At this point it is impossible to avoid theological language, for an adequate answer has to have some connection with how Jesus redefined the "kingdom" he came preaching.

One who thinks that Christianity means nothing or makes no difference has only to ask the indigenous people of New Guinea who have converted during the twentieth century. Up until very recently, their clans were engaged in perpetual feuding and murderous strife. Now the adults tell the young people in their culture how it used to be. The change is no laughing matter for them, nor is it something abstract and unreal. On the contrary, it is highly concrete. We in the West seem to be too far removed from such things to remember how it used to be for us. But it is not that long ago, nor is it fully over yet.

Of course, there is another option besides the theist, or to the thesis of God's fidelity. Nietzsche himself instantiates, in fact deliberately and dramatically acts out this option as a pioneer—either to prepare a way for us, or to send us back from a debacle and disaster for the human spirit. The rationale behind this non-theist alternative is given literary expression by Albert Camus in *The Myth of Sisyphus*:

> No one will live this fate, knowing it to be absurd, unless he does everything possible to keep before him that absurd brought to light by consciousness. . . . The lucidity that was to constitute his torture at the

same time crowns his victory. There is no fate that cannot be surmounted by scorn.[5]

The point is the traditional one that man's dignity consists in his knowledge, but now raised to an absolute value and supreme achievement in an otherwise valueless universe by the Enlightenment's distinctive will to furious non-deception. Since Descartes defined man as essentially a *res cogitans*, any advance to a clearer or more distinct idea automatically lifts the self up to its higher level, brings about a change that otherwise would never have taken place, and re-creates or reconstitutes the mind as a new and higher being. Critical activity thus becomes our principal means to demonstrate the freedom and dignity which critical (doubt as reduction) activity simultaneously wants to strike from our hands. The contradiction internal to this position builds to an intolerable level, where only going to the "end" of critical activity —if such exists—offers a way out, since if we stop anywhere short of this maximal point, the freedom, dignity, and value we thought we had demonstrated may prove to be vulnerable, unreal, and illusory. Hence the passion and indeed desperation behind Nietzsche's otherwise bizarre program.

God cannot be faithful, *nothing* can be faithful, in a "maximally rigorous" Enlightenment position. Or as Camus expresses it, it is better to know our fate, no matter how tragic or pathetic, than to suffer it like an uncomprehending brute. In knowledge consists our particular dignity, even a modest victory over whatever forces may attempt to deny or crush it. To reverse the Christopher Fathers' message, in this situation it is better to curse the darkness than to suffer it like an uncomprehending animal. Better to shake our fist at an unfair, malicious, or simply indifferent universe, if there is nothing else we can do. Better an appropriate response than no response at all. "Lucidity" becomes our only victory, but still a victory, where the comparative comforts of a less clear but also less dignified level of awareness are always available. Thus we must toughen ourselves for the rigors of this higher ethic, an ethic of knowledge, of the "most painful knowledge." Better to go out like an eagle than a goat; better to go out "with head bloodied, but unbowed."

The compensatory consolation Nietzsche offers us is to step into non-illusion, as a smaller, more isolated figure against a colder and more hostile landscape, perhaps, but still no longer deceived; to feel the chill, bracing wind of this elitist height and determined non-deception through a preemptive strike upon our deepest assumptions and most cherished hopes, with the possible added solace of believing that we are leading the way, in fact leading history, for where else is there for the human race to go, if and when anyone else should decide to go "forward?"

What Nietzsche offers us is the satisfaction of no longer accepting an illusion. This "lucidity" or painful knowledge, and the pride which naturally and appropriately accompanies it, are intended to sustain us, to be our substitute for the consolation we are presently getting by accepting our status as creatures—and the ultimate faith in the fidelity of God this dependency requires and calls us to. Well, we may admit that, if this is the only consolation available, then indeed we have to accustom ourselves to make it do. But given the self-contradiction in this position (i.e., demonstrating our freedom and dignity by being willing to deny both), is even this consolation available? More deeply, this is a posture whose foundations are fear of deception and desire to save our pride, rather than a primary concern for the truth.

Is there an element of weakness, of dependence, on occasion of powerlessness in asking the question about God's fidelity? Of course there is. But this doesn't mean the question is based on fear or some other irrational motive, but rather just the opposite, upon a finally clear-eyed and mature recognition of a real factor or condition of our existence, to attempt to deny which amounts to romantic self-divinization. We would have to be God Himself for this not to be the case. This is part of the question at issue—our status as creatures—not in the Christian sense of being formed by a loving God, but in the more primitive sense of not being a god ourselves, of not being the cause, justification, or explanation of ourselves.

The old man playing the Wizard of Oz and telling Dorothy not to peek behind the curtain in 1939 spilled into the popular mind what had until then been an academic virus or distemper. Since then we have been trying to "reenchant" our world, or put Humpty-Dumpty back together again—none too successfully. Rather it has gone the other way—the popular mind has become infected with the reductive cynicism, the determination to think the worst about a situation so as not to be caught off guard, a disease which up to then had been a kind of armchair, contrary to fact speculation by leisured professors. Perhaps it was inevitable that the West had to go through this period of curiosity and doubt as part of its fumbling, hesitant approach to maturity. The natural desire during adolescence to put at arm's length the convictions with which one has been raised and to look seriously at alternatives, if only to return to them more strongly—and no longer uncritically—later, was exaggerated by the modern Cartesian experiment into a permanent stance, into a deliberate elevation and exaggeration of doubt into an exclusively valid method. Diagnosing our condition and writing on the conditions of belief for a modern Western man, Paul Ricoeur puts it famously:

> We are in every way children of criticism, and we seek to go beyond criticism by means of criticism, by a criticism that is no longer reductive but restorative. . . . Does that mean that we could go back to a primitive naiveté. Not at all. In every way, something has been lost, irremediably lost: immediacy of belief. But if we can no longer live the great symbolisms of the sacred in accordance with the original belief in them, we can, we modern men, aim at a second naiveté in and through criticism. . . . This second naiveté aims to be the post-critical equivalent of the precritical hierophany.

Calling for a "conjunction of belief and criticism," and joining with a chorus of voices calling for a "reenchantment of our world" after the bankruptcy and self-evisceration of the Western Enlightenment, Ricoeur continues:

> Thus the second naiveté would be a second Copernican revolution: the being which posits itself in the *Cogito* has still to discover that the very act by which it abstracts itself from the whole does not cease to share in the being that challenges it in every symbol. All the symbols of guilt—chaos, blending, mixture, fall—speak of the situation of the being of man in the being of the world. The task, then, is, starting from the symbols, to elaborate existential concepts—that is to say, not only structures of reflection but structures of existence, insofar as existence is the being of man.[6]

In other words, after we have "hit bottom" from this exaggerated Cartesian experiment, we make several discoveries. The first has occurred in philosophy proper, where "anti-foundationalism" is the order of the day on all fronts—that is, a deliberate abandonment of the Cartesian experiment to find some indubitable or unshakeable foundation for knowledge, be this empiricist, rationalist, or transcendental. Our knowledge neither is capable of nor needs such a foundation. Demands for such a foundation were exorbitant and unrealistic in the first place. Philosophy has to tone itself down and adjust to what humans in fact do, rather than summon us to fulfill the lofty demands of a world we do not in fact inhabit.

Second, on the religious theme, we discern that the issue of God's presence or fidelity does make a difference. At a basic level, we recognize that we may carry on our joint program with the Enlightenment (toward justice, against corruption, etc.) *with* a theist motivation and sustenance as well as without one—in fact, it becomes questionable whether we can carry it on for long *without* a theist support because under the Enlightenment dispensation (in which we still for the most part live), which equates intelligence with doubt, any other grounds for hope or goal for effort seems to evaporate before our eyes. In other words, the critical project of the Enlightenment itself often pushes us toward this type of pessimism.

Ultimately, it comes down to the question of whether man can walk forward for long without a sense of the presence of God—and not for utilitarian purposes only, those of mastering and shepherding our universe as a steward, but as our deepest satisfaction and for its own sake, without which our life is not honest, truthful, or properly founded. That there is some ultimate cause of the universe, and that mankind is not it, should by now be painfully clear. The question arises whether we should make contact with it. Since with our technology-based leisure we have nothing else to do, why shouldn't we?

That is, beyond its utility as an "energy packet" for a project that is in many ways coincident with the Enlightenment program, there is a deeper reason behind recognition and praise of God for the fulfillment of our nature, that is, as an end in itself. For as creatures, our deepest fulfillment and ultimate project consist of turning from the delights of creation to its source, as a flower turns to bask in the light of the sun. In a scriptural setting (the psalms), it is our highest privilege and deepest satisfaction to be admitted within the heavenly court and to attend with the rest of creation upon the throne of the great Singularity, to lay down our gift and to lend our voices to the chorus which is perpetually chanting "Holy, Holy, Holy." There is a paradox or irony here, for technically we are giving praise to *God*, and yet it is *we* who are nurtured, it is we who grow, swell, and in general are perfected, for we are thereby performing the most powerful activity of which a creature is capable, directing our highest faculties toward their highest object.

According to Aristotle, the greatest pleasure accompanies the act of our highest faculty upon its most exalted object, so perhaps it is no surprise that the mystics tell us that in their prayer they often have no sense of effort or even of time passing, but are buoyed up by the rapture of coming within proximity of the heavenly court—and that we are all called to our share in contemplative prayer. If we do not engage in it, we are only cheating ourselves. Apart from sustaining us in any worthwhile utilitarian activity, its deeper reason is that it cultivates a sense of ourselves as creatures and of the fidelity of the god upon whom we depend.

The poet Stefan George wrote the best epitaph, and the most appropriate response to the desperate, urgent experiment that is Nietzsche's philosophy, in his poem *Nietzsche* (1900):

Du hast das nächste in dir selbst getötet
Um neu begehrend dann ihm nachzuzittern
Und aufzuschrein im schmerz der einsamkeit.
Der kam zu spät der flehend zu dir sagte;
Dort is kein weg mehr uper eisige felsen
Und horste grauser vögel—nun ist not:
Sich bannen in den kreis der liebe schliesst.

Thou hast destroyed what in thyself was closest
To tremble after it with new desire
And to cry out in pain of solitude.
He came too late who said to thee imploring:
There is no way left over icy cliffs
And eyries of dread birds—now this is needed:
Constraint within a circle closed by love. (tr. Kaufmann)[7]

Notes

[1] F. Nietzsche, *The Will to Power*, tr. W. Kaufmann, Random House, NY, 1967, Preface #2 and Bk. 1, 54.

[2] F. Nietzsche, *The Cheerful Science*, #285. Tr. W. Kaufmann in *The Portable Nietzsche*, Viking, NY, 1954, p. 98.

[3] F. Nietzsche, *The Will to Power*, #910; Random House, NY, 1967, p. 481.

[4] Aristotle, *Nicomachean Ethics*, 1158b35.

[5] A. Camus, *The Myth of Sisyphus*, Knopf, NY, 1958, p. 121.

[6] Paul Ricoeur, *The Symbolism of Evil* (tr. Buchanan), Beacon, Boston, 1969, pp. 350–357.

[7] Quoted in W. Kaufmann, *Nietzsche: Philosopher, Psychologist, Antichrist*, Princeton University Press, Princeton, NJ, 1974, p. 11.

CHAPTER 13

Lonergan and the Completion
of American Philosophy

At the start of the twentieth century, American philosophy, like the country itself, was an adolescent flexing its newly developed muscles. Such philosophy was still largely derivative from Europe, although there was a growing impatience with the dualisms and false oppositions which had beset European philosophy since Descartes. At the end of the First World War and after the building of the Panama Canal, the young country was surprised to find itself already a world power. Enjoyment of this new status alternated with bouts of isolationism and doubt that its wisdom might not equal its enthusiasm.

Henry James wrote novels depicting newly rich but naive Americans going to Europe, where they encountered for the first time a world of sophistication but also of jaded and cynical decadence. American pragmatism carried forward the national virtues of meliorism, "boosterism," and optimism, as well as an emphasis on concrete detail and efficiency. Thomas Edison and Henry Ford would soon show the world the results to be obtained from the team approach to problem solving and the assembly line. American pragmatism combined the naturalism, empiricism, and scientism typical of English philosophy with an interest in method and an exegesis of insight in problem solving that was distinctive and penetrating. The intentional aspect of cognitional activity, however, remained a contentious or vexed topic in American philosophy throughout the twentieth century. Initially it came under attack as introducing "psychologism" or endangering the objectivity of science, and the formalists attempted to expel it. In the postmodern backlash and attack on the modern search for "foundations" in all its forms, however, it has returned as an essential accomplice of language learning, especially of the "abnormal discourse" essential to scientific progress. The unfortunate influence of behaviorism, however, has kept intentional activity from being studied directly; a method-ological prudishness has restricted attention first to behavior, then specifically to linguistic indications of insight, thus confining study to the "tracks the animal left" rather than opening up access to the animal itself. This unwarranted self-limitation has led to an incapacity to elaborate a satisfying science of the subject that is not reductionistic or foundationalistic in one of the dated senses, and thence to the befuddlement or lack of clear self-definition that currently besets American philosophy. Caught between competing allegiances, its best chance for survival and intellectual self-justification consists of carrying forward its traditional and legitimate pragmatic program, while freeing itself from this self-imposed methodological restriction. Only a removal of this impediment will allow American philosophy to complete its program to elaborate a satisfying science of the subject, which is the only "foundation" for philosophy possible today—and, as it turns out, the only one philosophy needs.

Dewey's First Sketch of a Science of the Self

The dominant influences on American philosophy were ontological and methodological naturalism, empiricism, and scientism (respect for the results of science as "objective truth," and expanding the scientific method to embrace all knowledge). Dewey esteemed Hegel for stressing the importance of history, but he naturalized Hegel's dialectical development of Absolute Spirit into the progressive adaptation and control by individuals over their environment, in accordance with Darwinian categories, to increase satisfaction. These allegiances were only loosely compatible. Specifically, empiricism had led, in Hume, to skeptical conclusions concerning the foundation for scientific generalization, thus endangering science's claim to embody objective truth. Similarly naturalism, using a vocabulary of nerve impulses and response to stimuli, provided scant resources to ground the claim to universal validity normally associated with scientific theories. Dewey skillfully parried these thrusts by stressing, not science as a result, but science as a method. That is, he stressed the hypothetical nature of scientific theories, their probing, falsifiable, instrumental, and approximative character. His interest fell principally on the method itself, and his major contribution to philosophy was a first articulation of the diverse elements and stages within human cognitional activity. If he removed the supports for esteeming science as "objective truth" in a timeless classical sense, he took advantage of this loss or concession to emphasize by compensation the element of originality and novelty crucial to the ongoing practice of science; implicitly he thrust intentionality forward as the critical engine and traditionally assumed or over-looked the source of cognitional progress.

It was Hume who first proposed that we locate the foundations of human knowledge, not in "clear and distinct ideas" or logic, but in a science of human nature. Dewey's discovery of "patterns of inquiry" in his "experimental logic" is a major American contribution to such a science. Dewey subscribed to a program of methodological and ontological naturalism in which the "scientific method" would be expanded and applied to all areas of inquiry. Going beyond the descriptions of Bacon and Mill, Dewey situated rational or scientific activity within the context of a problematic situation arising for a sentient organism. The purpose of inquiry is to resolve this troubling situation by actively transforming it in accord with an experimental idea. Such an idea allows the subject to "re-see" or reinterpret the situation in terms of realities or relationships not previously discerned, which open up strategies for action that will alter the situation and remove its troubling aspect. The resulting scientific theories do not frame timeless verities, but rather are projected solutions to historical problems, without the universality and invariance traditionally attributed to the former.

Anti-Psychologism

In the first half of the twentieth century, American philosophy was subject to a number of influences seeking a firm foundation for the objectivity of knowledge, principally science. In Europe, a new wave of irrationalism stemming from the philosophies of Schopenhauer and Nietzsche, together with the *Zeitgeist* of the late Romantic movement which moved toward pessimism, aestheticism, and decadence, roused a number of thinkers to return to traditional theories of epistemology and to reinvigorate them. Science itself was not immune to these destabilizing forces; Einstein's General Theory of Relativity overturned the assumptions of classical mechanics which had seemed invulnerable to change, and the paradoxes of transfinite mathematics opened the possibility that simple arithmetic might harbor contradictions. Firmer foundations were wanted, and these were sought either in logic, in supposedly invariant transcendental structures of the mind, or in the bedrock of empirical sensation. In England, Russell and Whitehead attempted to reduce arithmetic to logic, neo-Kantianism flourished at Marburg and elsewhere in Germany, and at Vienna neo-positivism commanded allegiance. All of these programs would have an influence on American philosophy, as occasionally a philosopher from one or the other of these movements came to teach in America and influenced a new generation of students.

What unified philosophers from diverse orientations, such as Frege, Husserl, Brentano, Carnap, and the Wittgenstein of the *Tractatus*, was an opposition to *psychologism*, or a naturalistic study of human cognitional activity that failed to attend to or justify the scientific claim to objectivity. For them such a psychology was only half a psychology; it failed to examine what was significant about human psychology, its claim to truth. In short, *psychologism* was a psychology which had given up any ambition or pretense of being an *epistemology*. As a naturalistic science, it could take its place as a subordinate discipline within the newly developing behavioral investigations, as a branch of nervous activity. In a time of crisis in the foundations of knowledge, however, when new and stronger normative standards separating truth from error were looked for, it was unacceptable as a final word on the psychology of human knowing. For this a philosophy of foundations was needed, and this gave rise to a succession of programs in American philosophy during the mid-twentieth century.

Foundationalism

In a sense, foundationalism is nothing new in modern philosophy. A series of foundationalistic programs have defined Western philosophy since Descartes' attempt to defeat hyperskeptical doubt in the second *Meditation* by uncovering an unshakeable foundation for traditional knowledge. Descartes' proposal of the self as a "clear and distinct" idea which would serve as such a foundation attracted few followers, but his *project* and practical redefinition of philosophy as the search for an indubitable foundation for knowledge (in contrast to the classical standard of invariant causes) was accepted by philosophers of other persuasions, and has made foundationalism synonymous with philosophy in the modern period.

Descartes pursued a rational reconstruction of knowledge based on the traits which characterized the experience with which he vanquished the arch skeptic, the experience of himself which he found to be "clear and distinct." Hume professed to be unable to discover himself anywhere in his experience; and anyway clarity and distinctness were primarily psychological traits which could accompany in principle *any* idea which we find resolves a puzzle for us; they are thus not infallible indicators of truth. The empiricists thence pursued a reconstruction of knowledge based on sense experience. Roused from his dogmatic slumbers by Hume's skeptical results, Kant reasoned backward to uncover what he claimed were universal and necessary structures of the mind; since these "transcendental" categories may validly be applied only to an object of possible experience, they may also serve as normative criteria by which to separate knowledge from illusion. Each of these programs identified a privileged level of experience, whether rational ideas, sense experience, or transcendental *a priori* concepts; by attempting to trace candidates for knowledge back to these strata, one could separate truth from error. In the alarmist "conspiracy theory" atmosphere created by Descartes' deliberately provoked and methodically cultivated contest with the supreme skeptic, the traditional corpus of knowledge must either be rejected or reconstructed on one or other of the "foundations" proposed by these three principal programs of the modern period. All moderns are foundationalists; they differ only in their candidate for a sure foundation for knowledge.

This program was extended and intensified during the twentieth century backlash against psychologism. Frege joined Russell and Whitehead in attempting to trace arithmetic back to formal logic. Husserl through the *epoché* of his phenomenological reduction tried to find invariant and necessary structures of the constituting ego. The most novel and impressive example of foundationalism, however, was the attempt by the early Wittgenstein, and later Carnap and the followers of the Vienna Circle, to set up a formal linguistic system that would trace all acceptable propositions back to a set of "atomic sentences" or intuitively validated primitive statements, rational or empirical. The logical rules for such a system would be carefully chosen in advance; once the rules were specified and the axioms set, the system would generate all the propositions which would be considered true. Statements from metaphysics or religion which could not be translated into this formal system would be dismissed, not so much as wrong as merely meaningless. It was hoped that by this method a host of pseudo-problems which had bedeviled philosophy and Western culture generally for hundreds of years could be caused to evaporate.

Common sense and the various natural sciences were to be re-constructed on a base of privileged linguistic units and the rules specifying their proper combination. A critical methodological step takes place here in the modern treatment of intentionality. Concessions to a behaviorist model which effectively screens the subject and its intentional activity behind a repertoire of external activity were made in the interests of scientific accessibility and verification. The contents of the epistemological base are no longer the private "ideas" open to the introspective gaze of a solitary subject. While these are not denied, they are not available for inter-subjective examination by the scientific community; hence they cannot serve as a satisfactory base for a trustworthy elaboration of truth functional discourse. Linguistic units, by contrast, are public and accessible; yet at the same time they are undeniably charged with intentional content. Could they not serve as an acceptable replacement for the private mental contents of traditional modern foundationalism, both rationalist and empiricist, thereby capturing what we mean by "intentionality" and simultaneously conforming to the contemporary naturalist craving for a unitary scientific method that would validate all forms of respectable discourse? If we cannot capture the elusive animal of intentionality for critical examination, could we not study the "tracks" the animal, and only that animal, could leave, and still elaborate a penetrating, complete, and satisfying science of intentionality on that basis?

Anti-Foundationalism

Anti-foundationalistic stirrings can be found in Wilfred Sellars' rejection of the "myth of the given" in favor of the epistemic priority of propositional knowledge, and in Quine's rejection of a strict analytic/ synthetic distinction in favor of a holistic approach whereby a web of beliefs is tested collectively rather than sentence by sentence—both ways of rejecting the foundationalism of traditional American and English empiricism. Quine's anti-foundationalism goes back to Dewey's rejection of the quest for certainty in favor of pragmatic criteria for truth. The more radical anti-foundationalism of Richard Rorty, however, must be traced back to the influence of the later Wittgenstein. The Wittgenstein of the *Philosophical Investigations* and the posthumously published *On Certainty* had undergone a profound alteration in his attitude toward language from the Wittgenstein of the *Tractatus*. No longer was language to be reconstructed on the basis of some privileged but supposedly undeceiving foundation. There was no such foundation.

As a general orientation, language needs no correction from any perspective outside of language itself. If certain sentences strike us as puzzling or nonsensical, this does not necessarily mean that they should be culled out or subjected to linguistic extermination. Rather, the fault may lie with us, that we do not yet properly understand the role they play within the "language game" of which they form a part. The practitioners of a language apparently experience no such embarrassment or confusion. To learn a language is not to be confronted in an intuitive, undeniable fashion with the entities which that language is "about," as Augustine thought, but rather to learn the "rules of the game," the role or significance attributed to various kinds of statements—a role which may differ significantly from a statement's apparent or literal interpretation. Rather than attempt to dictate to and make language over some ideal but unrealistic model, we do better to adopt a more humble attitude, to give language the benefit of the doubt as *already having* meaning, and attempt to delineate and comprehend the various mutually irreducible language games which speakers may legitimately engage in. Against the foundationalist assumption of concealment, Wittgenstein insists that nothing of philosophical importance is hidden.[1]

Of course, nonsensical statements are still possible, and inappropriate questions may still be posed, as when radical doubt is brought against basic beliefs; but such psychological episodes can take place only when we forget how language is *used*. Indeed, this fact supplies one of the principal employments and justifications for philosophy in a post-foundational age: the therapeutic task of reminding us of how words are normally or correctly employed, so problems based on such an exaggerated or hyper-inflated sense may not be solved but rather *dis*solved. "The reasonable man does not have certain doubts," writes Wittgenstein.[2] "Giving grounds . . . justifying the evidence, comes to an end—but the end is not certain propositions striking us immediately as true, i.e., it is not a type of *seeing* on our part; it is an *acting*, which lies at the bottom of the language game."[3] "But the end is not an ungrounded presupposition: it is an ungrounded way of acting."[4] In his second phase, Wittgenstein insists on seeing language games as embedded in a common form of life: "I did not get my picture of the world by satisfying myself of its correctness; nor do I have it because I am satisfied of its correctness. No: it is the inherited background against which I distinguish between true and false."[5] In this new appreciation the project of foundationalism which has dominated modern philosophy loses its rationale. As Rorty puts it, "The cases in which doubt plays no role are cases in which we do not let doubt play a role—not cases with respect to which we are in a different psychological state."[6] As Wittgenstein writes: "(D)oubt gradually loses its sense; the language game is just like that"[7] and "My life consists in my being content to accept many things."[8]

Rorty extends Wittgenstein's therapeutic role for philosophy in a wide-ranging attack on any species of foundationalism. Philosophy has no particular subject matter over that of the special sciences. There is no ground for philosophy assuming a superior posture over the other sciences. Each is relatively autonomous, is capable of discerning truth from error within its own domain, and requires no guidance, oversight, or policing by philosophy. Philosophy is reduced to being one voice within the ongoing conversation of mankind and should revise its ambition from that of evaluating the whole to chastening this inveterate temptation to rule and to keeping the cultural conversation lively and zestful.

There is a refreshing release that comes from accepting Rorty's sweeping anti-foundationalism. Common sense and scientific discourse need no longer be "normalized" and regularized, reconstructed on the basis of one or another privileged level of reality, experience, or language. There is no such privileged level that may act as a "foundation" for the others. All the language games that have established themselves on pragmatic grounds are equally valid, and which ones we engage in, and which new forms of discourse are allowed to arise, are questions to be decided on grounds of enjoyment rather than whether the basic terms can be put into contact with a putatively privileged stratum of experience, the "really real." In a democratic, rainbow revision of a previously monochromatic, single-stratum ontology, and as an overthrow of the Cartesian epistemology of concealment, the terms of *all* language games that can establish themselves culturally are respected as indicating something real. The foundation of knowledge is groundless belief. As Wittgenstein writes: "It is so difficult to find the beginning. Or better, it is difficult to begin at the beginning and not to try to go further back."[9] "Going further back" was what foundationalism was all about. On the contrary Rorty can now write: "Let a thousand discourses bloom!"[10]

At the same time, it may be charged that the linguistic behaviorism of the later Wittgenstein and Rorty continues an evasion strategy together with the earlier formalist or foundationalist approach to language which effectively screens and conceals the intentional subject that is the source of language. Indeed, so powerful is the continuing fear of the charge of psychologism, embarrassment, and confusion over Hume's reduction of the self to a congeries of disparate psychic episodes, and dissatisfaction with what Quine calls the spectator view of the self that went together with foundationalism—that is, the post-

Cartesian view of the self as a "ghost in the machine" (Ryle) that receives something immediately or as "given"—that the ambition of contemporary anti-foundationalist linguistic behaviorism, like its earlier formalist and foundationalist counterparts, is to develop an encompassing or satisfying theory of language which makes no mention of private mental states, psychological episodes, or the intentional self at all. Post-foundationalist linguistic behaviorism attempts to "explicate meaning without truth conditions, truth without extralinguistic sources of truth value, and knowledge without intentional relations between persons and objects."[11] Restricting itself methodologically to such a narrow resource base, however, threatens the project with a lack of power or comprehensiveness—that is, it may not be able to reach or justify important regions of linguistic activity.

Rorty himself points out one such area where the function of intentionality cannot be overlooked or eliminated. Following the breakthrough work of Thomas Kuhn in his *Structures of Scientific Revolution*, Rorty distinguishes "normal discourse," where there are shared criteria of agreement and the rules of the language game are familiar and clear, from "abnormal discourse" where a revolutionary proposal or a paradigm shift has occurred. In the latter the discourse is strange, we are unsure how to evaluate it, and agreement on criteria is provisionally lacking. Foundationalist linguistic philosophy concentrated on science as normal discourse, as an achieved fact, with its propositions "founded" and reconstructed on a privileged level of base concepts. This is science normalized and systematized, immune to change, ready to function as a definitive and final map of the world. It is science in its Sunday clothes, ready to sit for a family portrait. Science as it is *practiced*, however, is something different—dynamic, not static, scruffier, messier, with tears in its clothes and yet a gleam in its eye. Science is perpetually unfinished, with significant sectors of data currently without satisfactory theoretical explanation, and punctuated by unpredictable but regular upheavals where its most basic assumptions are called into question and data fall into new and unexpected arrangements along previously undiscerned axes.

To invoke linguistic behaviorism as a sufficient explanation of how language operates is to freeze civilization in the already established language games of normal discourse, to preclude advance to new forms of language where the rules are not yet clearly worked out, and to fail to explain (or to engage in only a "hand waving" type of explanation) the most interesting and characteristic aspect of science, the advance to a new theoretical grasp of the material. An open admission and adequate treatment of intentionality is unavoidable as a revised "foundation" for an adequate science of language, because the only way abnormal discourse can be "normalized" is for significant segments of the population to "catch on" or to "see the point" behind revolutionary proposals in our interpretation or "reading" of complex situations, in science and elsewhere. When such agreement ultimately takes place, the proposals are accepted as an advance and perhaps the work of genius. When such agreement does not take place, the proposals are viewed initially as puzzling and ultimately dismissed as nonsense.

Without insight or intentionality we have no way of explaining how new language games arise which are embraced enthusiastically by large segments of the population, nor the powerful hold they exercise over their devotees after they have overcome sometimes formidable resistance. After having evaded intentionality methodologically for several hundred years, and having tried in vain to locate the "foundation" of knowledge elsewhere, this recent progress in our appreciation of how science really works makes this "oversight of insight" no longer tenable; both a relaxation of our allegiance to behaviorism, or the restriction of scientific discourse to publicly verifiable data, and a "paradigm shift" in our search for a "foundation" of knowledge, become methodological correctives whose avoidance or postponement can no longer be justified. Wittgenstein explained both the difficulty and the need for this step by the "hiddenness of the familiar": "One is unable to notice something because it is always before one's eyes. The real foundations of his enquiry do not strike a man at all . . . we fail to be struck by what, once seen, is most striking and most powerful."[12]

Lonergan

There is one contemporary philosopher who has developed a sophisticated study precisely of the intentionality of the inquiring subject. As has been argued by Michael H. McCarthy in his *The Crisis of Philosophy*,[13] the Canadian philosopher Bernard Lonergan has put forward not only an epistemology which distinguishes satisfactorily the various and irreducible stages of cognitive resolution, he has done so without the methodological constraints which have bedeviled and compromised the work of previous philosophers in the Anglo-American tradition. The result is a more penetrating and comprehensive retrieval than Dewey's of the crucial role of intentionality in the recurrent and distinctive human process of cognitional resolution. Further, this is precisely the kind of contribution of which the dialectic of the Anglo-American tradition in philosophy stands in need to bring it to synthesis and completion.

This is not the place for an exhaustive presentation of Lonergan's theory, but the main distinctions he makes may be rehearsed.

A recurring and self-reinforcing cycle of experience, understanding, and judgment structures the way human beings negotiate their way about the world. Experience is not a passive intuitive exposure to immediate data; it is structured by preconceptual desires and the results of past cognitional activity. A thoughtful inquiry frames the questions by which subjects engage their environment in a dialogue. Insight does not occur in a vacuum; an exploratory question anticipates what kind of intelligibility one might find in a situation. Tension increases as alternative schematic models are explored. Until insight occurs, the answer to an absorbing question eludes the subject. "Insight is a preconceptual event that consciously unifies and organizes the data of experience the subject is investigating. In the act of understanding, the cognitive subject either grasps an *intelligible unity* within the data or grasps a pattern of *intelligible relations* among its various elements."[14] This is not to say that insight is always correct. It requires the third stage of critical testing and judgment before our grasp on previous theories is relaxed and we shift our allegiance, always somewhat tentatively, to the novel interpretation. "Certainty" or the powerful psychological force of the new arrangement of data, as when the different parts of an optical illusion "tumble" into a novel pattern, or a move suggests itself in a chess game, is no guarantee of its ultimate appropriateness. We have to look around the board and explore other consequences of the move, before we declare that it is the best one.

Observations

There are two relevant points to be made when approaching American philosophy from a classical (pre-foundationalist, or classical foundationalist—the foundation must be invariant but not certain) standpoint.

It is important to note that, while respecting science's claim to represent "objective truth," this evaluation represents a step down from what Plato and Aristotle meant in contrasting "knowledge" with "opinion." Indeed on Dewey's appreciation, science would fall more under "opinion" than under "knowledge," since it is inherently revisable and approximative. Even apart from the pragmatic theory, we can say that mathematical science is not knowledge as the Greeks understood it. Knowledge consists of a causal explanation that is unchanging (if not certain, which is a modern requirement). Mathematical science does not conform to this requirement. This may strike us initially as a setback, but it can also be experienced as liberating, for nothing significant that science traditionally has done for us has been lost.

It appears today that there will always be some data which even our best theory of a given domain will not be able to explain. Further, any given theory, no matter how complete, is potentially revisable and replaceable by a theory which calls into question one of its basic assumptions, if the second theory is more accurate or comprehensive in its predictions. Our best move here is perhaps to "bracket" the question, or adopt an agnostic attitude on whether science will ever be completed or able to deliver a full account of the world. There is no point in judging what there is no need to judge. This certainly is science's ambition; however, failing this or if it does not happen, nothing important in the concrete *results* of science will be lost. Everything that science has done for us would still be in place. Such a "full account" may function as a kind of unrealizable ideal or asymptote, which science is always approaching, but which it may never reach. Still, we are constantly getting better accounts, more powerful and comprehensive theories "along the way." Whether or not we reach our ideal makes virtually no difference. Thus in terms of our lived experience, it is immaterial whether we may one day have in our hands a final "map" of the world; our experience until that (perhaps infinitely distant) point will be the same either way. By the principle of the "identity of in-discernibles," the two realities are the same. Perhaps another way of saying the same thing is that any such ultimate "explanation" of the world will be philosophic, and not scientific.

A related but distinct point is that basing everything on the inquiring subject as Lonergan does "saves" everything philosophically that was "saved" by the classical Greek metaphysics that based itself not so much on an anthropology of the inquiring subject as on an unchanging causal account of the objective world. Whatever insights of classical metaphysics were valid before are still valid now. The new theory can reach or "generate" all the truths the old one could; it just begins further back, and is oriented toward a different experience, that of experimental science, which was not distinguished from philosophy by the classical mind and whose structure and working the major philosophers of the twenty-first century are concerned to explore.

Finally, on the topic of the contemporary interest in exploring the interface between philosophy, artificial intelligence, and psychology, the attempt to "explain" consciousness is to be traced back to the fact that, in the Cartesian understanding of man, (bare) consciousness—not knowing—is the unique trait that distinguishes man from a machine. It is, however, the lowest aspect of human intelligence, the mind "idling" or running in neutral gear, so to speak; it is completely atypical, in no way distinctive or revelatory of the mind's characteristic activity, which is knowing an independent object. The current interest in "explaining consciousness," while perhaps relevant for physiological psychology, is the most recent in a long line of false leads or red herrings—or "perennial chestnuts"—for philosophy, most of which are variations on the mind-body problem, by which modern philosophy has shunted or distracted itself from what is truly significant or worth explaining—the mind knowing an independent object—and whose success can be traced to the continual modern refrain: "Let's go back to the beginning, Descartes." The debate is over whether or not one can develop or deduce the "ghost" from the "machine," to use Gilbert Ryle's famous terms, rather than doing epistemology proper. Further, this way of posing the project of philosophy is not being true to Dewey; it is giving a "test pattern" in place of the cognitional traction and muscular engagement with life which for him is characteristic of the human mind.[15]

Conclusion

In this article I have attempted to describe a trajectory, an internal dialectic, within twentieth century Anglo-American philosophy. Beginning with a reaction against psychologism, which threatened the objectivity of science and appeared to require a retrieval and reinstatement of intentionality, philosophy was diverted into linguistics by a methodological behaviorism which pulled up shy of treating anything so private and controversial as the subject. The reaction against foundationalism went in the opposite direction by showing the inadequacy of the foundationalist view of the self as a disembodied mind in immediate contact with a mythological "given" in the so-called "spectator theory of truth," and thereby showed the need for philosophy to develop a more dynamic, sophisticated, and flexible model of the self.

In the later Wittgenstein and Rorty, however, anti-foundationalism was again thwarted by linguistic behaviorism and the consequently impoverished resource base from developing a satisfactory theory of the knowing subject. This self-imposed methodological restriction ham-strung the official project to develop an account able to handle the variety and richness of linguistic activity. An anti-foundationalist theory of the self—not the "ghost in the machine" of Descartes and the moderns, but an inquisitive, probing, and fallibilistic self as suggested in Dewey's picture of the problematic situation in which every cognitional operation originates, and described more adequately by Lonergan's discrimination of the three phases of inquiry as experience, understanding, and judgment—becomes no longer optional, but is now a mandatory development, once philosophy faces the need to do justice to such significant data as revolutionary science and the "abnormal discourse" by which new stages of cultural awareness are reached.

Notes

[1] L. Wittgenstein, *Philosophical Investigations*, tr. G.E.M. Anscombe, Macmillan, NY, 1953, p. 435; hereafter "PI."

[2] L. Wittgenstein, *On Certainty*, tr. D. Paul and G.E.M. Anscombe, Harper and Row, NY, 1972, pp. 4, 24, 56; hereafter "OC."

[3] OC 204.

[4] OC 110.

[5] OC 94.

[6] R. Rorty, "Cartesian Epistemology and Changes in Ontology, in Contemporary American Philosophy," ed. J.E. Smith, Allen and Unwin Ltd., London, 1970, p. 283.

[7] OC 56.

[8] OC 344.

[9] OC 471.

[10] Michael H. McCarthy, *The Crisis of Philosophy*, SUNY Press, 1990, 2. 216; hereafter "McCarthy."

[11] McCarthy 217.

[12] PI 129.

[13] See above note #10.

[14] McCarthy 266.

[15] The project to "explain consciousness" is beset by several conceptual difficulties. How would we know when we had "explained" it? What would such an explanation look like? What model or criteria would we use to distinguish a "description" from an "explanation?" In other words, the project transposes to a variation of the "perennial chestnut," the mind-body problem, for the project reduces to that of deciding what level of primitive or undefined category we must start from to "reach" consciousness that will count as an explanation. It seems impossible to escape one or another form of reductionism; indeed, the project is a call to reductionism.

CHAPTER 14

Jesus, the High Fidelity of God

I n 1922, Rabbi Leo Baeck produced the first of two articles which contrasted Judaism with Christianity by saying that Judaism was a "classic" religion, whereas Christianity was a "romantic" religion.[1] To appreciate this distinction, one must know something about the Romantic movement which was determinative in the formation of German literature and indeed German culture generally, in reaction to the French "classic" or "neoclassic" culture. Without going into a full-scale historical discussion, we can make the following point.[2] The classic tends to emphasize structure and order; it is comfortable with hierarchy, tends to trust reason over the emotions, and approaches religion in terms of proper social relations in contrast to aesthetic individualism or religious mysticism. The romantic by contrast finds structure and order stultifying, characteristically seeks to breach hierarchy, views reason as betraying or at least failing to keep pace with the emotions, and tends to view the essence of religion in terms of key experiences which are almost invariably individual and may frequently be described as "mystical." Often a "romantic" phase of culture follows upon a "classic" phase, which it presupposes and to which it is a reaction; "romanticism" is associated with youth, while the "classic" is associated with maturity.

It is not difficult to see what elements of Judaism and Christianity might make Baeck identify the former as "classic" and the latter as "romantic." Rather than contest this comparison, which strikes me as valid as far as it goes, it might be more valuable to consider what strengths and weaknesses these contrasting profiles give Judaism and Christianity as religions which must eventually engage the full human experience or situation and minister to the human heart. It is at this level that an evaluation of their adequacy must eventually take place.

A "romantic" religion runs the danger of being accused of being sentimental, more easily manipulative than a classic, in the sense of playing upon the emotions rather than appealing through our reason and leaving us independent in our reaction. On the other hand, a "classic" religion can be held to be insufficiently sensitive to the power of the emotions released in our response to the transcendent, of being insufficiently respectful of symbol, and to the wealth of meaning, emotive as well as cognitive, that can be conveyed by religious ceremonies. Understood in these ideal forms, neither description seems appropriate to either Judaism or Christianity, although certain forms of each have approached one extreme or the other.

Nevertheless, I submit that an element of truth must be granted to the description of Christianity as "romantic" as compared with Judaism. However, to be honest, one must also add that, on the key human experience of suffering, Christianity would appear to have certain strengths as a consequence of this characterization. Christianity can appear truer or more adequate to our experience, in the sense that its central religious ceremony emphasizes that the savior has tasted whatever sorrows we have experienced, and more. Jesus was from the beginning appreciated by the evangelists through Isaiah's image of the suffering servant. Israel interprets this image—with some difficulty—as applying to itself as a whole, but still within Judaism the question remains, why must Israel suffer so? In Judaism, Israel suffers, but God is not usually said to suffer—except by Israel's infidelity. God is faithful even when Israel is unfaithful. By the covenant He gives the Law, and expects Israel to obey, to be faithful; He allows her enemies to punish her when she is unfaithful. History presents the spectacle, however, of Israel suffering when there is no clear sign of unfaithfulness. In Christianity more explicitly, Christians suffer, and God suffers. This is a key difference, and the latter can be said to be more "romantic" than the former.

However, one must also assert that this makes the Christian liturgy potentially more powerful than the Jewish liturgy—in fact, on this issue the Jewish liturgy can raise a problem for the participant. For the Christian liturgy allows the participant to undergo an experience and come to a kind of resolution which is denied or unavailable to the participant in the Jewish liturgy. The "secret revelation" or disclosure that can take place in every religious ceremony is not how "good" God is—this is the official or "public" proclamation common to all religions —but rather that the liturgical space and movement provide a "sacred canopy" in which the participant is protected from outside threats to which he or she must normally muster a defense. This freedom or protected zone allows the participant to turn, recognize, and come to terms with aspects of his or her situation which they normally must ignore or suppress because they are "impractical" in the sense that we cannot do anything with them or about them—they are just part of the evil of the human situation—of being a Christian, or a Jew, etc. We have become so inured to these difficulties that we scarcely recognize the pain they cause us; yet they extract a real price.

Liturgy allows us the luxury of taking off our "street face," but also invites us by the same security to turn to address aspects of our situation which we normally keep from our conscious selves. Without the assurance of the love of God, we could not engage in such a meditation that might otherwise leave us at the mercy of our unrestrained emotions and also makes us exposed and vulnerable to ridicule. Liturgical space and time cuts off outside stimulation and encourages the participant to turn inward, to reflect and bring to the surface events and emotions which they do not normally consider. By association, and without becoming morbid, this ceremony provides a shelter in which we may recognize the extent of evil or pain in our personal or public lives, the things we are angry, ashamed, or sad about from our personal or collective past—all the things that are "useless" in getting on with the essential affairs of life, but which weigh us down and color our dispositions when we come to the major or minor decisions of our lives. They affect the "quality" of life—that all important but intangible reality we are trying to improve for our children. Liturgy provides an unparalleled and otherwise unavailable opportunity for growth and personal integration.

The Jewish ceremony, which stresses God's fidelity when Israel is faithful, the deliverance of Israel from her enemies, and the gift of the treasure of Torah, invites such a reflection while rendering the resolution of the problem of suffering problematic. Sorrow or anger seem acts of ingratitude and hence out of place, a cause for embarrassment in the presence of the gift of the Law. One must settle this first, before one comes to temple. What is valid in the experience is the suffering caused to Israel by the resistance of the nations to the message of monotheism, announced through the Hebrew people; however, the disproportionate nature of Israel's suffering, personal and collective, together with no obvious infidelity on Israel's part, renders God's behavior puzzling at best. The "sacred canopy" exists which extends the invitation for the "impractical" reflection on evil, but no clear direction for resolution is indicated. This raises the delicate but unavoidable issue of God's fidelity, and it is here that I believe a Christian must mention Jesus.

The Christian mass supposedly dates back to the Last Supper. Perhaps it more properly goes back to the experience of the disciples on the road to Emmaeus, for the mass has the same two elements—the reading and explication of scripture, and the re-enactment of the last supper, looking forward to Jesus' sacrifice the next day. Several metaphors or similes have recently been proposed for interpreting the event of Jesus which extend or take us beyond the Christological titles presented in the New Testament and the creeds. Besides appreciating Jesus as Lord, messiah, Son of God, Son of Man, Word of God, visible image of the invisible God, we have recently been invited to meditate on Jesus as the "icon," the "face," or the "parable" of the Father. While I am not insensitive to the novel aspects of Jesus raised to our attention by these descriptions, I would like to suggest that we go back to an older, if seldom used, title as the more central. It is more central, I believe, because it is basic to the others in the sense of containing them all, while itself being contained by none of them. This is Jesus as the fidelity of God—or the "high fidelity," if you like, since he alters what we had been led to expect, although it can be said to be prefigured in the scriptures: Jesus as the faithfulness of God to the promises made to Moses on Mt. Sinai and renewed regularly through the prophets. The other titles expound different aspects of God's fidelity to these promises, while none of them can be understood without them.

Without this background in the Old Testament promises, many of the descriptions of Jesus in the gospels and epistles must seem at best poetical exuberance or rhetorical flourishes. With them, they become intelligible and acceptable. For example, in the gospel of John, the Jesus who in Mark's gospel is appreciated most deeply according to the suffering servant typology of Second Isaiah, the faithful witness whom God will justify, is elevated to become a cosmological principle present at the world's creation and to whom it will return at the end of time. What has happened here? There is clearly interpretation going on, and legitimate interpretation or development of doctrine, when one sees that the author is appreciating the fidelity of God as coming to fruition in Jesus, who in some ways is the "end" or goal of creation, the fullest and definitive disclosure of the divine nature in our presence, whom (as Duns Scotus among others would later say) the Father foresaw and loved *before* the creation of the world, for whose sake he *made* the world, and according to our orientation toward him the world will eventually be judged. The Johannine language becomes permissible against this background, but only against this background. Cut free of it, the titles become fantastic and invite rather the gnostic interpretation of an aloof or hostile creator god, from whose mistakes we are rescued by a distinct and higher "savior" god, who only appeared as man to give us the true account of our "fall," and to make it possible for us to return whence we came.

Early on, the Church had to face the heresy of Marcion, which held that the New Testament cancels and does away with the Old and that Jesus can be appreciated apart from the Old Testament. While sensitive to St. Paul's statement that with Jesus the promises initially made to the Jews have been extended to the gentiles as well, and that in a sense all creation, even on the natural or philosophical level, has been groaning and longing for the completion of the divine initiative begun in creation in a final and complete disclosure, a defender of the titles of Jesus must still insist that they are acceptable only against the background of that initiative and thus presuppose fundamentally the activity of God as this is set down in the Old Testament. In a sense, we must all adopt the patriarchal narratives as our own "family saga," we must all become "cultural semites," if we are to become authentic Christians. Jesus was not primarily a wonder worker to be compared with other magicians and workers of extraordinary feats during his time, such as Apollonius of Tyana; such signs as he is recorded as performing were not done for their own sake but seem rather carefully chosen by the evangelists to illustrate and back up the claim that with Jesus the final, definitive form of God's intervention, and the eschatological phase of his kingdom as the fulfillment of the promises, is breaking in.

"Fidelity" is a fundamental topic in the scriptures, but for rather complicated reasons, for it dovetails through the story of Jesus in interaction with his Father, with his disciples, with Peter, with the Jews, with the Romans—and with the reader—and results in the formation of rather powerful questions and ironies. This is not the place to go into all of them; most the reader can identify readily for him or herself. What must be said here is the main point that Jesus had to decide how (or *if*) the Father was being faithful *to him*, who had distinguished himself by proclaiming to the Jews—against apparent evidence—that God *was* being faithful to his promises. The essential power and effect of the gospel story comes about through these questions and ironies. Cut off from that background, Jesus becomes a prophet of a confused message of liberal/progressive/revolutionary political and social upheaval who encounters an unfortunate demise. That the fidelity of God was seen by the evangelists as central to Jesus' message is clear from the way the plot of the gospel is patterned on the second chapter of the *Wisdom of Solomon*, quoted by Matthew, where the faithful servant of God, who "claims God as his father," encounters the resistance of the "godless" who must change their conduct if they are to come to believe that God is indeed being "faithful."

On the other hand, from the Christian perspective there is a danger in the "classic" position of a depiction of God that is too transcendent. This danger is present in the Hebrew, Islamic, and also in the Greek philosophical depiction, in the latter of which it is openly asserted that God must be changeless and can only be engaged in the highest activity and that directed toward the highest object—he is and must be "thought thinking itself." Since the Christian thinkers of the Middle Ages could not rebut this description, the principal burden of scholastic thought became that of showing how the two depictions were compatible (God could know us *while* knowing Himself, as an effect or possible likeness to himself). Plotinus had developed the rudiments of this device because he recognized that Greek philosophy suffered from a more fundamental or acute deficiency as a consequence of its excessively transcendent portrait of God: there was and could be no explanation of why there is a world at all. There should only be God knowing Himself. The Greeks could reason from the world to a "first cause" or "unmoved mover," but after they had reasoned "up" to such a being, they could not reason back down again. In fact, they could only demonstrate how it was *impossible* to reason back down—thus God *could not* make or know a world. Thus, embarrassingly, Greek philosophy ended up proving the *opposite* of what it set out to prove—it showed clearly that a rational account of the world is impossible.

The Jews and the Muslims rather easily appropriated the Greek notion of God, since it was close to their own;[3] the Christians had greater difficulty, because of their more "romantic" portrait. The Pauline/Augustinian strain, stressing the embarrassing discrepancy between the extravagant outpouring of divine love manifest in the passion and death of his "Son," and man's fallen condition after "original sin," offended the Greek axiom that love should be proportional to its object, and that the higher never inclines or "stoops" toward the lower—rather, it is for the lower to "convert" and rise toward the higher. The Christians had a difficult time reconciling these rival accounts; their solution came in suggesting that there can be a form of "motion" *not* based on lack or need, but on over-fullness or generosity, and the related point that there can be forms of perfection *higher* than that of being a "substance"—unmoving, independent, insensitive, or invulnerable to anything outside.

To respond to the main point of Baeck's contrast, the "romantic" emphasis of Christianity has the effect of making our suffering no longer the scandal it would otherwise be. That is, the regular re-enactment of this "myth" or deed of God on our behalf undeniably has the psychological effect of checking any tendency to dwell excessively upon our own sufferings and complaints, it embarrasses and silences such a tendency by placing it next to the tragic sufferings of Christ, more psychological and spiritual than physical, and also opens the possibility of bestowing significance upon our sufferings by associating them with the redeeming sacrifice of the savior, thus rescuing them from the futility, the "useless passion" that a philosopher such as Jean-Paul Sartre assures us we are. Such a strategy of resolution is not apparent in the Jewish liturgy, and indeed would be less available in any "classic" religion. It is important to recognize that one need not subscribe to the truth of either Christian or Jewish beliefs to note the different psychological effects produced by the principal religious ceremonies.

So when I write about Jesus as the "high" fidelity of God, I am not talking about an improved sound system. Rather, it is to suggest a return to the traditional appreciation or Christian suggestion about Jesus as the altered, unexpectedly ennobled and ennobling form in which God has been faithful to the demographic, dynastic, and territorial promises He made through the ages, starting with Abraham, through Moses and the prophets, to the Hebrew people. We expected God to be faithful to His promises, but not in this way. It takes us back; it is breathtaking and unnerving at the same time. We are initially not sure we like it, because it puts claims upon us we had not expected and are not sure we can follow. If holiness consists in "becoming like God," this inevitably poses the question "Can we follow Him?" This conformity undeniably involves more of a stretch in a "romantic" religion than in a "classic" religion.

Notes

[1] These articles, written in 1922 and 1938, have been collected in *Jewish Perspectives on Christianity; Leo BAECK, Martin Buber, Franz Rosenzweig, Will Herberg, Abraham J. Heschel*, ed. by Fritz A. Rothschild, NY, Continuum, 1996, pp. 56–92, with a helpful introduction to Leo Baeck by J. Louis Martyn.

[2] For a good historical discussion stressing the philosophical differences, see Isaiah Berlin, "Hume and the Sources of German Anti-Rationalism," included in Isaiah Berlin,

Against the Current: Essays in the History of Ideas, Oxford, Oxford University Press, 1981, pp. 162–188. See also Chapter 1, "The Terms Classic and Romantic," in Irving Babbitt's *Rousseau and Romanticism*, Boston, MA, Houghton Mifflin, 1926, pp. 1–32.
[3] The Jewish synthesis with Hellenism occurred primarily in Alexandrian Jewry. Posidonius had already cast Moses in the role of an eastern sage, probably on the basis of what he read in Hecataeus of Abdera. Philo built on this foundation and presented a "mosaic philosophy." F.E. Peters speculates that Numenius, who had a decisive influence on Plotinus, may have been Jewish; in any case, Numenius found that Plato was nothing more than "Moses speaking Attic Greek." See F.E. Peters, *The Harvest of Hellenism; a History of the Near East from Alexander the Great to the Triumph of Christianity*: NY, Simon & Schuster, 1970, pp. 300–304, 586.

Epilogue

The Enlightenment myth that Greek philosophy was a free-standing, fully achieved and finished temple that was vandalized and quarried by world-weary, insecure religious fanatics to become pillars in their own cathedral will no longer stand up to critical scholarly examination. Parmenides' frozen convention of True Being made it impossible for the Greeks ever to explain the presence of changing beings. In fact, Greek philosophy is characterized by a series of palace revolts against this convention, never quite successful, because unwilling or unable to question the basic truth that comes down through Parmenides: in some sense the deity *is* finished, complete, unmoving, needing nothing, and directed exclusively on Himself. Plato tries to inject the notion that the Good is naturally self-diffusive, and Aristotle says that when every being becomes adult or complete, it naturally seeks to produce another like itself; but ultimately these philosophies bow before the Parmenidean convention of True Being, and this interjects a *systematic* incompleteness into their attempts to replace the mythological accounts of the changing world with something that could be defended as "rational."

The pressure and competition of Judeo-Christianity, together with the eastern mystery cults, pushed Plotinus, the last great defender of the classical tradition, to come up with the two devices that could solve the problem: that in knowing Himself, God could simultaneously know indirectly everything that is His effect or that depends upon Him, and, more critically, if His love for Himself is sufficiently intense, this self-love would not constitute an *impediment* or barrier to His producing other beings, but on the contrary would lead Him naturally to want to produce a being able to appreciate this goodness and reflect it back to Himself. Plotinus did not exploit these inventions sufficiently to overcome the force of the Parmenidean convention; however, after a promising start His attempt to escape or to interpret the convention in this revolutionary way fails, and his philosophy is sucked back into the static coils of "True Being," where the world can only be the necessary but unintended side effect of God's self-knowing and self-loving. Ironically but not surprisingly, it was the partisans of Judeo-

199

Christianity, with their activist or dynamic views of the deity, who recognized and exploited these devices to the full, thus bringing to "completion" the project of the West.

The substitution of methodic doubt for the wonder and comprehensive integration of knowledge that defined philosophy for the ancients led to a search for defenses against Descartes' "evil demon"—space and time for Leibniz and Kant; but ultimately nothing could prevent the slicing away of the transcendent deity as a potentially deceptive idea and the transfer of its functions to the finite but developing subject, newly invested with semi-divine faculties guaranteeing the unity of experience by Kant. This economical simplification which identified the finite subject as the universe in its cognitive mode, or a developing absolute, was the basis for the Romantic sequel to the classical project, and is our current settlement. Many of the conflicts of the last three centuries, however, are due to competing "romanticisms," or the eruption of the divine in our midst, in nationalism, artistic genius, scientific messianism, economic ideology, or various liberation movements. Unresolved tensions between freedom and determinism, between reduction and adequacy, and between fantasy and reality, together with Nietzsche's call to an unremitting and fearless critical examination of our most fundamental and deeply cherished assumption, render this Romantic solution fragile, precarious, and questionable in our day.

INDEX

A

Adam, xiii, 48, 49, 52, 55, 62, 71, 72, 75, 77, 78
Aeneas (SEE Ennead)
altruism, 29, 37, 51, 52, 56, 63–65
amour-propre, 55
Anselm, 75
anteriority, x, 130, 135, 136, 143–145, 147
anti-foundationalism, 174, 182, 184, 190
antithetical, 129–131, 143, 146, 147
Apollonius, 195
apperception, 88, 103–110, 113–117, 120, 124, 127, 128
Areopagus, 45, 66, 70, 170
Aristotle, 3, 8, 30, 32, 33, 43–45, 56, 59, 60, 63–65, 67, 104, 116, 118, 119, 122, 152, 154, 170, 175, 176, 188, 199
Atomists, 8
atonement, 24, 46, 49, 54, 55, 70, 75
Augustine, 46, 49, 54, 55, 65, 70, 71, 74, 75, 78, 183
Ayer, ix

B

Bacon, 179
Baeck, 160, 191, 197
belatedness, x, 130, 136, 140, 144, 146
Berryman, 148
Blake, 131, 137, 138, 140, 142, 148, 165
Bloom, xiii, 130–148, 151, 157, 165, 184
Burckhardt, 1

C

Calvin, 62
Camus, 171, 172, 176
causal efficacy, 84–86
certainty, xiii, 92, 93, 98, 182, 187, 190
Chateaubriand, 1
Christ, xiii, 1, 9, 10, 11, 22–25, 27, 51–53, 55, 57, 66, 67, 72, 73, 75–78, 138–141, 163, 168, 170, 171, 197
Christianity, xii, xiii, 1–4, 6, 8–12, 13–15, 19, 22, 24–27, 43, 44, 48, 56, 60, 62, 63, 66, 67, 72, 147, 156, 160, 165, 167, 171, 191, 192, 197, 198, 199, 200
conatus, 82, 83
consciousness, xii, 4, 11, 67, 106, 109, 114, 115, 132, 142, 144, 145, 147, 171, 189, 190
Constantine, 13, 26
contradiction, x, xi, 54, 61, 83, 111, 112, 118–124, 127, 128, 152, 172, 173
convention, xii, xiii, 8, 29, 36, 38, 50, 53, 62, 65, 138, 154, 158, 199
creativity, 30, 85, 86, 152

D

Dante, 139
Darwin, 44
David, 1, 15–17, 21, 23, 159, 161–163, 168
Derrida, 130
Descartes, xi, xiii, xiv, 82, 100, 101, 105, 117, 126, 127, 155, 172, 177, 180, 189, 190
Dewey, 178, 179, 189
Diderot, 63
Dilthey, 1
Duns Scotus, xiii, 38, 41, 42, 46, 47, 50, 56, 57, 59, 60, 65, 67, 75, 78, 194

E

egotism, 29, 51, 52, 55, 56, 63–65
Einstein, 179
Eliot, 1, 136
Endo, 168
Enlightenment, x–xiii, 1–4, 42, 43, 53, 55, 56, 59, 60, 62–67, 72, 127, 132, 133, 141, 147, 156, 167, 172, 174, 175, 199
Ennead, 33, 35, 38, 67
Erasmus, 42, 127
external objects, 81, 85, 86, 89

INDEX